CHACOKIA

Chaco, Cahokia, Cities & Ceremonies ~

Bundles & Blood Lines Centuries Ago

Jay Miller, PhD

2018 © 2016

Contents

Contents

cnts ii   NA iii   intro iv   SW vii   Edits viii

Chaco

1   Chaco phenomenon
2   Keres
5   Chaco Canyon
25 Pre Chaco
35 Post   37 Summary
40 White House
44 Turning Sun
45 November SE corner
48 February NE corner
49 Implications
50 Acoma SE
52 Battle
55 Fires
56 Beyond ~ Katsina   65

Chahokia

66   Mississippians
69   Hub
72   Downtown Core
73   Monks Mound
75   Azimuths
77   Mound #72
80   Byers 06
83   Milner 06
84   Emerson 97   85 Great Lakes chart
86   Illiniwek
87   Busk 91 Busk Today   88 SE chart
98   Cherokee
102 Pawnee
105 Siouians chart 105 timeline 106 Omaha 107 Hidatsa 108 Crows
108 HoChunk
110 Osage   112 temple
115 Mandan Okeepa Day 1 ~ 118 2 ~ 120 3 ~ 121 4 ~ 122
124 Cityscapes & Cultures 126
127 Bib 158   159 Index 162
        iv map v SW 15 town plans 16 Bonito 26 slab rings
        73 Monks 85 Lakes 88 SE 105 Siouans 105 timeline 115 Mandan Rites
footnotes #1 – #110

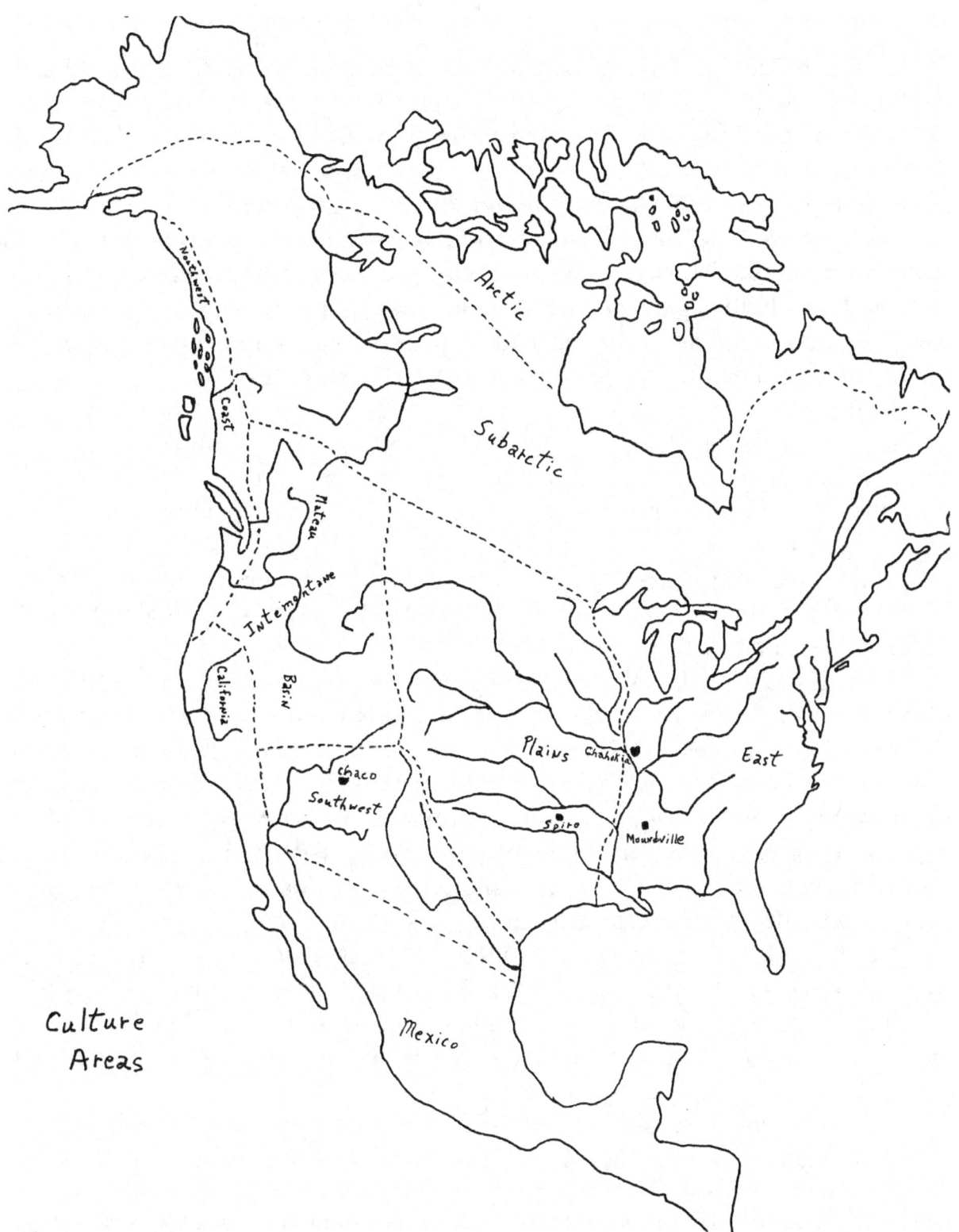

Culture Areas

Chaco 🖤 Spiro ● Moundville ■ Cahokia ♥

Introduction

Chaco circles & Cahokia squares, dating in the same Medieval Warm ~ Neo-Atlantic (AD 950-1250) era, are a study in opposites. Both are organic outgrowths of their regions, attracting wide contacts as pilgrimage centers. My intent herein is to repeople them with plausible ceremonies & tribal ethos to return them to past glories of the Americas. In the Southwest, Chaco belonged to Keres, a Pueblo language isolate, whose religious chambers are kivas – rock, round, below ground; in the Midwest, Cahokia belonged to Mandan & Dhegiha Siouians, with temples – built square beside free standing poles set high on mounds. A primarily celebate situation among Chaco priesthoods contrasts with celebratory sexuality among Siouians, termed "walking with the buffalos".

Both came to rely on maize ~ corn,[1] priestly theocracy, political kinship, clans, towns & tribe (Neitzel 1999, Holley & Lekson 1999). Life was organized in terms of age, gender, bundles & blood lines, matrilineal ♀ for the SW & patrilineal ♂ for the MidWest. While there was never any doubt that banded masonry pueblos, even in ruins, were human made, the earthen mounds of the Mississippi floodplain were long assumed to be geologic remnants, until systematic excavations revealed for all to see – basket loading & alternating light ~ dark layers that were obviously not natural.

During their heyday a *pan pax* ~ peace seems to have been in effect since violence was selective & "surgical": military maneuvers to gain captives for sacrifice or to expand access to resources when trade was somehow compromised. A key clue to both elites & their youthful guardians ~ enforcers is filed teeth, a permanent badge with origins in ancient Mexico (Holder & Stewart 1958, Perino 1967, Turner & Turner 1999). Chunkey games (Culin 1975: 420-527) spread with missionary zeal, kept Cahokia troops agile & fit. At Chaco, kickstick races along roadways provided similar fitness training and spiritual focus.[2]

Comparison of Southwest & Southeast "great towns" (Neitzel 1999) noted eleven archaeological topics: a) Timing & Scale, b) Time Span, c) Population, d) Built Landscape, e) Focality, f) Site Planning, g) Sprawling Nature, h) Unique Monumental Elements, i) Circumscription, j) Growth & k) Decline (Holley & Lekson 1999). We will seek plausible anthropological ones.

Yet appalling insensitivity pervades these comparisons by archaeologists wearing blinders. While the entire Southeast has the useful cover term of

---

[1] Of especial note, Missouri tribes grew 50 varieties of maize, mostly of the six worldwide types = dent, flint, pod, popcorn, flour, & sweet corn.

[2] Hohokam of southern Arizona relied on MesoAmerican derived ball courts, which also served as venues for ceremonies like the Wikita world renewal, featuring hand-carried floats portraying wished ~ prayed for rain and aspects of healthy environments.

Mississippians, reflecting its huge unifying river, shared Mobilian jargon, and Muskogean ~ Gulf language stock; the expulsion of these slave-owning tribes to Oklahoma, where ethnographies were written, is never addressed. Its long indigenous ethnohistoric record in Spanish, French, Swedish, and English was severed by a "voluntary" US policy in the 1830s.[3] While the arid Southwest lacks both a dominant river or single cover term, its diverse native communities do remain in their homelands, layered by successive migrations into the region by Numics and Athapaskans.

Moreover, these scholars rely on hopelessly flawed analogies, mired in pervasive US individualization, progress, & democratic ideals, denying native expressions of rank, kin, and privilege so obvious in the basic ethnography, especially among Pueblo theocracies. Regretfully, "chiefdom" is used abundantly, but "theocracy" is avoided in favor of "rituality". Southeast leaders, living atop mounds, were obviously political & corporate; Southwest priests, always secluded, most especially after persecution by Spanish Catholic inquisitors, still act through war captains, appointed yearly to prevent their usurping of authority. Indeed, "crying blood" & agile troops foiled competitors via strategic trauma & human sacrifices. In all, these were never egalitarian societies, despite a glib conclusion by those who did not do their homework & kept their heads in the ground.

As they began during optimum climates, so their endings coincided with the beginnings of the Little Ice Age ~ Neo-Boreal (1300-1870). Given the blown apart, explosive shattering visited upon the Americas by European "discoveries", ethnographic analogy suffers from a lack of appreciation of the vast complexity that once characterized Indiens (Indies not India) & this must always be borne in mind during any scholarly undertaking. What amateurs, Bureau of American Ethnology & Boasians recorded were pale fragmented shadows ~ shades of what the Americas had been, thankfully saved for posterity but needing dirt archaeology to better grasp these past wonders. Given the forceful outward scattering of native cultures, revealing clues may well be far flung so ethnographic analogies must be equally wide ranging.

In all, each American hub seems to belong to a language stock, such that Ohio earthworks were Algonkian, strongly Shawnee; Moundville was Muskoghean, identified with Creeks as was Etowah; Spiro was Caddoan, strongly Kichai; Chaco was Keresic; & Cahokia was Siouian, mostly Dhegihan & Mandan.

---

[3] Divide, dispossess & conquer is the rule, with such present day consequences as the newly federally recognized Poarch Creeks in Alabama destroying the holy site of Hickory Ground to build a wealthy casino against legal challenges by the huge Creek Nation removed for almost 200 years to Oklahoma in support of venerable Hickory Ground and its Mikko relocated there.

While Keresans & Siouians are our primary focus for Chaco & Cahokia, our net of comparative analogies is necessarily cast widely because of the explosively flung devastation Europeans caused in the Americas. Given serendipitous reports due to luck, dedication & diligence, best cases are nonetheless widely scattered. Only Hidatsa specify cosmic aspects of pottery making as a contest between sky Thunderers & underworld Snakes. Lenape trace their creation from a primordial Cedar tree growing from the back of the World turtle, bending down to spark first Woman to life & reaching up to enliven first Man. Similarly, datura use at Cahokia, if not also Chaco, receives detail & context in terms of Toloachi cult instituted by Chungishnish in southern California.

At the crux of all endeavors is contact with, access to, harnessing & renewing cosmic power, generically herein termed *puwah*,[4] with tribal equivalents cited whenever possible – Mandan *xopini*, Crow *maxpe*, Creek *puyvkeca.*, and Keresic *iyaanyi*. These efforts especially concern bundles ~ power packs devoted to particular causes & concerns. They are all necessary because *puwah* drains through its constant use, especially during times of threat, danger & exertion to the person ~ bundle ~ clan ~ guild ~ tribe. Thus a recursive circuitry − maintained by prayer, ritual, dicta & sacrifice − imaged as a spider web of intersecting rings & rays − channels its flow to reenergize during healthy ~ creative ~ festive occasions.

Today, ethnographic analogy works best for archaeology when it is understood that tribes, especially those once chiefdoms and theocracies, are shadows of their prehistoric complexities, still faithful to broad basic patterns & sometimes reflecting aspects of greater wholes blown apart by European devastations. Comparisons are therefore needed from across the "New World", with subsequent wider reaches across the whole world to begin to piece together the resilient cultures of the Americas in all of their variety and vitality.

---

[4] Conceptually all-pervasive, its many names include, among Subactic Athapaskans: *zhaak* 'grace' = Tutchone, *nadetche* = Sekani, *ink'on* = Dogrib ~ Dene Tha, *nitsit* = Kaska (Lanoue 2007: 253 #1).

SOUTHWEST Peoples

PUEBLOANS
Aztec-Tanoan Stock
 Tanoan Family
  TEWA
   Ohkey Owingeh ~ S Juan
   Santa Clara
   San Ildefonso
   Nambe
   Tesuque
   Pojoaque
  TANO (Southern Tewa)
  Hano (at Hopi)
  TIWA
  Taos
  Picuris
  Sandia
  Isleta
  TOWA
  Jemez
  Pecos (at Jemez)
 Numic Family
 HOPI
  First Mesa
   Walpi
   Sichomovi
   Polacca
   Hano (Tano)
  Second Mesa
   Shimopovi
   Shipaulovi
   Mishongnovi
  Third Mcsa
   Old Oraibi
   Kyakkotsmovi (New Oraibi)
   Hotevilla
   Bacavi
   Moenkopi

Penutian Stock (?)
 ZUNI

OTHERS
Hokan Stock
 Yuman Family
  QUECHAN (Yuma)
  COCOPA
  MOHAVE
  MARICOPA
  WALAPAI
  YAVAPAI
  HAVASUPAI

Aztec-Tanoan Stock
 Uto-Aztecan Family
  Piman
   O'OTAM (Pima)
   TOHONO O'OTAM (Papago)

Na-Dene Stock
 Athapaskan Family
  NAVAHO
   Eastern
   Western
  APACHE
   Llanero
   Chiricahua
   Mescalero
   Jicarilla
   Lipan
   Western
    Tonto
    White Mountain
    San Carlos
    Cibicue(Coyoteros)

ISOLATE
KERESIC
Eastern
 Cochiti
 Domingo
 San Felipe
 Santa Ana
 Sia
Western
 Acoma
 Laguna
 Awatobi ?

Edits

Editorially, text & punctuation are herein steamlined so '&' replaces 'and', dates in 1900s & 2000s drop their century after first citation & equivalents are shown between ~ tilde.

Quotation "marks" remain inside final sentence punctuation.

For Chacoans, Keresic is the language, Keresan is the inclusive & Keres is the generic term.

For Cahokia, as needed, regional charts summarize likely tribes, languages & culture areas.

Derived from a crucial concept in native grammars:

Tysic is <u>T</u>ime <u>S</u>pace <u>C</u>enter with vowel letters pointing down & up, fusing all these dimensions like the "deictic" feature of most native languages.

Chaco Phenomenon

Culminating all facets of Keres culture, spanning the period from AD 850 to +1150, Chaco Canyon was the pan-Keresan center & glory of Southwestern prehistory (Hewett 1936, Jackson 1887, Gladwin 1945, Gillespie 1979, Gwinn Vivian 1990, Sebastian 1992, Miller 2015).

Today, this isolated canyon in west central New Mexico consists of over a dozen greathouse ruins & hundreds of smaller Bc-unit ruins scattered within a region set apart from other Anasazi[5] populations. During occupation of Chaco Canyon, major features of Keresan society were defined architecturally. Matrilineages occupied the smallhouses throughout the region, while the leaders of major clans occupied the greathouses, both at outliers near clan lands &, in the case of important clans, in the canyon itself, where public ceremonies like those sponsored by the Antelope or Corn clans with fetish bundles at Acoma (below) took place. Males, initiated into family priesthoods, used the small kivas as their chambers. Both clans & priesthoods, arranged into alignments of kiva wings, cooperated in the use of great kivas as overall integrative mechanisms.

O
S   Pueblo I > 800 II > 1000 III > 1300 IV> 1800 V > today
H   Basketmaker II > 400 III > 750 AD
A   Archaic   > 7,000 years ago
R   PaleoIndien   +15,000 years ago
A

Near the center of distribution of Oshara tradition ~ ancestral Keresan sites (Irwin-Williams 1973), the canyon itself runs East & West, providing an ideal Keresan context. Over two centuries, the "Chaco phenomenon" during Classic Pueblo III had a key role in the integration of all Keres & exchange of information & goods among all Anasazi groups & Toltec Mesoamerica. Moreover, the emptying of Chaco coincides with the rise of Mesoamerican trade networks centered at Casas Grandes in modern Chihuahua (Lekson see all).

In his masterful survey, The Chacoan Prehistory of the San Juan Basin, Gwinn Vivian (1990) summarized the history & theories of prior research, particularly broader perspectives on the Chaco Basin region, before presenting his

---

[5] Anasazi is now out of favor, meaning 'ancient enemies' in Navaho, ironicly derived from Navahoes working as ruin excavators and stabilizers, financially oblivious to such taint.

own theory of Chaco development. Yet, by drawing his boundaries in terms of geography, cultural differences were obscured.

His perspective was further limited by looking only at the Eastern Anasazi record, rather than the entire northern Southwest. Since Keresic speakers were settled among both Eastern & Western Anasazi, important aspects of prehistory were ignored. Moreover, while Vivian (90: 437) quoted Robin Fox on Keresan links to the Chaco, together with "a shift from lineage-based 'unit houses' to segmented villages composed of multiple sibs to unplanned towns incorporating matriclans & patrimoieites," full articulation of Keresan society in terms of matriclans, priesthoods & dual kiva wings is slighted. Thereby lost are links of smallhouses with matrilineages, small kivas with priesthood chambers, greathouses with clan icons, fetishes, leaders & great kivas with integrative kiva wings.

Rather, Vivian was particularly concerned with issues of environment & climate in the basin &, in terms of these survival issues, contributes a great deal. As he noted, Chaco canyon was advantaged over other parts of the basin because of its size & access to rain runoff from both head & side drainages (90: 2). The canyon itself was a divide between primarily marine sediments to the northeast & land deposits on the southwest (90: 16).

Keres

From Void, *Tsityostiinako* ~ Thought Woman created Keresan existence. Their world, a 4 layer cube, originated from a blood clot, which grew into a Woman with head to the east, feet to the west & arms to the north & south. Layers arranged from top to bottom are Yellow, Turquoise, Red & White Worlds, with Yellow World at the center connected to their primordial White womb, *Shipop*[u], an underworld passage where life emerged & dead return. Working through 2 sisters, U & N, Thought Woman animated & named each of these worlds. While seeking its center, Keres built several towns along the way, especially at White House, where major esoteric priesthoods were instituted – devoted to Managing, Curing, or Protecting people & where men & women quarreled over who contributed more, separating for 4 years until women deferred to men. Katsina, immortals bringing rain from the West, were insulted ~ offended & attacked until subdued by Twin war gods, *Masewi* & *Oyoyewi*. Withholding rain, causing prolonged drought, a chaste & humble young man danced to lure Katsinas back, who gave humans permission thereafter to embody Katsinas with masks & regalia.

In time, White House itself dispersed into smaller communities, becoming modern towns of Cochiti, San Felipe, Santo Domingo, Santa Ana (Tamaya), Sia, Acoma & Laguna (*Kawaika'a*). With the arrival of the Spanish in the 1540s, native religion was persecuted & forced into increasing secrecy. In the process, many Keres converted to public Catholicism, hence many towns are named for the patron saint assigned to their church by early Franciscans.

Keres have long lived in pueblos, apartment-like buildings built around open plazas. Before that, their ancestors lived in pithouse villages. Dug into the ground, kivas serve as chapels & churches. Within houseblocks, smaller chamber kivas are used by their special priesthoods.

Men & women shared work when building a town. After masonry foundations & heavy timber framework were set by men, women finished the building, applying a coat of plaster & polished adobe floors. Completed houses belonged to women & their matriclan. By occupation, men were farmers, hunters, weavers, metal workers, warriors & ritualists; women were housewives, cooks, potters, basket makers & auxiliary ceremonialists. Most vital is irrigated farming of maize, beans & squash, supplemented by cotton & amaranth. Women tend small kitchen gardens that might include tobacco. Other activities involved gathering pinyon pine nuts, fire wood, building materials, medicine plants & raw materials for trade goods.

During birth, the right hand is used for ritual gestures because associated with the category of Woman. During childhood, youngsters played at adult tasks & roles. At puberty, children of appropriate age & gender are initiated into Katsina cult & pledged to secrecy. During all death events, left hand is used because associated with Man. A soul returns to primordial *Shipop*[u] for later rebirth to another set of parents.

Each Keres town (*pueblo* in Spanish) is governed by priesthoods, arranged into matriclans & integrated by two kivas variously called East/West, Turquoise/Pumpkin & Inside/Outside. A man joined a priesthood ~ guild because of kinship obligations, a personal vow, being cured by its members & thus learning some of its ritual, or being trapped ~ caught by it under special circumstances. Women might help the doctors, but they "never doctor; they brew medicines & they make yucca suds to simulate clouds or to wash the head ritually, all functions close to their ordinary economic ones" (Parsons 1939: 132). Some priesthoods go so far as to forbid women to associate with them in any capacity.

The head of the most powerful priesthood, usually Flint Knife, was Town Priest (cacique). Though husband & father, "she" was installed wearing the garments of a bride & thereafter addressed as "mother" since "her" primary duty was to fast, pray & meditate for the good of all in that town. Complementing the cacique was the Country Priest, now replaced by two war captains named for the miraculous Twin boys. Both Town & Country leaders had aides & messengers.

All of these officials were advised by a town council composed of male heads of households, retired officials & native priests. All positions relied on legitimate access to esoteric (sacred & secret) knowledge for community & world welfare, derived from full detailed knowledge of the origin saga.

All of the Pueblos are justly famous for the complexity of their rituals & dramas, based on their farming calendar with a series of feasts, public dances, private displays, masked incarnations & return foods thanksgivings. Current repertoire has added fiestas, feast days, patron saints & Masses derived from the Spanish Catholic Church.

Keres culture was intensely anthropomorphic, engendered as Man / Woman mediated by Mind – as Consciousness. After analyzing features of Keres kinship & mythology, Claude Levi-Strauss (1967, 75), French father of structuralism, saw "a system of polar oppositions," while Robin Fox (1967: 69) concluded Keres "seem to see the society as composed of a series of opposites." Man included a sacred language, white ceremonial costume, turquoise color, kivas, the boy Twins & war captains, priesthoods, left, Sun, animals, death & the directions of north, east & above. For Woman, these were the ordinary language, black costume, yellow paint, houses, U & N sisters & the cacique, matriclans, right, Earth, plants, birth & the directions south, west & below.

Men & women, in accordance with gender duality so pervasive in all of Keres culture, have differential access & control of *iyaanyi*. Men are able to attract & direct "power," with adepts being able to concentrate it in ways proportional with their rank & grade in priesthoods. Women, unless they act very much like men, are unable to attract, control, or concentrate it, presumably because their "natural" responsibilities to life, home & family distract them from the "cultural" life of prayer, meditation & fasting that is necessary to maintain good relations with power. For example, at the Solar rites to Turn the Sun (below), men pray for their own access, while women pray that *iyaanyi* come to their kinsmen instead. Yet women have other vital links to *iyaanyi*, indeed giving it life. While men are able to attract, direct & control power, it remains actively kinetic – highly mobile & fluid, pulsating with definite rhythms like music: "One of the most effective ways of obtaining & using supernatural power is by singing" (White 1962: 114).

Song pulsates with power & allows humans to manipulate it. *Iyaanyi* is most like sun beams, radiating out from a center & moving in absolutely straight lines that can be angled but not curved by using reflective surfaces like quartz crystals or the sheen of shell, stone, or mica.

Therefore, power can only be concentrated, revived & renewed by the cooperation of both men & women because *iyaanyi* is closely associated with life, functioning as a vital force whose source & summary is androgynous Consciousness Deity. As men & women are both necessary to the creation of life in its most viable forms, so they are also able to concentrate & renew power through their own respective abilities.

This renewal of generic *puwah* requires cooperation & union of men & women in ways that are neither sexual nor extraordinary. Men are protectors & teachers to instruct it of their wishes, while women nurture & cuddle its icons to give it strength & support. In all, *puwah* is least influenced by any reek of mortality (coitus, birth, death) & most compelled by acts of kindness, support & good intentions from the community & its leaders, especially in drum & song.[6]

Chaco Canyon

In tracing the history of research in the canyon, Vivian observed that while there was an early tendency to focus only on the canyon greathouse ruins (Chaco Core) & to regard them as cultural experiments ~ deviations from Northern Pueblo history, present researchers assume that the Chaco Phenomenon "was an indigenous development with roots in the late Archaic" (90: 7, 13). Moreover, persistent attempts were made to link together central greathouses to define some sense of a larger Chacoan community. For example, Edgar L. Hewett, neglected Chacoan theorist, considered Pueblo Bonito, Chetro Ketl, Pueblo del Arroyo & Casa Rinconada one single town (90: 52). As early as 1881, Lewis Henry Morgan noted that the same town plan was used for Hungo Pavi in the canyon & for Aztec West along the Animas River. Indeed, recent surveys suggest that there may have been a low wall around the four Core sites of Pueblo Bonito, Chetro Ketl, Pueblo del Arroyo & Pueblo Alto (90: 447, 482).

While tracing the Chacoan development from the Archaic Oshara of AD 500, particularly in terms of the growth of the great kiva, Vivian nevertheless noted considerable experimentation ~ creativity within the canyon & basin as evidenced by architectural redesignings. In particular, the rectangular Northeast Foundation built to the southeast of Bonito in 1070-75 suggests a break from the D-shape that long dominated the ground plan of this central greathouse (90: 56, 284).

Vivian was particularly concerned with tracing the increasing recognition by researchers that greathouses & smallhouses were occupied by the same people at the same time, both in the canyon & in the basin.

Past theories to explain difference between great & small houses, always emphasizing the latter, invoked immigrant colonists, Mexican traders (*pochteca, trocaderos*), turquoise trade, cultural progressives or conservatives, different languages, wealth differences, complex ecology & levels within administrative hierarchies (90: 395, 407).

---

[6] Sacred clowns, of course, as anti-social avatars, rely on sexual humor for much of their repertoire. Even more involved with biological functions are witches, the very essence of anti-social forces.

Before their excavations & surveys, the National Parks Service Chaco Center argued for a redistributive network centered on the Core, but, after excavations, pilgrimages into the Core for "consumption events" seemed more plausible, intimating "compensation for ritual services was construction labor on great houses to enlarge accommodations for future pilgrims" (90: 408). Smallhouse excavations also suggest craft specializations, particularly in turquoise, by these farmers were trade for food from outside the canyon (90: 415).

While Vivian recognized a common Archaic origin for both great & small houses, he saw their difference as primarily related to social organization. The smallhouses, which he attributed to the Cibola system to the south, were each occupied by a localized lineage, presumably of women (90: 446). "Cibola social relationships were embedded in the lineage & functioned through the lineage for the duration of the Chacoan presence in the Basin" (90: 449). For greathouses, "two systems were present in the Basin from at least 400 … [& that] organized on the basis of dualism … became a critical factor in the evolution of Chacoan-San Juan nucleated communities in the Chaco Core" (90: 491).

Others, moreover, have suggested that greathouses at Chacoan outliers were built & occupied by a "selectively male colony" intermarried with local women (90: 76), which, over time, whether ancestral (organic within the cluster) or scion (added later), formed a "Halo" around the western two-thirds of the basin.

Unlike prior scholarship which had noted a break between PaleoIndian & Archaic occupations of the Southwest, some of the latter may have remained in the region & adapted to a foraging economy about 7500 years ago. By the Late Archaic of 5000 years ago, a pronounced seasonal round had developed (90: 84), with some evidence of maize growing about 3000 years ago (See Timeline).

While Vivian did not consider Archaic (Picosa) variants outside the later Eastern Anasazi region, after the transition from the Archaic to Basketmaker II, he carefully considered subregional variants for each time period. Since the Archaic, these variants went from 2 to 4 examples, with a distinct overlap occurring in the canyon & leading to the flourishing of the Core.

With reliance on the farming of corn, beans & squash about the time of BC/AD, foragers moved into upland mountains & farmers took over the floodplains & lower elevations (90: 120). While the use of slab linings was traced from pithouses to surface rooms, no special attention was paid to their significance. At a Lupton site dated around AD 800, "Brownwares were primarily associated with D-shaped pit houses with benches, but most graywares were found in circular, benchless pit houses" (90: 148), which suggests Mogollon ~ Cibola inspiration for the D-shape that later became so important for indicating priestly or religious sites. In the north, great kivas were becoming more common.

As canyon population grew, resource use fluctuated, depending on supply, particularly of varieties of game animals & lithics (90: 215-7, 314-18, 378-91). With the elaboration of sites in the Canyon after AD 920, social mechanisms devised to balance population density with resource availability included "task diversification & specialization within & between settlements, variable settlement patterns & exchange within established networks" (90: 168).

Surveys found 50 or more outlier sites (90: 234), both ancestral & scion, around the basin, but only about half had great kivas (90: 234, 243). Since each of the seven modern Keresan towns has a dozen or so clans (7 x 12 = 84), clan ownership of outliers seems likely. Only the most important clans, such as Corn & Antelope sponsoring major rites at Acoma (below), had greathouses in the canyon.

Within the canyon, three great kivas were located at Casa Rinconada, Kin Nahabas & site 29 SJ 1642 east of Wijiji (90: 249, 251). (Two others have been mentioned & a few more are likely). Such great kivas served as the integrative mechanisms for district & regional communities of greathouses.

Small ~ chamber kivas were distinguished as Chacoan (90, Figure 6.15) or Mesa Verdean (1990: Figure 8.4), along with hybrid kivas, combining features of both, during the Late Bonito. The Chacoan had "low, wide benches, horizontal log pilasters, subfloor ventilator, slab deflector & roofs laid directly on the wall top or … cribbing beginning on the pilasters" (90: 161). The Mesa Verdean had a keyhole shape & "were deep, had a ventilator & firepit arrangement & roofs supported on masonry pilasters set on an encircling bench" (90: 230). Tower kivas set into upper stories also became more common through time. In all, Vivian (90: 289) diagramed five kiva types for Chaco & the Anasazi. Since modern Tewa believe the keyhole shape of their shrines, which developed from kivas, funneled power into that space, the Mesa Verdean kivas seem to have been concerned with the upper world realm, as the Chacoan ones concentrated on the under earth & *Shipop*[u]. Tower kivas, presumably, accessed winds, spirits & *iyaanyi* from the sky.

In his own research, Vivian (90: 307-313) found evidence of water control systems in seventeen of twenty-eight drainages leading into the canyon, in addition to waffle fields & other special gardens. While water supply was a crucial concern of life in the canyon, the symbolic importance of such fields should be noted. To this day, the quality of a native priest among the Pueblos is measured as much by the success of his cures as the bounty of his crops. A "good" priest must also be a good farmer to prove the virtue of his links with spirits & the land.

Vivian (90: 169) contributed his revision:

Bonito Phase (1080-1225)
Late (1120-1220)
Classic (1020-1120)
Early (920-1020)

He thus argued against McElmo as separate or intrusive settlers in the canyon. Instead, the McElmo sites like Kin Kletso were seen as a logical development from experiments by Chacoan leaders. Though "It is assumed as well that the building of great houses was rooted in cultural precepts that were expressed conceptually in architectural plan & form" (90: 265), Vivian did not suggest what those precepts were (though Lekson & Cameron suggest McElmo shifted to communal pueblos as known ethnographically).

While builders had a master plan in mind, that plan changed over time. During the Early Bonito Phase, the basic unit was the suite of living & storage rooms, which then shifted to roomblock & finally, by Late Bonito, became the entire ruin (90: 269, 365). According to Stephen Lekson (1983), who computed four stages for building episodes on the basis of the number of persons & the length of time needed, a 30-person crew could build Bonito in 21 months, although a third of that time was devoted to felling & transporting timbers, probably in the late spring & early summer when "labor could be pooled from several great houses" (90: 273), unlike the model of Lynne Sebastian (below) which presumes that each greathouse acted alone, despite obvious great kiva. Acoma clan-sponsored rites (below) suggest how such pooling or recruitment was possible by designating initiation godparents.

The typical building sequence began with an arc of central rooms which was then doubled in size by adding first an east wing & then a west one to define a plaza (90: 278, 280, 291). This sequence argues that the orientation of the east side was the community & that of the west one was male specialized.

Continuing a practice as old as the shift from pithouse to kiva & to surface room, Late Bonitos moved functions "into separate buildings, where previously they were undertaken in different portions of a single structure" (90: 296). This transition can be seen in the construction (90: 285, 374) of Pueblo del Arroyo (1065-75) & Wijiji (1100-15) before final sites (1100-15), when "Ceramic imports were more noticeable during the Late Bonito phase as a result of the appearance of Chaco-McElmo Black-on-white, a carbon paint type that contrasted sharply with earlier mineral paint types not only in the pigment used but in design style & rim decoration" (90: 381).

"Several Chacoan growth models purport that the Late Bonito variant became more complex during the first half of the 12th century ... [&] involved a concentration of energy in the Chaco Core, where population was massed in settlements with more restricted & precisely defined boundaries" (90: 487)

The most distinctive addition to Late Bonito architecture was the tri-wall behind Pueblo del Arroyo with a central kiva & twin rings of 6 inner rooms & 10 outer ones, dating from the early 1100s & recalling later office rooms of the Tiamunyi ~ Keres town priest.

The appearance of block towns & carbon painted wares in the canyon indicated increasing priestly isolation or retreat, as noted by Lynne Sebastian & can be traced in a similar progression from plaza greathouses to block units found in Manuelito Canyon (below).

The loss of the bracketed or enclosed plaza meant that public functions were curtailed. The core of the community & the template for the modern Keresan towns was defined in the McElmo or Late Bonito as a block of rooms with paired kivas, like those of the modern East & West town kivas. Later, except for important religious centers with a circular plan as at Tyuonyi, the aggregation of people during Pueblo IV was marked by towns arranged as a series of these housing blocks divided by street or open-ended plazas, like the modern Keresan communities.

After four decades of apogee, Chaco unglued:

System disintegration rather than collapse may most aptly describe the process involved during the twelfth century if the term is understood to represent a change in composition through separation into constituent elements & not the complete loss of cultural & system identity. There is no reason to suppose that the basic social elements that served as building blocks for Chacoan culture did not survive in subsequent modified forms of Puebloan culture. If this was the case, the task becomes one of identifying those elements in the twelfth century forms (90: 333-34).

The last Puebloan occupation of the canyon, before Navajo arrival, was indicated by a Cibola ~ Zuni glaze ware site dated to AD 1300-50 (90: 389).

Because of its age, complexity & richness, Chaco has received considerable attention, although not as a religious center. Trade & tribute dominate interpretations, rather than a proper appreciation for respect, reverence & ritual. Only Fritz (1978) has paid close attention to hints about the ideological system manifested in the ruins. As a healthy relief from testable & material aspects of prehistory, he reminds us that culture plays the vital role of providing "conceptual memory" in adaptation systems, serving as an organizational framework & control over content during long-term information processing, ranging from rules for private behavior & public conduct to elaborate symbolism relating to meanings.

Fritz's point is well taken, although it has been little heeded. Looking specifically at Chacoan architecture as an iconic code ~ grammar of design elements reflecting important cultural concerns, he sought an ideal order. In its own terms, devoid of any ethnographic analysis or comparisons, he found that Chacoan world view consisted of a cosmos with differentiated elements "dynamic yet bounded & restrained" (78: 41). These patterns are expressed as symmetrical & asymmetrical relations that crosscut each other, with symmetry involving phenomena which were "located in the east & west & were defined by axes aligned roughly north-south," while asymmetry involved those oriented north & south "defined by axes aligned roughly east-west" (78: 41).

For example, central greathouse ruins are Wijiji, Una Vida, Hungo Pavi & Chetro Ketl to the East; Pueblo Bonito, Pueblo del Arroyo, Casa Chiquita & Penasco Blanco to the West. In all, he posits a balance of 4:4, if Kin Kletso is ignored & Pueblo Alto is substituted for Late Bonito dated Casa Chiquita. There is ample justification for these substitutions since the McElmo construction & dating put Kletso & Chiquita after the heyday of the canyon (Vivian & Mathews 1964).

Asymmetry was also characteristic of the canyon & of its ruins, together or separately. For example, the greathouses were built on the north side of Chaco Wash, but most of the smallhouse Bc units are on the south side. Asymmetry also applies in terms of a center / periphery opposition in that towns in the canyon bottom have more kivas & complexity than those above the rim or further away. In addition, there are distant outliers, presumably associated with regional great kivas & seasonal concentrations, connected with the Chaco by straight sections of roadways (below).

In all, placement of Chacoan ruins most suggests a Keres context of center \ inside / outside ~ core \ rim / halo in terms of Bonito, Chetro Ketl at the center \ Pueblo Alto, Tsin Kletzin at the rim / nearby outliers along the Chaco Halo. Certainly, demography & lapses in the transmission of esoteric theological knowledge make problematic such direct continuity between all Chaco ruins & all modern towns.[7] At its height, Chaco was the elite center of a theocracy, not just a marketplace, however egalitarian. In particular, except for the grand pilgrimages during the year, the greathouses were more like monasteries because of the ceremonial chastity required during fasts & retreats. Chacoan priests did live with their families, however, when not engaged in rituals in their chambers.

Fritz interpreted other reasons for these differentially balanced relations, deciding symmetry represents a society based on equality within a "closed system of balanced duality" (78: 50). Citing Dee Hudson on measurement systems at Bonito, he argued for different social groups, like moieties, on the West & East, in

---

[7] Miller (1972) draws explicit parallels between each ruin & a modern Keres town, but, to judge from reader reactions, my intentions were misunderstood. In lieu of tracing direct continuity from Chaco ~ regional towns to specific Keres towns, my aim was overall town relations.

part because the basic unit of measurement at Bonito was equivalent to 20 inches on the West & 29 inches on the East. Significantly, the eastern measure was the larger, making it more inclusive. The row of rooms down the middle of the ruin used both sets of measurement, supporting its integrative role.

Fritz related asymmetry more plausibly to "control within a hierarchically organized social system" (78: 51), with "managers" on the north side at the locus of sacred power & "managed" on the south. Yet his own data indicates that both the north & the east were loci of ritual attention. For example, the east side of Pueblo Bonito had most of the kivas by a ratio of almost 2:1.

For the great kiva sanctuary of Casa Rinconada, he noted that the north / south orientation correlated with one of darkness / light & moisture / heat, but he phrased these as a sacred / mundane association that seems inappropriate for a great kiva at Chaco, rather like misidentifying a chapel as a parlor in the Vatican.

While he linked the underground ramp at Rinconada with rituals of origin & return, modern Keres data relate it to *Maiyanyi* earth spirits, suggesting it may have actually been used only once at the consecration of the building to draw spirits & power into the structure before that passage was sealed over to retain them & *iyaanyi* inside.

This explanation is probable because the subfloor feature was not found until a year after the excavation was finished. Students later visiting the site noted its outline in cracks on the settling floor. Yet, as currently seen, this feature is shown to tourists as part of the functioning kiva, despite the fully plastered floor that hid it from its contemporary users & archaeologists for so long.[8] Ellis (1952) provides another ethnographic parallel from Jemez for this argument where a similar passage into each kiva is blocked off after its consecration.

As I have learned from other native groups, particularly the Tsimshian, the effectiveness of ceremonials relied in large part on the absence of many of the townspeople for part of the year. During this free time, priests (and their helpers sworn to secrecy) devoted much time, labor, thought & attention to designing & building the equipment (Cf Vivian, Dodgen & Hartman 1978) needed to amaze an audience during dramas, rituals & displays, helping to assure continued devotion. Given the size & complexity of Chaco, together with a period of dispersed summer farming on plots scattered throughout the San Juan Basin, a similar separation & conjoining by season probably effected the canyon.

Moreover, Altschul (1978) has considered the wider context of this so-called Chacoan phenomenon by looking at it in terms of the larger San Juan River drainage. The area north of the river is cut up into many plateaus & mesa fingerings, with a deep water table, many springs & heavy summer thunderstorms

---

[8] Similarly, wall niches with offerings were plastered over while Rinconada was in use.

allowing for floodwater farming. The area to the south is more dry, less bountiful & more divided into planes of plateaus, cliffs & deep valleys that are broader than those in the north. Within the Chaco, the south side with the Bc units parallels the general pattern of growth & construction for the entire San Juan region, while the north half shows "areal consolidation in a few large centers" (A78: 116). In the process, two features became closely involved in this consolidation: great kivas (sanctuaries) & waterworks.

Most researchers have argued for the beginning of the great kiva about AD 900 as part of the increasing social control suggested by the size & complexity of the early greathouse ruins. Once, great kivas were thought to be a uniquely Chacoan development, but excavations near Zuni, New Mexico; Allentown, Arizona; & Lowry, Colorado also revealed sanctuaries. Such sanctuaries are probably a Keres innovation, reflecting the community focus for both regional populations outside the canyon & of ritual congregations within it. Since Keresans lived over a wide area of the Southwest, with Chaco as their heart, it is not surprising that sanctuaries are found throughout the area, but most heavily concentrated in the canyon.

Recently, archaeologists argued that the great kiva served as a redistributive center, a store & supply house for self-entrenching political leaders. As a cross-cultural generality, such a statement has merit, depending on how terms are defined, but it does not consider its long development from the central hearths & springs of Oshara. The likelihood, then, is that the sanctuary was built to attract & retain large reservoirs of *puwah* for the benefit of an extensive community. If food & supplies were stored in adjoining rooms, this probably added sanctity.

Following the hydraulic theory of Karl Wittfogel, many have argued that the motivation for strengthening the priesthood in Chaco was the need to regulate the waterworks in the canyon. While some features of this network are long recognized, the work of Gwinn Vivian (1990) has revealed much of its elaboration.

Throughout the San Juan, water control systems are concerned with either the conservation of rainfall & other water sources, or with the diversion of rain runoff. Conservation was used in the northern region, requiring little management. Diversion, on the other hand, was characteristic of the Chaco, requiring coordinated management to effectively use networks of ditch laterals & switches. Controlling such diversions gave Chacoan priesthoods increased authority.

Wittfogel & Goldfrank (1943) have discussed modern Pueblos as representative (if minor) hydraulic societies, with continuity from this prehistoric pattern. For the Keres, however, priesthoods ~ fraternities ~ cults have little to do with the control of irrigation systems, except for their annual blessings during the Spring ditch cleanings. In the modern towns, the official in charge of irrigation is called the *mayordomo*, a Spanish title although the role is clearly aboriginal.

Rather than supporting a common pan-Keres use of the Chaco catchment system, each Keres town now has its own official. The evidence for anything like a central official occurs only at Santa Ana where a native priest has the role that the mayordomo has in all the other communities (White 1942: 106). This man is appointed annually by the Town Priest to manage the irrigation system, but he does not have the ability to penalize. His distinctive insignia is a fine meal ground up from white beans, used while he prays. In short, he is a special priest with a unique insignia, suggesting an antiquity that could stretch back to the Chaco.

The location of Chaco at the heart of Keresan population density – reflected by the sanctuaries in other areas & its trade relations to the East for Cerrillos turquoise & to the West for trachyte (sanidine basalt) tempered pottery from the Chuska Mountains (Harris, Schoenwetter & Warren 1967, Windes 1977a) & other ceramic styles from the Little Colorado region – was facilitated by a system of roads now mapped (Hayes 1981: 45). "There are no sweeping curves or lazy bends in the Anasazi roads. They are straight for long stretches. When it is necessary to change direction, it was done with an angle" (81: 46). As these roads deal with the Outside, they are appropriately manly, angular & lineal to harness light-beam-like *iyaanyi* power.

Another use of these roads could have been as kickstick race courses, played by teams which often compete for miles. Since training of troops was always an aspect of these great towns, as chunkey was advanced by Cahokia (next section), Chaco young men would have been encouraged to engage at distinctly Keresan two-billet male & female kickstick (Culin 1975: 668). Each team kicks one of the engendered billets along tan agreed upon course, which included religious aspects of helping the Sun along its own course & success for the winning gender.

Outlying ~ satellite ruins surround Chaco in all directions, again indicating that it was the heart of Keres territory. Over time, however, as centralized authority was entrenched in Chaco, communities on the fringe, at Lowry in the north & others to the south, moved closer toward the canyon & road terminals. Thus, later towns at Aztec & Salmon in the north & in the Nutria valley to the south should be viewed as relocated districts.

Moreover, some people may have been settling in the canyon itself, founding Bc units. As is clear from the surveys of the San Juan & larger Anasazi region, these smallhouses were consistent over the entire area, representing the organic growth of local populations. The greathouses, by contrast, can be traced back to the ceremonial centers like the paired pithouses with associated community ring, occupied by family lines whose men filled priestly offices, which increased in number & authority as part of larger demographic trends. The moiety-like characteristics of the greathouses with East & West wings, therefore, derived from these earlier pairings of leading families.

The smallhouses & the greathouses were contemporaneous in the canyon. Gladwin (1945: 123) once argued that they only dated from the same time because timbers from the small units, his Hosta Butte phase, were removed & reused in the large ruins, his Bonito Phase. His feisty claims to novel interpretations of Chaco have not, however, proved correct. Hosta Butte & Bonito existed side by side, but with very different densities of occupation. "The Hosta Butte pueblos averaged 10 rooms. The Bonito Phase pueblos averaged 288" (Hayes 1981: 32).

Gwinn Vivian (1970) examined a number of hypotheses for the Chaco & found two particularly plausible ones: 1) Hosta Butte units were occupied by localized lineages & Bonito ruins by moieties, 2) Chaco was a ranked society with Haves in great pueblos & Have-Nots in small ones. Paul Grebinger (1972, 1975) pursued the latter theory, arguing for a pristine rank society in the canyon with the greathouses located on best farmland until deforestation, changes in rainfall pattern & over population led to "collapse".

While these general arguments have comparative merit, it is important to push the ethnographic analogy with the Keres since it adds depth & complexity to interpretations. Also, Keres patterns closely approximate many features of Chacoan society, showing Chaco to be a climax of Keresan integration. Such analogy is especially culturally relative, lacking obvious ethnocentrism of American culture so rife in recent academic theory. In all, Chaco was the likely Keres focus for several centuries.

Earlier work on Chaco concentrated almost entirely on the more spectacular greathouses, which are indeed impressive, yet both Bc units & great houses add strength to any argument that they were occupied by ancestral Keres. After all, a culture so fundamentally dualistic as the Keres should be expected to produce two distinct ruin plans. As clusters of rooms, the Bc units would have been lineage family homes, with little religious symbolism, while the D-shaped, clan-owned greathouses with curved outer walls would be womanly, combining manly lineals with a womanly curve.

Further examination reveals, however, that most later greathouses began as a row with side wings, a bracket [shape, which only later had the outer curved wall added. Yet, the four earliest greathouses began as room arcs in a C-shape, with a straight outer wall added later. Peñasco Blanco, the first, became an oval; while Bonito was planned & built, after at least one false start, as an integrated D-shape. Significantly, the earliest masonry consists of sandstone slabs laid flat between masses of adobe mud, giving yet another expression of slab / clay complements. Later still, the masonry gained greater strength when sandstone bands were built as a veneer around an adobe rubble core, stone on the outside & adobe inside.

Four greathouses were built between AD 860-940. Three are well known; the fourth at the East Community between Bonito & Pueblo Pintado is recent.[9]

Chacoans situated three large buildings at key locations where major side drainages enter the canyon; Una Vida, across from Fajada Butte & near Gallo Wash; Bonito, across from South Gap; & Penasco Blanco, on the bluffs overlooking the confluence of the Chaco & Escavada Washes (Frazier 1986: 175).

The next major stage, from 1020 to 1050, was at Pueblo Alto, Chetro Ketl & Pueblo Bonito (additions). Architectural forms begun in the 900s were continued (86: 176).

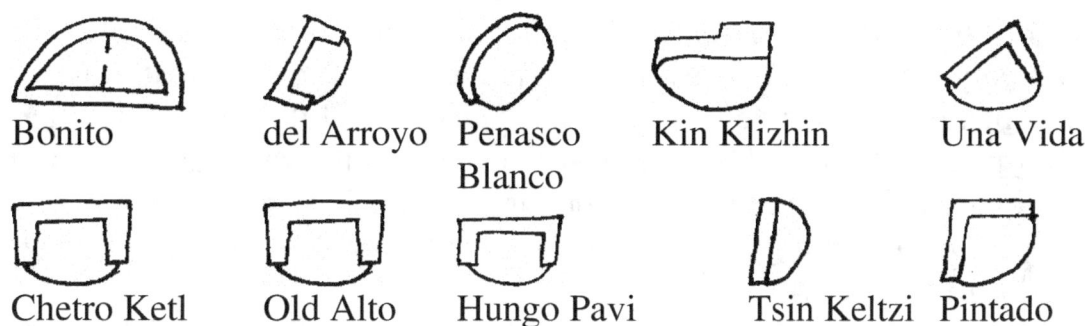

Bonito   del Arroyo   Penasco   Kin Klizhin   Una Vida
Blanco

Chetro Ketl   Old Alto   Hungo Pavi   Tsin Keltzi Pintado

These construction phases & later developments suggest an ancestry for the pan-Keresan context. Within the canyon, paired towns were built, a manly & a womanly one, while on the rim of the canyon was built an outside town. Bonito is the only one within the canyon to be consistently male during the entire occupation. Initially, the inside womanly town seems to have been Una Vida, then Chetro Ketl located beside Bonito. Peñasco Blanco is special as an outside circular town with a very long occupation & spectacular views in all directions.

Except for the later Bonito & Chetro Ketl mating, other greathouses seem to have been passing through a developmental sequence from C to D, depending on the amount of power, position & priestly leaders residing therein. During the 1050s, towns were planned as an angular "[" that finalized as a D. In all, the directional orientation, date & placement of the ruin within the canyon should reveal its position within the Man / Woman context. For example, as a northern half circle, Bonito would be manly; as a southern half, Chetro Ketl would be womanly. Likely associated clans would be Sun for Bonito & Corn for Chetro Ketl because of their importance among all the Keresans.

---

[9] Four, rather than three, earliest towns, of course, fits with Keresan & Puebloan number symbolism. U had charge of four towns in the four directions after coming into this upper world, before people moved to White House. The East Chaco Community greathouse was discovered by Tom Windes & is known as 29 Mc 560, its Navajo name is "the house next to the place where red ants have gone" = *Kin doo walachii yoo iina*.

While the greathouses were undoubtedly Keres, not all of the Bc ones were. With both an indigenous population & others moving in from the periphery, mixing occurred. For example, Łeyit Kin (Dutton 1938) does not seem Keresan because of its predominance of carbon paint & Mesa Verde styles, suggesting ties to the north through kinship, trade & immigration. At least some units were occupied by ancestral Towa, since Jemez elders have legendary accounts of the Pe'lush, whom Florence Ellis (1953: 163) suspected were ancient Chacoans.

Further, while each of the towns had at least one great kiva, or perhaps, a sanctuary at each of its two seasonal locations, Pueblo Bonito & Chetro Ketl seem to have had two in use at the same time, with the remains of a third also reported from each. The likelihood, then, is that both were occupied year around, while the others had only their celibate priestly hierarchy as permanent residents. Representing Inside & inclusive, the East sanctuary served the town, attracting & renewing *iyaanyi*, while the West one was Outside, exclusive & concerned with regional manly activities. Over time, people drew away from the canyon for more of the year, staying at farming locations & eventually avoiding, except for pilgrim priests, the Chacoan center core.

As yet missing is any discussion of the *hotcanitsa*, the office of the modern Town Priest & the heart of every Keres town. Basically, its origin traces to the plastered pithouse closely linked with the slab ring at late Basketmaker centers. In masonry pueblos, it was a site centrally located for solar & astronomical observations along the skyline, such as the room row down the middle of Bonito. Later, it achieved independent existence as the triwall structures noted at Pueblo del Arroyo (Vivian 1959: 84), Aztec & elsewhere along the San Juan River.[10] One proposal is del Arroyo was built by a splinter group who left Bonito after disagreements.

This schism seems plausible. To this day, the work of the Town Priest is to pray, meditate & fast for the good, peace & wellbeing of "her" townspeople. At council meetings, no anger or bitterness can be shown because this would disrupt the good thoughts of the cacique. If hostilities erupt, "she" must leave the proceedings. If the people founding del Arroyo did so after an angry departure, it would be very fitting for them to build a triwall office for their cacique, outside the town walls, as a calm haven from strife. At Cochiti, a new office was built whenever a Tiamunyi was installed, for "her" use, thereby allowing changes of style & design to influence the development of this building.

The major task of priesthoods is to keep things running as smoothly as possible. The sense is that any anger, insult, or malice causes bad thoughts, which

---

[10] Tri-walls are clearly a feature of the San Juan River & northern basin, where they are fully integrated into regional site plans.

linger in nooks & crannies of the village to cause further harm & upset. Greathouses with full D-shapes must have contained great power, where every thought & action had to be monitored carefully. Feuding would thus offset this highly delicate balance with the cosmos.

The triwall with central kiva & double ring of rooms, an inner & an outer one, is an apt form for representing the entire community in the care of Town Priest &, as such, logically conforms to the requirements of a *hotcanitsa*. As further indication of stresses that the late occupation of the Chaco was undergoing, triwalls were located outside of their towns. Over time, however, they merged into the community as the modern sanctuary of the cacique. When times were bad & the cosmos not cooperating, community relations must have suffered & the Town Priest needed his special building away from the community so as to better concentrate on better relations with cosmic forces.

Neil Judd felt that the greathouses with their enclosing walls were built to be defensive, but there are few indications of warfare at this time. Rather, the greathouses were defensive only in the sense that they represented Keresan unity in the face of encroachment by speakers of other languages. That greathouses were built as religious preserves makes sense in terms of the all-pervading importance of religion in Puebloan societies. Each greathouse was probably built to be an eventual repository of power, accumulated over time through its priests & rituals, until the outer curved wall was finally added to retain this amassed *puwah*. In the process, the town took its place in the context of the overarching hierarchy headed by Bonito & Chetro Ketl.

Massive surveys, excavations & analyses by the Chaco Center of the National Park Service have added to our understanding. All of these contributions, of course, are unabashedly materialist, concerned with artifacts, economy & politics in ways that are meaningful only to an Euro-American audience.

After hopeful beginnings, multi-culturalism, including alternative symbolism, has become largely shunted aside in Southwestern archaeology. Even while seeking only universal, albeit academic, laws about the development of human societies in response to internal & external criteria, the Puebloan archaeological record can also serve to explain how modern Pueblos emerged over thousands of years. Archaeology & ethnography complement & enrich, despite comments such as

The situation at Chaco is remarkable for a number of reasons, the most significant being that there are no analogs for Chaco among the modern Pueblos & perhaps none in any contemporary society, that the tremendous growth of Chaco was so short-lived & that the amount of labor invested in nonessentials such as beautifully decorated masonry veneers [plastered over] must have been enormous (Cordell 1979: 149).

Chaco & Keres allow us to explore what has long baffled scholars: their particular blend of matrilineages in clans – based on the mother-child bond, of priesthoods – based on that of father-son & of town kivas – based on both of these bonds along with other choices & spiritual linkages. All rely on sacra, such as icons, fetishes & bundles.

Theories guiding the renewed research in the canyon & beyond provide only materialist explanations based in the economic, trade & political sectors. The grandeur of the greathouses & the dense scatter of other ruins bespeak complex society, probably a chiefdom held together by redistribution in which goods & services went up the ranks while decisions & gifts came downward.

But this theory fell apart in the aftermath of excavations because findings were not so simple. Pueblo Alto, sampled as a representative greathouse & the end of the Great North & other straight roads, indicated intermittent population concentrations in the canyon. Since rooms were bare, except for a few connecting rooms ~ suites with hearths for cooking & warmth, population estimates were seriously reduced. Two of these household suites had

> stone- & adobe-lined hearths, storage pits, mealing bins for grinding corn & special niches for food ... pollen & burned seeds from food plants indicated that food was processed & eaten in those rooms. The floors ... had been replaced many times, [and] were badly worn – presumably as the result of heavy domestic use (Lekson, Windes, Stein & Judge 1988: 104).

Further, the estimated 100 people who lived at Alto left 150,000 broke pots in the trash mounds over a sixty year period. At 250 pots per person a year, this figure astounds. Yet these pottery sherds were not scattered evenly throughout the trash. Rather, they occurred in layers as though every so often people gathered together to smash pottery, probably as part of the feasting & ritual of a world renewal ceremony.[11]

Chaco, instead of being the political hub of a vast chiefdom, now seemed more like a pilgrimage center. What held it together was a network of exchanges bringing in food, goods & services in return for ritual uplift & blessings. These

---

[11] Aspects of this wholesale destruction of old items for replacement by new ones, yearly renewing the Pueblo world, occur at Zuni Shalako, with more direct Keresan ~ Acoma parallels below.

services were sometimes substantial, including quarrying sandstone slabs for walls & carrying trees 60 miles from the Chuska Mountains for beams.

This network was in place before the Chacoan florescence of AD 900-1130. The "great kivas, non-local [traded in] ceramics, minerals & lithics" begin in Basketmaker III & continue because Chaco was a "cultural response ... to adapt effectively to a stressed, semiarid ecosystem of low productivity & low predictability" (Schelberg 1982: 2, 278). Three levels were involved: villages – basic producers of food or goods, outlier greathouses – arranging their transfer & central greathouses (like Pueblo Bonito) – coordinating & receiving these materials but not dominating this trade.

Lynne Sebastian (1991, 1992) looked at Chacoan leadership, curiously disembodied, as an aspect of this regional exchange of goods, services & information. The system grew, for her, as interactions increased, due to food exchanges, periodic aggregations & cooperative building projects which occurred during times of drought & increased stress. Scholars find this amazing because, usually, during environmental crisis & food failures, people share less or not at all. Given the strong communal ethic of Pueblos, however, such sharing & cooperation was & is expected, reinforced by the threatened accusations of witchcraft for hoarding ~ being selfish. Indeed, while recognizing that Pueblo leadership, now & in the past, relied on the ownership of ritual knowledge, Sebastian is remarkably silent on obligations of a leader to his or her community.

Her study of leadership complexity, rather than leaders themselves, relied on five criteria: settlement pattern, site hierarchy, differential distribution of artifacts, burials & water control devices. Based on size & attention, Chacoans were divided among the greathouses ~ Bonito ruins; the Bc ~ Hosta Butte smallhouses; the outliers, both home-grown or imposed (called ancestral / scion), copying greathouses on a smaller scale; & the later McElmo block units. Interlinking these were the formal roadways, line-of-sight signal stations, earthen mounds & network of masonry shrines. Everyday items like pottery & stone were shared evenly by Chacoans, but not luxury goods – since turquoise, shell, copper bells, macaws, mosaic inlays, jewelry & more varied foods predominated in the greathouses, often associated with prestigious burials. Instead of irrigation channels, water control in the Chaco captured & distributed runoff from infrequent rains though a series of check dams, diversions & stairways slowing flows. To be effective, this network needed centralized authority to quickly marshal labor as it rained.

Because the environment was harsh, she argued, mobility & flexibility were better adaptations than developing complexity. Previous archaeologists argued that complexity allowed redistribution, leveling out regional resource fluctuations for the benefit of all Chacoans, especially the elite. Yet the periodic "consumption events" when many pots were smashed discredited any such smooth evening out, although movements of goods & services up the ranks continues to be cited as initial motivation for the Chacoan system. Yet, seen variously as a form of social insurance or of welfare, Sebastian noted that moving people around was easier than transporting goods throughout the San Juan.

In the interest of increased production (92: 100), Chacoans could use either of two strategies: land extensive or labor intensive. In the canyon, intensive was used, relying on building water channels to capture & direct rain runoff. While not an irrigation system, successful use needed central authority to quickly coordinate human efforts during rain storms. Land extensive use relied on a variety of fields in many locations to maximize harvest potentials.

Indeed, the greatest influence on Chacoan development was fluctuating rainfall patterns. Chaco building started during a drought, then construction resumed during a time of above-average moisture & was abandoned after sustained drought. Each greathouse, therefore, served to express leadership success at recruiting followers while assuring legitimate succession to "his" position by acting as "father" or "mother's brother".

While the first greathouses (Peñasco Blanco, Pueblo Bonito, Una Vida & East Community) began during decreased rain, all others were built when the climate was favorable. Finally, early in the 1100s before the abandonment, construction was limited to "arcs of rooms enclosing the plazas at these sites" (Sebastian 91: 128) – which can be interpreted as "finishing off" the town by holding *iyaanyi* within, although Sebastian saw instead closing up & looking inward at each site.

Overall, she saw a shift, about AD 700, from foraging mobility to settlements to allow for the overproduction & storage of crops as hedging against crop failures. During the 900s, Chaco began because regional hardships allowed canyon residents owning productive land to apply generosity to become regional leaders, with followers laboring to build specific greathouses. Because Chaco Canyon was surrounded by desert, population concentrated along the bottomlands. After this burst of building activity, however, most greathouses remained the same for a century.

Such concentration was significant because "Pueblo III outside the San Juan drainage was a time of population expansion & growth" (Cordell 1979: 144), suggesting that Keresans were being further hemmed in.

After AD 1040, building resumed during better 1050-80 rainfall, providing leaders with new appeal, perhaps in terms of competing cults based in the priesthoods & greater ethnic identity. Former greathouses were renovated with repeated, massive additions & new ones were built, but usually with only one story, as at Pueblo Alto & Arroyo. During AD 1050-70, great kivas, both integral & isolated, were built & renovations concentrated on "rear-row rooms, upper stories over existing rear-row rooms & massed blocks with many interior & few exterior rooms" (Sebastian 92: 122, 123).

Distinctive core & veneer masonry of finely banded slabs of sandstone suggests public work projects of modern Pueblos, but the outcome of Chacoan style was so architecturally sophisticated that another, now lost, procedure must have been involved. Though this banded masonry required some skill, these buildings match the characteristics of most public architecture: labor intensive, able to be built in stages & impressive enough so that every worker could feel a sense of pride (92: 126).

We do not know where workers lived while building greathouses & outliers, so finding their homes, if any. should be instructive. In terms of modern Pueblo logic, such large construction projects would have required a religious & communal inspiration. If wearing masks & dramatic rituals (Vivian, Dodgen & Hartmann 1978; Geertz & Lomatuway'ma 1987) required special or privileged initiation, unlike the more general ones now held for the Katsina cult, training of young men for such a Keresan cult may have involved labor for greathouses, roads & other public projects. Keeping these boys together & busy served the community & enhanced the fame of Chaco, even as they played kickstick along the roadways.

After AD 1100, before the catastrophic drought of 1130-80, "activities at the great houses seem to have turned inward, with the plazas being enclosed, the trash mounds falling into disuse & the space within the structures being more heavily used for domestic activities" (Sebastian 1991). From 1100 to 1130, "trash deposition shifted from extramural mounds to abandoned rooms & kivas; that the source of imported black-on-white decorated ceramics changed, as indicated by the shift from mineral-painted to carbon-painted types; & that faunal procurement shifted from an emphasis on deer to an emphasis on small mammals & turkeys" (92: 132). Outside the canyon, however, among distant members of the community, construction projects continued.

During the 1200s, people moved back to the canyon, but without complexities indicated by greathouse & great kivas. Since the McElmo blockhouses are now thought to have overlapped with final original occupation, rather than a century later, their use as storage bastions seems likely.

Looking at the entire span, Nancy Akins (1986) tackled the sensitive issue of burials in the canyon. When estimates for the population number of Chacoans ranged from 5,000 to 10,000 people, concern was expressed that only about 200 burials had been found. Reviewing excavation & catalogue records, however, she found reference to 663 burials, with evidence for 464. Now that estimates range between 2000 & 5000, this total seems more appropriate. Given that Keresans lived scattered throughout the San Juan, however, those who died while visiting the Chaco may well have been taken home for burial.

Akins found that Chacoans were not well nourished. In a fascinating study of parasites, Akins (86, Appendix E ~ Reinhard & Clary) also confirms a dense & untidy population in the canyon, but ceremonial requirements to fast & avoid water might help explain these findings. Both men & women buried in rooms at Pueblo Bonito, the central Great House, were taller – suggesting they were better fed than those buried in the Bc ruins. Moreover, greathouse burials were formalized, more elaborate & better supplied with luxuries, indicating that they outranked ordinary people. While bones indicated dietary stress & some malnutrition, effects of fasting rather than food shortages was not considered.

Of particular note for the Keresan association of men & death with the left was Bonito burial 14,[12] surrounded by thousands of turquoise beads & other jewelry that emphasized the left over the right side (Pepper 1909). For example, while his right wrist was wrapped with 617 beads & 168 pendants, his left had 2384 beads & 194 pendants. Similarly, the right ankle held 322 beads & 5 pendants, but the left one had 434 beads & 8 pendants. In all, Room 33 with a dozen burials included 24,932 beads, 512 pendants, 451 mosaics, 15 effigies & 1,052 fragments (Akins 68: 115). It is no wonder that most archaeologists believe that Chaco rose to greatness by controlling the manufacture & trade of turquoise throughout the Southwest & into Mexico, although they fiercely debate the extent of the Mesoamerica connection.

Since turquoise continues to have great spiritual & practical value among the modern Pueblos & Keres still name one of their kivas after it, the final word should be that of Gwinn Vivian (90: 490), preeminent scholar raised in the canyon, "The Chaco system did not collapse, it simply readjusted."

In hindsight, therefore, Keresan matrilineages resided in the Bc (Hosta Butte) villages, town wings aligning clans & priesthoods were focused on the great kivas, both inside & outside the canyon & coordinating priesthoods in the clan-owned Bonito greathouses managed relations between humans, spirits, animals & environment. Since modern caciques can never leave their towns without causing spiritual harm, high priests were probably also fixed to the canyon. The general population, however, remained mobile, farming town lands away from Chaco, presumably with manly towns to the north in the San Juan & womanly ones to the south in the Cibola. The modern two kiva system, thus, developed from twin seasonal & geographical locales of the same town. The East ~ Turquoise Kiva was located at the greathouse in Chaco canyon; while the West ~ Squash Kiva was at

---

[12] Since 14's skull had a fresh gash on the right parietal & his left femur had cuts or chops, he died violently (Akins 1968: 116-17).

the farming site. When people stopped going to Chaco, these kivas joined together at the regional town. The building of a great house, therefore, did not represent the success of a leader ~ leading family, but, instead, indicated that the prosperity of a clan region was being shared within the canyon.[13] Since clans owned land, each greathouse was under the nominal authority of the elite women & men of the clan providing agricultural produce.

The crux of this system & of Keresan genius was the evolution of the priesthoods, their gift to the Southwest. Beginning as family specialties centered in the religious chambers ~ small kivas that developed from the pithouse, Chaco provided the means to systematize & coordinate these specialties into an overall cosmology. In the process, men with the best memories were trained in the details of esoteric lore & learned, by pooling information, about the resources near the localities of their respective farming towns.

These same priests made pilgrimages to ancient sites to visit shrines & leave offerings, adding time depth to their knowledge. Hence, in all, Keresan priesthoods, which thrived in Chaco & still sustain Keresans, were the secret to their cultural success since they embodied the collective memory deified as the head & heart of the Keresan pantheon.

In all, then, Chaco Canyon was the fulfillment of Keres development & the mold that created the modern situation. Aspects of Chacoan invention can still be found among the Keres, particularly at Cochiti & Santa Ana, along with other towns. Among the most significant of these traces are the possible relay points for fire signals strategically located along the rim of Chaco canyon. These call to mind the ritual reported only for Acoma called "Shuratsha Lights The Fire" (White 1932: 94), held every five years under the sponsorship of the Corn ~ Maize clan (below). Features of the ceremony are comparable with Zuni rituals of the Boy Fire God & may also have ancient Mesoamerican parallels & sources.

The link between clans & rituals among the womanly Keres towns probably goes back to Chacoan greathouses. The importance of religion, even in the domain of kinship, cannot be overemphasized. It is in this strong light that the Chaco must be understood, not in terms of the amassing of goods & position, but rather in the acquisition & controlled sharing of *iyaanyi*. For example, Keres ancestors may have built the elaborate network of roads in order to direct enhanced power from the greathouses into their regional communities, mimicked by runners transversing these routes.

While Gladwin (1945: 65) noted practical reasons for continued use of the pithouse as kiva, he slighted religious concerns when writing of Red Mesa Phase:

---

[13] My analogy here is overseas Chinese sending money back to Hong Kong to lavishly renovate a family temple. Another was European towns devotely building of their own Gothic cathedral.

It would be very easy to say that the people lived in surface rooms all of the time & that pit-houses had now become kivas, but the question at once arises as to why a family (and the houses were rarely large enough to shelter more than a family) should want a kiva all to itself any more than a modern family should want a chapel next to the living room. To a people who had only recently emerged from subterranean dwellings, the old pit-houses (protokivas?) must have had a good deal to offer in the way of coziness & warmth on cold, stormy nights in winter.

In a culture where religion pervaded everything, the sacred / domestic dichotomy implied by Gladwin, just like the sacred / mundane one of Fritz, is not useful. Rather, the functional situation probably involved women & children occupying the rooms & men spending most of their time in the kiva chambers, as reported in early Spanish records & confirmed by separate male & female housings for much of Western America. In terms of modern America, the question of why a family would want a chapel nearby is of the same order as asking why a Anglo family would want a bank account, since both store accumulations needed for continued wellbeing. In short, aspects of gender & culture explain the Chacoan situation much better than do appeals to Euro-American tenets. Food & goods were accumulated, not for their own sake, but as outward manifestations of spiritual success, as with the Christian concept of grace. Further, Gladwin (1945: 152) argued that Chaco collapsed because too much time had been devoted to "gilding the lilies" of architecture & not enough to producing food. Carrying this idea further, elaborations of Great Kivas may imply a top-heavy priesthood more dependent on prayers & ceremonies than hard work to assure good crop returns.

Yet this distinction is meaningless in Pueblo culture since people are quite sure that both ritual & hard work together bring in good crops, but hard work alone is bound to fail. Labored control of knowledge accessed *iyaanyi* & thereby assured success. Since power, knowledge & life equate, these determining factors allowed talent & ability to be successful.

Pre Chaco

Chaco organically grew from Keresic distinctiveness as the Oshara tradition (Keresic for "sun") evolving from eastward migrating Archaic camps with an especially large central hearth that lead to integrative great kivas, to pithouses, often paired by walls of manly slabs or of womanly adobe, through arcs of stone rooms behind a pithouse ~ men's lodge ~ kiva that develop into greathouses & today's communal pueblos. Each & all of these groupings were ~ are inspired by sacred items ~ bundles, inherited through bloodlines within matriclans & via priesthood ~ cult ~ fraternity initiations conferring a perfect ear of corn as individual insignia, as well as group sacra such as left bear paws mittens, crystals & medicine bowls. These priestly leaders directed all social & religious activities, as well as population shifts into Chaco, up to Dolores River in the 800s & back to Chaco for the apogee.

As an aside, Al Hayes (1981: 58) observed

Great kivas had their origin in the distant past, but in Pueblo III, the circular firepit was pulled out of the floor & raised in the form of a rectangular masonry box & the earlier subfloor pits that flanked it were built as masonry vaults above the floor.

His brief mention of this transition belies the important cultural attitudes revealed by these actions.[14] Among Keres, buildings set into the ground were circular – in keeping with the consistent symbolism of Earth Mother, while those built above the ground were angular – appropriate for Father Sky & the manly Sun. Further, as sanctuaries were reflections of community solidarity, it was fitting that they have both manly (square vaults) & womanly attributes (round hearth) within an overall circular shape.

In some of the Chacoan great house ruins, there are both great kivas & tower kivas (circular great kivas built within a square room on an upper story). These different kivas were intended for the worship of & access to power associated with the earth spirits like the modern Maiyanyi in the case of sanctuaries & for that associated with sky ~ rain spirits (like the modern *Shiwana*) in the instance of tower kivas. This seems appropriate in terms of present Keres belief & practice. As such, this pattern is different from the kiva-tower combination in the Mesa

---

[14] The opposition of round / square is important among all Pueblos. For example, in Arizona, among Hopi ancestors, "in most areas of the state, round belowground dwelling structures were replaced by rectangular aboveground ones between A.D. 700 & 1000" (Martin & Plog 1973: 34). Charles Adams (1991) argued that square kivas became important in connection with the spread of the Katsina cult after AD 1300.

Verde, which suggests that immortals were being drawn from the air into the kiva much as modern Tewa shrines are sometimes called "airports" for spirits (Ortiz 1969: 24).

In addition to Chacoan sites, great kivas have also been found in the so-called Chacoan outliers, such as Aztec (Morris 1921-8), Salmon & Lowry ruins to the north or at Nutria & Cebolleta Mesa to the south. Presumably, these reflect town ~ community integration on a seasonal basis, with the Chacoan ones used predominantly in the winter & the others during Spring & Fall farming.

Regions	Slab Rings	Benches	Masonry
SW Colorado	Ackmen (81')	Cahone (43')	Lowry
NE Arizona	Brokn Flute	Juniper Cove	
Cibola (Zuni)	Whitewater (37')	Nutria	
Animas River		La Plata (63')	Aztec
Chaco	Shabik'eshee (40')		
	Salt Point		

Returning to Basketmaker sites, there are clearly many more pithouse villages than have been identified because their antiquity has meant that they have been silted over, built upon, or utterly destroyed by nature or man. What sets them apart, however, is evidence for ceremonial centers associated with an emerging class of priests. This situation was earlier suggested by Vivian (1959: 85), whose "incipient theocracy" was an

> Inference from the specialization in ecclesiastical architecture ... whether disregarding or taking into consideration the possibility of external influences from the Meso-American region, we see throughout the Chaco & Mesa Verde area that ... basic, town-dwelling, agricultural pattern with its religious emphasis upon agriculture, had become well established.

Vivian (1959: 85) hedged, however, by arguing that "such a theocracy never developed into an identifiable, priestly ruling class & that a priestly ruling class was not in evidence as such at the time of European contact." But he had in mind Pueblos like the Hopi, who are usually but erroneously regarded as egalitarian (Whitely 1988: 64-70). While priestly control of knowledge still constitutes the basis for ranking among the Hopi, who were never centralized, the modern Keres give every indication of an earlier period with an intertown theocracy that can still be glimpsed among the modern towns. Further, this hierarchy was not noted by Europeans because Catholic religious persecution warned the Pueblos to keep their priesthoods a closely-guarded secret for their own protection. Until the coherent, consistent duality in Keres culture was appreciated, logical intertown organization among Keres could not be understood.

While some inspiration & details for much of Puebloan agriculture & ritual came from the south, particularly Mexico, ancestral Keres probably met these influences not as pawns but as masters of their own fate. Internal consistency of Keres culture & its reflection in ancestral sites suggests that Mesoamerican features were integrated into the earlier patterns, rather than forcing a new one to be made of whole cloth. In short, the Keres as Oshara & later peoples controlled their own assimilation of foreign traits, rather than being dominated by them.

In the period before AD 1000, these traits filtered through the Mogollon, whose "great lodges" probably functioned as community buildings from AD 1 to 600. At its most distinctive, a great lodge was kidney (rounded D) shaped with a stepped entry ramp (Wheat 1955: 58), a form contrasting with slab rings. Further, the ramp itself may have been inverted by ancestral Keres to make it distinctively their own.

Unfortunately, the best example for this is Casa Rinconada, several hundred years later, where a buried walkway slopes up to emerge at the center of the floor. Assuming that this feature was a development from earlier examples during the intervening centuries, a comparison, therefore, can be drawn, especially in terms of Maiyanyi earth spirits, who are enticed into the kivas at certain times. The possibility, hence, is that the sloped entry into some Keresan sanctuaries deliberately reversed the entrance ramp of some Mogollon great lodges. The sanctuary passage sloped upward \ into the center, while the lodge ramp rose / toward the outer wall.

While each settlement probably had its religious leader(s) ~ family line of ritualists-curers, there were also large ceremonial gathering areas, the loci for various regional groups. Each of them had a slab enclosure that served to represent regional cohesion. As the symbolism of sky / earth, square / round, winter / summer & fire / water served the interests of integration within the total environment, so that of stone / clay & West / East helped to capture the integral differences within the human community. All of these oppositions, of course, were reflections of paramount Man / Woman categories, as can be seen in the construction & arrangement of Keres pithouses.

In the early days of Southwestern archaeology, Alfred Kidder referred to such habitations as "slabhouses," & thought they were a distinct tradition. Such insight into diversity was unusual since Kidder & others of his time recognized only a single umbrella ~ all-purpose Anasazi tradition. Here, inadvertently, he did identify a distinctive feature of ancestral Keres construction – the use of such sandstone slabs, as one side of an articulated contrast with use of adobe, clay, or mud. In the Basketmaker Period, such mud was usually mixed with wads of vegetive material, reaffirming its symbolic links with plants, women & softness.

In short, the use of stone slabs was an aspect of manly contexts, while that of clay & slabs was associated with womanly ones. Hence, slab rings as religious buildings were associated with men, while houses of stone & adobe were linked with families, particularly women as housekeepers.

Indeed, concern with gender was a prominent feature of ancestral Keresan architecture. In contrast to the saucer depressions of Mogollon & later Navajo Reservoir pithouses of ancestral Tanoans, the deeper Oshara pithouses had low partitions, often of standing stone slabs, called wing walls ~ radials, separating the quadrant between the door & hearth from the rest of the floor. Since grinding tools have been found in this section, it was female work area. In the rear of the house were stone-working debris & tools associated with men.

As the door often had an eastern exposure, women were located in the East & men in the West. Further, a hole is sometimes located in the west section of the floor. Now known as the _sipap^u_,[15] such an opening in modern kivas serves as a channel to the underworlds, the focus during rituals, offerings & prayers. Since pithouses became kiva chambers with this opening intact, direct continuity with the modern _sipap^u_ is indicated.[16]

Domestic activities gradually moved to the arc of rooms behind the pithouses, developing from the rows of storage cists of an earlier period. At Ackmen-Lowry, these arcs indeed ran East & West in slab / mud pairs, with the rooms entered through roof hatchways.

> The arrangement of these various kinds of rooms was as follows: a row of slab-lined rooms running East & West; to the south of them, a row of pole-and-mud-wall rooms; to the south of this double row of above-ground rooms, the pithouses (Martin 1939: 462).

Bullard (1962: 175) generalized from such sites to trace the evolution of pueblo multi-story architecture:

> The bringing together of slab lined storage rooms into arcs ~ rows behind the pithouses led to the development of surface architecture, so that by the end of Pueblo I true masonry multiroom surface structures were built.

---

[15] _Sipop_ or _shipap^u_ is one of the religious terms that the Hopi & other Pueblos borrowed from Keresic, with a capitol letter for the primordial underworld home, lower case for a kiva hole.

[16] Variations in _shipap^u_ shapes have not been studied. Keresans make deep, tunnel-like holes, while Tewa make broader, shallow basins, as appropriate for people who emerged from a lake.

Increased use of surface structures as dwellings led to a gradual shift in pithouse function from domestic house to ceremonial ~ communal chamber.

Thus, by the end of Pueblo I, the earlier gender spaces divided by wing walls became separate buildings. Such a transition to surface apartments stands apart from that noted by FHH Roberts (1930) for the Piedra district of Colorado, where pithouses with sloping walls were jammed together to form a connected block of rooms behind a single kiva.

These domestic units, according to Cordell (1979: 100), provided private space that allowed hoarding & limited access to produce, imposing inequality. Since Puebloan ranks are based on the control of knowledge, however, privacy is best achieved by leaving the community rather than retreating behind walls. Again, her argument is European rather than Puebloan.

As Paul Martin mentioned, not all of the rooms at his site had slab walls. Some were made of jacal, again, in keeping with the inclusivity of Woman, especially within domestic spaces. This attribute of the womanly, having the qualities of both genders, also appears in the pithouses within some (or all?) of ancestral Keres sites that seem to have been ceremonial centers. At these sites, at least, the roles of Inside & Outside Priests would have been passed down family lines, perhaps as stem kindreds or patrilines that stood in contrast to the localized matrilines in the households, linked into clans (Davenport 1959, Steward 1937, 1970, Service 1968). As each priesthood owned icons of great power, so too did important clans have fetishes handed down from its ancestors. Parsons (1968) regarded this fetish-house-clan linkage as a fundamental aspect of Puebloan society. When combined with the priesthoods, such a double descent system was a logical beginning for elaboration into that of modern Keres.

As a consequence of this, pithouses, at sites with great kivas (chart, p 26), seem to occur in pairs with one slab lined & the other plastered with adobe clay. Presumably, the first was the dwelling of the family of the Outside Priest & the latter that of the Inside Priest's wife & children. The actual situation was more complicated, of course, but their contrast is obvious. Future Basketmaker excavations, hopefully, will pay attention to this important but overlooked detail of intracommunity pithouse variation.

Unfortunately, if such variation was noticed, archaeologists typically assumed that it had only a practical function. Thus, Bullard (1962: 149-50) argued that slab lining served to reinforce weak walls or to hold back sandy soil. While this may have been the case occasionally, the consistent contrast between slab & clay as a feature of pithouse architecture implies meaning.

At Shabik'eshchee, the twenty-odd pithouses seem to represent two separate occupations with a break between them. Roughly half of the houses have wing walls, while the others lack any dividers. Similarly, about half have slabs along the walls, although Roberts (1929: 16) thought that all of them had been slab lined before some had their linings removed for reuse elsewhere. This deconstruction seems unlikely, however, because some walls had only a coating of clay plaster & no evidence of slabs ~ slab imprints. While pairs of slab & adobe pithouses could be listed by comparable size, shape, orientation & internal features,[17] such dualism would not be conclusive without better excavation records.

One clear example, however, shows definite pairing – Pithouse M, also called the double house (Roberts 1929: 49-52), since the structure had two hearths, two partitions & two deflectors. It was oriented southeast-northwest, with a slab deflector & entry on the southeast. The walls were lined with slabs, with an adobe partition near the door & a slab divider toward the west where a *sipap*[u] was located just in front of it toward the center of the room. The firepit, south of the door, "had small stone slabs covered with plaster for its interior facing .... The one at the north had been lined with plaster" (29: 51). Thus, the 19 x 16 foot room indicates a joint occupancy, with slab deflector, slab firepit & adobe radials near the door; *sipap*[u] toward the rear; & slab partitions & adobe hearth at the back. Each hearth group, therefore, combined slabs & adobe in different ways, with adobe more prominent toward the East & slabs emphasized toward the West. Pithouse M suggests expediency at the start of the reoccupation of the site.

Recently, at least two other canyon sites (#724 at AD 760-820, #1360 at AD 850-1030, especially AD 950-1010) have also indicated occupation by paired ~ double families (Vivian 1990: 158) like Shabik'eshchee. Since two women & three infants were buried on the floor of Pithouse B at Site 1360 (90: 199-202), matrilocal residence seemed likely. "Most of the stone & bone tools were on the bench & 75% of the pottery was on the bench or behind the wing walls, leaving the central floor area for living & [food] processing. Pottery behind the southern partition was primarily large-volume containers used for storage, whereas most vessels stored on the bench were smaller. Based on the diversity & quantity of the pottery (24 vessels), these presence of paired sets of decorated bowls, pitchers & ollas, almost equal sets of culinary vessels & some spatial distribution of paired vessels within the house [Peter] McKenna postulated that at least two families had occupied the structure" (90: 202).

---

[17] For example, Miller (1972: 48) pairs 16 of the pithouses dug by Roberts as Slabs: O, H, L, F-1, N, F, D / Adobe: I, E, K, B, Q, G, A, C, P); C & J were made of poles & branches; M is the double house discussed. Recently, two more pithouses (Y, Z) were excavated by Alden Hayes (c1973).

At Broken Flute Cave, the pithouses had radials made of mud foundations with a horizontal log or vertical slabs set along them. The front of many of the houses had eroded away, so complete construction details were lost. Of note at this site are two features. First, on the eastern side, was a slab ring "constructed of a single row of sandstone slabs set upright" (Morris 1980: 40). Second, directly across from it on the west was Pithouse 9 (80: 35) with walls coated with mud, a radial composed of mud & logs ending in slabs to the cliff edge & a deflector of pine slabs. This deflector, a feature of modern kivas, indicates a ritual significance for Pithouse 9, as do the number of wood & clay figurines found in its fill.

Incidentally, the significance of the deflector as a sign of a religious building recalls an argument between Edgar Hewett (1943: 222, 289) & Jesse Walter Fewkes. Hewett argued that the so-called deflector & ventilator shaft were really an altar & passageway. Fewkes, whose opinion gained currency with the support of Neil Judd, held that the shaft merely brought fresh air into the kiva, while the slab deflected it away from the fire. The evidence from Broken Flute Cave, however, suggests that Hewett was more correct culturally. Further, this interpretation has been confirmed by modern Keres priests who visited ruins & commented on these kiva features (Hoebel 1953).

Hewett spent his life in the Southwest paying careful attention to the natives of the past & the present, noting "the religion of the Pueblos, as of all their cultural relatives, rests on two basic ideas: namely, belief in the unity of life as manifested in all things & in the dual principle in all existence, fundamentally, male & female" (Hewett 1943: 74). Clearly, Hewett had been listening to some Keres, most likely during his excavation of Tyuonyi (43: 218-31, 1909), the important protohistoric Keres site in Rito de las Frijoles, now Bandelier National Monument.

In terms of the flow of *puwah*, the so-called ventilator shaft served to direct power down & through the kiva wall to the so-called deflector where they rested in this altar. As the different types of kivas developed, each performed a different function in terms of harnessing power.

For the Classic Pueblo III, two kiva types are well known. The so-called Chacoan kiva is round with a low, wide bench, a subfloor vent shaft, a slab deflector & a roof of cribbed logs forming a dome. The subfloor vent probably relates to the inverted ramp of the sanctuary, as the slab deflector also implies strong continuity from Oshara.

The Mesa Verdean kiva has a keyhole shape, six or more pilaster supports for the cribbed roof, a wall vent & a layered masonry deflector. It is not as obviously congruent with Keresan tradition & probably had Tanoan origins.

The best example for the use of slabs & plaster in paired pithouses is Whitewater Group 2 with its slab ring, slab lined cists & six pithouses (numbered 12, 13a, 13b, 14, 15, 16). Based on details of size & layout & superimpositions of later buildings over earlier ones, there are three pairs of pithouses at this site. The earliest pair is 13a & 14 as both were small & built over. Pair 12 & 13b were close in placement, size & orientation, although 12 was later remodeled by the addition of a bench, throwing into question its tree ring date of AD 844. Pithouse 13b was lined with slabs, but 12 had only a plastering of adobe. Pair 15 (with a date of AD 857) & 16 had nearby granaries, but those northwest of 15 were square & those beside 16 were oval. Appropriately, 15 had a plastered over stone slabs (Roberts 1939: 135), but in 16 "The walls of the main pit were not lined with slabs; they were simply covered with a thick coating of plaster" (39: 151). Thus, squares & slabs of 15 were manly; the ovals & clay of 16 were womanly.

This pairing of pithouses around a ceremonial slab ring suggests communal cooperation among priestly leaders. As Fox (1967: 165-185) reconstructed Keres kinship terminology, male relatives were distinguished by whether they were related through the father (-*mu* males) or through the mother (-*wa* males) (67: 171). Such terminology probably arose under conditions where paired pithouses & later block units were participating in marriage alliances over several generations.

"Good" families would have passed particular curing techniques, sponsored by an animal spirit, down patrilines. Thus, men of certain families became famous for their abilities to perform ancestral treatments. Given the animal patrons of the six directions & the combinations of songs, medicines & goals; a wide variety of shamanic techniques were available, providing the context for the development of the small kiva or chamber that became associated with particular priesthoods when these were formalized at settled villages &, later, institutionalized in the greathouses of Chaco canyon & the outliers. Over time, the ancient shamanism became "professionalized" as the priesthoods of the modern Pueblos.

In keeping with the exclusive dimension of the manly, these finer distinctions separated out males related through the father (also with the Outside Priest) from those males related through the mother & having womanly associations with the Tiamunyi Inside Priest. In all, slabs relate to the male sphere of religion, spirits, warfare & power, but slabs + plaster express community, economics & children. Buildings of jacal & adobe plaster seem to reflect the womanly in some more restricted female sense. As the inclusive category, however, Woman had no reason to distinguish different degrees of genders.

Of all female activities, ceramics probably has had the greatest bearing on archaeological research because it is both durable over time & sensitive to cultural fads & fluctuations. Here, too, the Oshara & ancestral Keresans set themselves apart from other contemporaries by the use of mineral & glaze paints & of the linebreak gap decorating the rim, both reflecting associations with women.

Again, this interpretation contradicts previous views in Southwestern archaeology, where it is assumed that the darker, harder & more lustrous mineral paint was always preferred, regardless of cultural preferences, so those people in areas without access to iron or lead had to make due with carbon paint, ignoring the possibility of trade to supply such minerals. In practice, the preparation was the same for both mineral & carbon paints (Hawley & Hawley 1938). A plant, often Rocky Mountain beeweed (tansy mustard at Hopi), is boiled down to a sludge to make the basic carbon paint. A pulverized ore, usually iron or manganese (lead for glazes), is added to the carbon base to make a mineral paint. Of the two, mineral paint more closely reflects the inclusive quality of Oshara-Keres womanhood, blending soft plant with hard ore. In modern Keres Pueblos, mineral paint is reinforced by the use of crushed stone as the clay temper. This addition was inconsistent over time, however, because affected by regional trade.

For example, Santa Ana was making sand-tempered Puname Polychrome in Pueblo IV when Sia was making a basalt-tempered version. Both used a hard material for temper, but the difference between sand & basalt was more important for intra-Keres town expressions than for intercultural differences.

More confusing, perhaps, was the use of carbon paint on much of modern Cochiti pottery, a very manly town likely to underplay the female associations with pottery. The reason, however, was historic.

First, very few local painted ceramics were made in Cochiti in the period 1700 to 1800. Most were imported from San Ildefonso, or made at Cochiti by Tewa potters in completely typical Tewa style. Second, whatever pottery was made by the Cochiti themselves during this period remained distinctly different from the contemporary Tewa wares (Harlow 1973: 46).

These Tewa were living among the Cochiti as refugees & as affines, so their women continued their own ceramic traditions while also profiting from their economic specialization as suppliers of pottery for the town. Once aware that women of another cultural tradition were involved, the situation at Cochiti confirms the association of Keres women with mineral paint & Tanoans with carbon styles. Incidentally, it also serves as a warning against assuming that only one cultural group occupied a site. As we know from the present, members of different pueblos are often surprisingly friendly with each other, visiting back & forth or living away from home for years at a time. This pattern is in no way unique to the present.

Another feature of pottery made by Keres women through the centuries is the addition of a painted line around the lip of a vessel except for a small gap ~ linebreak left between the two ends. While often interpreted as a symbolic opening for the passage of spirits or an escape for any misfortune associated with the pot or potter, "Of historic groups, until recently the Hopi used it consistently, as did the Zuni. It was standard at Keresan Acoma, Laguna, Zia, Santa Ana, Santo Domingo & Cochiti" (Chapman & Bruce Ellis 1951: 265). Further, Ellis followed Morris & Burgh (1941) in linking the gap to an ancient fertility cult, centering around the Basketmaker II burden basket & intensifying during Pueblo II in the Chaco-Gallup area. He quotes Zuni data from Frank Cushing to the effect that a closed line would snuff out the subtle source of life.

> The potency of the completed circle as a trap or a prison is widely believed in today in the Southwest ... Among the Keres & southern Tiwa the stick-scratched or cornmeal-traced circle is used to capture recruits for Koshari or Kurena societies, to guard the corral during the hunt, to imprison witches or renegades against tribal custom. The belief is recorded that if a man puts his hand into the mouth of a cooking pot while on a hunt he will become lost, always walking about in a circle ... At Santa Ana ... the break formerly was an intimate & personal affair to the potter, which had to do with the well-being of her family – its continuation & health (51: 274, internal references omitted).

As these examples illustrate, the closed form was a manly one, associated with male activities of hunting, protection, ritual & restraint. Actually, it is more often square than circular in this context. As the manly is a closed category, so the womanly is an open one, having its own characteristics, along with those of the manly to give it (her) completeness. It is in this sense, then, that the gap ~ linebreak is to be understood as Keresan. Once originated, however, like so much else that was Keres, it was adopted into other Pueblo cultural traditions by the Hopi, Zuni & Tanoans. Yet, like a word borrowed from another language but meaningful only in terms of its origins, the line break best makes sense for the Keres, who continue its use within their own logical system.

Keres show long & sustained progress among Oshara Keresan ancestors through a series of overlapping foci ~ nexi beginning with the central springs, larger hearths & cavernous gathering places of the San Jose & continuing through slab rings & masonry sanctuaries. Each nexus served to integrate larger senses of community. In addition, there were a series of internal differentiations expressing similarity & difference among humans as men & women, conceived of in the broadest possible terms within a humane universe. Among its expressions were the general oppositions of seasons, winter & summer camps related to animal hunting & plant gathering, together with the more specific ones of slab / clay & of West / East.

In each case, West & slabs were more delimited, while East & adobe clay were more variable ~ mixed, often including male traits. The prime motivation was increasing access to & control of *iyaanyi*. Presumably this is why the Oshara began to enclose spaces with slab rings, divide off the male & female activity areas in the pithouses &, later, move into small kiva chambers & surface room blocks, intensifying male access to power.

Kivas added ventilators & altar slabs to direct & retain some of the power attracted to them, together with clay & stone effigies kept there for the same purpose. Presumably, as sky & earth spirits, Shiwana & Maiyanyi were recognized as manly & womanly. Other strategies were devised for attracting their power into the plaza or a tower kiva. Chambers, derived from pithouses, served the specific purpose of housing ceremonies for the curing of internal & external diseases. These rites were family traditions passed down through sons, with those associated with the leading families including features of the others, much as Flint priests now undergo initiations into other priesthoods in addition to their own so as to know "all the secrets." Pervading all of these relationships is reverberating Man / Woman as the organizing principal of Keres culture, the echo that provided consistency, uniformity & continuity.

Post Chaco

In the light of Chacoan readjustment rather than a collapse, an orderly withdrawal best fits with evidence of continuity into modern Keres. Indeed, there is the distinct possibility that Keresans, having built up the canyon & enclosed the major ruins as D-shapes, assumed that Chaco would continue to serve as a huge transformer ~ power relay station for their continued wellbeing.

Towns ~ smaller kin groups seem to have left by two routes. The womanly towns went south & east, following the modern course of highway 66, as noted by Ellis (1950). The migrations of Santa Ana were particularly complicated, according to oral tradition (Ellis 1967: 41). They moved near Santa Fe & the Galisteo Basin before coming into the Rio Grande & noting the farming potential of the Bernalillo area, where they are now. Migrants split up, however, some settling Pa'ako in the Sandias & others living first near Sias & then Acomas. In time, these wanders came back to the east, joined with those from Pa'ako & founded today's Tamaya, along with farming colonies along the Rio Grande.

The manly towns went north across the San Juan River to the Animas River near Aztec Ruin, before clustering around Tyuonyi in the Rito de las Frijoles, still claimed & visited by Cochiti & its neighbors as an ancestral site.

The Rito duplicates Chaco in that it also is a canyon running East & West, filled with both smallhouse ruins & the great circular village of Tyuonyi, occupied between 1350-1450 (Hewett 1943: 218-31, Smiley, Stubbs & Bannister 1953). The circle of Tyuonyi, together with six similar ruins near Zuni (Spier 1917: 323-4,

Table XI) & *Tebugkihu* (Fire House) near Hopi (Mindeleff 1891: 57) suggest that priests leaving the Chaco fulfilled their ideal town plans. While these circles represent the womanliness of the town, such closed circles retain as much *iyaanyi* in their new locations as possible, analogous to the use of slab rings & sanctuary kivas. Significantly, Tyuonyi had only a long passageway through the East side to gain entrance to the plaza, allowing power to enter but not leave again because the western side was closed.

Oshara Keres returned to their earlier pattern of having religious leaders reside within the lay community, not separately as they had at Chaco. Intracommunity secrecy, so common today, must have then become strongly entrenched. Each priesthood had its separate chamber removed from the bustle of daily life, with the town oriented around its Inside & Outside Priests & East & West kivas, together with the off-limits office of the Inside Priest where esoteric rites were conducted in regular series for the benefit of all.

It was in this situation of priest & people sharing the same community that the laity came into their own with the adoption of the Katsina cult, influenced by Mesoamerican prototypes. Priesthoods continued the cult rituals of old, conducted in the seclusion of their chambers with an occasional night of public performance or curing in the kivas, while the laity had the more visible & public Katsina held in the plaza during the summer farming season &, perhaps, similar rites held in the community kivas during the winter. In time, Katsina eclipsed or blended with the *Shiwanna* cloud spirits of the sky, while the *Maiyanyi* earth spirits, if they included Animal Deities as well, were retained by the priesthoods for their special regard.

The story of the fight with the Katsina at White House may represent a consecration of this period. It is important that the fight ended with a compromise that allowed men to embody Katsina by wearing masks. If the Katsina cult reflects any Mesoamerican stimulus, then early Katsina could represent professional (*pochteca*) traders & other visitors. As legend makes clear, however, Keres met them on their own terms & from a position of relative strength. As Keres once pilgrimaged to Chaco for rituals, now the Katsina spirits visited from the West.

Settlement in the Rio Grande drainage brought a return of prosperity & relief from environmental stress so that the old preplanned communities with outer walls were abandoned for the modern lineal houseblocks built around open-ended plazas. Impetus for this must have arisen from anxiety by priests that they could not maintain the close regulation of thoughts, actions & sexual restraint required of laity & priests if rituals are to be effective. Hence, they focused their concern on discrete ritual enclosures, rather than unmanageable community at large.

When the Spanish arrived to stay in 1540, this pattern of internal secrecy & special chambers became accentuated by Inquisition & repression by Catholic clergy & Spanish soldiers. Traditions of the past moved, therefore, into less public circumstances. By the time of Spanish *entradas*, all of Keres towns were in their present locations, including Awatobi among the Hopi.

Only Laguna has been debated, since one reading of Spanish documents suggests it was founded by Rio Grande Keres refugees in 1699. This is unlikely because their dialect is close to Acoma Keresic (not a mixed amalgamation), Ellis (1959) has shown its in-place archaeological development & Fox (1967) has indicated the town's organizational stability, as does overall town context. Thus, 1699 probably dates the founding of its Catholic church, not Laguna itself.

In Pueblo IV, Keres shifted from mineral paint to glaze, following its development in the Little Colorado, among Keresan (possibly Awatobi) ancestors, where Katsina cult was also emerging. For several centuries, the Rio Grande Keres made & used glaze ware, but this mixture of stone (lead ore) & plant sludge was only a variant of Keresan paint styles. The East-West orientation continued, at least for ruins associated with town priests.

Near Cochiti, the Alfred Herrera site (LA 6455), occupied between 1400-1500 & using glaze wares, was built in two sections with adobe walls laid on cobble foundations. The east sector included a large kiva & the west one had two small, deep kivas, but there is no indication whether they were used at the same time or if one replaced the other (Lange 1968: 73-110). Appropriately enough, the site was named for a recent Cochiti leader, since the implications are that this site was a ceremonial center for a more dispersed ancestral Cochiti population.

The combination of stone / adobe continues in the walls of modern Keres homes built in old styles. Men still do the stone work & place the heavy timbers before the women build the adobe walls & plaster them (Parsons 1939: 38). At Cochiti, the lower portion of each wall is stone & the upper half is adobe (Lange 1968: 65), continuing a tradition several millennia old.

Summary

This, then, is a short summary of Oshara & Keres archaeology within the Anasazi tradition. As very ancient migrants from the Hokan area of eastern California, the Oshara entered the northern Southwest as strangers & (I suspect) their linguistic peculiarity set them off from the beginning, encouraging them to act defensively by instituting a more centralized organization than their neighbors. Initially, this was a leading family who had responsibility for the largest hearth in a San Jose camp & for group rituals in the largest available shelter.

Eventually, population increase coincided with farming & greater sedentarism. Leaders emerged as priests & natural sacred places were augmented by slab enclosures. Multiple ritual nexi ~ loci emerged until those in the centrally located Chaco took precedence. Here, full import of Man / Woman symbolism became expressed in terms of slab / clay, stone / plant, winter / summer, lineal / curved & West / East pairs. Chaco functioned as a sacred reserve, with the laity visiting for major winter ceremonials & as members of spring & fall work parties assisting resident priests & novices with construction projects & elaborate rituals. During summer, most people were living at their farming plots across the basin.

After Chaco, aspects of its ritual society were reestablished at various circular ruins in the larger region. Eventually, once power was again accessible & predictable, the community lost its outer perimeter as priests localized their concerns within manageable areas. Meanwhile, laity joined in ceremonialism by elaborating the Katsina cult & rephrasing the role of ancient deities.

This was the situation when Europeans arrived & it continues in a similar fashion into the present, with a marked increase in the need for self-protection through secrecy & exclusion.

Keres culture, as reflected from Oshara to later traditions, is a patterned totality; much more than a random assortment of traits & details at various times & places. Decisions to regard a site as Keresan rest on the same sorts of criteria as those for determining if a date is acceptable for a particular level or site. If a tree-ring, carbon 14, or archaeomagnetic date from a site is inconsistent with what is already known about its pottery, architecture, or lithics, as dated at other sites, that date will be rejected unless other reasons are found for its inconsistency. A date of 800 for a Classic Pueblo III ruin is impossible, unless its source is a reused timber or a slabhouse beneath.

Hence, total configuration has to be considered, not just a date, or only pottery, or only style of architecture. Our preceding discussion outlines those artifact developments that are consistent with the evolution of Keres culture, not as radical changes through time, but as permutations of the tension of Man / Woman so crucial for this culture & its member towns. If culture has a steady course through time, than Keres can claim a respectable antiquity, sanctified in memory.

Its consistent aspect has been centering the culture in terms of an overlapping series of relationships which expressing paramount concern with gender. Centralized authority that became fully realized in Chaco continues into the present as the theological control of each town, while the network of intertown relations seems to survive in ritual interaction & initiations, despite the lack of an obvious overall polity. Modern centralization appears most clearly not in the rituals or social structure, partially because data are slim, but rather in the study of Keres law (Hoebel 1969: 98, 115-6).

Keres influence beyond their own towns is reflected among other Pueblos & neighbors like the Navaho, Ute & Apache. Yet other Pueblos also had climaxes of their own. After Chaco, the next zone of cultural flowering was Mesa Verde in Colorado, which lacks Keresan diagnostics, although some Keres may have been living there as affines or ritualists. Mesa Verde was probably the Tewa center, favored by moisture & terrain for a few centuries, before its inhabitants moved down the Chama River into the Rio Grande.

After this, the next peak was in the Kayenta among some Hopi ancestors, influenced by resident & refugee Keres on Antelope Mesa who later lived at Awatobi & nearby towns. People drew in to the lower Black Mesa area because its seep springs guaranteed a water supply during the most arid years, allowing Hopi to develop their dry farming techniques. Hopi accepted all migrants into their area provided each could first prove they had a ritual for bringing rainfall. Once again, the basic explanation for all acts among the Pueblos, as elsewhere in Native America, was a paramount concern with religion, expressed through *puwah*. All else was tangential to this (Hewett 1943: xiii, 24):

Reviewing the literature of the Southwest, one is impressed with the substantial scientific & historical reports of the latter part of the last century, the more analytical though less convincing technical studies of recent times" [are, however, flawed because they failed to appreciate for Native America that] "The life thus evolved was preeminently aesthetic & religious, though these activities were so intimately organized with the industrial life & the social order that the result was a completely integrated culture.

CHACO CANYON =
KASHKACHRUTYA ~ WHITE HOUSE

While the Keresan Origin Saga is a complex statement about their existence, it also includes a historical sense that increases throughout the narrative. Beginning in *Shipop[u]* & the underworlds, people emerge & set about ordering life after the founding of White House. With *Shipop[u]* as precedent, the sequence of events in White House,[18] continuously fluctuating between prosperity & disaster, roughly correlates with the improved archaeological record from Chaco Canyon ~ mythic White House. Similarly, a coordinating dual leadership is suggested by John Gunn (1917) of Inside (*Hochaiyanyi*) & Outside (*Sahte Hochaiyanyi*) Priests, also called *naiya tsraikatsi* & *nahiya*.

Keresan religion, their premier institution, was bound up with the observance of particular natural cycles, such as those of stars, animals, crops & the span of human life. Overarching all these cycles, however, was the command to keep "'the universe moving' – the general & typical Pueblo concept of relatedness in the universe & reciprocity between man & nature," as Edward Dozier (1970: 153), Santa Clara anthropologist, expressed it so well.

While hunting, farming, curing & life cycle rites are held when needed but involve only concerned segments of the population, Momentum rites, by their very nature, involved the entire community in its most formalized guise under the control of its full complement of priesthoods.

According to the saga, the institutions begun at White House constituted a series of sacred centers from which customs built outward. First off, a kiva was built to remind everyone of *Shipop[u]*. Then the Town Priest ~ Tiamunyi was installed as a man in the guise of a woman. From this moment, more & more authority & power passed to males, from generic to specific. Hunt Chief was put in charge of the larger domain, then the Country ~ Outside Priest took office to guard the boundary between town & territory.

The priesthoods received their final form & took command of society while espousing the outward forms of prayer, fasting & nocturnal cures. Koshari & Kwirena coordinated all of the public social activities, along with a covert desire to prevent selfishness, greed, or other forms of witchcraft.

---

[18] Simon Ortiz (1994: 65, 72), Acoma poet, spells it *kashkahtruutih* & adds "And at Chaco, I've realized there is no past & no present … To the Acoma people & other Native Americans, time & place are linked, a sacred continuum in which human consciousness is inter dependent with creation & its process. From the beginning to the present, nothing is left out because the Pueblos insist the purpose of knowledge is to clarify & to demystify."

Men ultimately concentrated their authority after quarrelling with the women, whose positions became seriously eroded. By phrasing the argument in terms of the relative merits of crops versus meat ~ plant / animal, attention was deflected from the greater concern with cosmic harmony & momentum. That women retained great power is indicated by the monstrous offspring they continued to produce. That men successfully usurped power is shown by the birth & triumphs of the war Twins, who reset the balance of the world in terms of an asymmetry of genders in which Woman is unmarked & Man is marked. Since men & women met in different kivas, the implication is that there were paired great kivas or, alternatively, men met in a kiva in a greathouse, while women met in a Bc chamber. On the whole, paired great kivas seem more likely.

Of note, to still quarreling, men moved "across the river," perhaps the Chaco River itself, to thrive by themselves with sustenance from animals. If Chaco Canyon is White House, its ruins interlinked into a pan-Keresan network, then the idiom of the separation of men from women may mark the beginning of the greathouses as priestly retreats sustained not only by the meat of game animals but also by the transfers of *puwah* enabled by the animal patrons of these organizations. Another interpretation of the split between men & women is that it also marked the independence of the manly towns, separating clans from priesthoods, as distinct from an earlier shared womanly pattern attributing priestly offices to specific clans.

The return of the women represented the reintegration of the larger network to include seasonal & gender-related aspects. Town lands beyond Chaco Canyon were now a link between a priestly greathouse & a local administrative outlier, associated with women, domestic space & clan fields.

This integration was the context for the "constant solemnity & fasting" that characterized life at White House when the Twin brothers were vanquishing the monsters. Needless to say, such discipline probably coincided with the rise of a militaristic stance represented by the war Twins, who eventually had their excesses curbed for the benefit of all. By implication, defensive efforts increased in the interest of protecting trade goods & routes, along with an increasingly coercive centralization by the priests. Indeed, the renovation & expansion of Chacoan greathouses, a century after their founding, seem to correlate with the saga of Twin brothers ostracized during the saga's first half. Chacoan phenomenon was now set, including the final arrangement of monuments, both in the canyon & at outliers, along with roads, formal stairways, mounds, ramps & other earthworks (Sebastian 1992: 33). The addition of upper stories & sheer-sided outer walls as facades implied, also, an "elevation" in sanctity of the buildings.

Prosperous & content, the priests proposed a release for people in fun dances, games &, most decisively, gambling. Katsina were mocked not once, but twice, sending droughts both times. Such episodes directly related to the rainfall fluctuations so typical of the canyon, providing a mystical connection between Keres behavior, moisture, crops & deities.

As suggested by Sebastian's computer simulation (1992: 28, 30), four Pueblo I communities (near West Mesa, South Gap, Fajada Gap & upper Chaco Wash) began building the first greathouses (Peñasco Blanco, Pueblo Bonito, Una Vida, East Community) during a time of drought as a special plea for divine assistance. Their success with above average moisture patterns led to the renovations a century later, along with the additions of Alto & Pueblo del Arroyo. Indeed, then as now, the amount of rainfall at a pueblo spoke to its moral condition.

After the first mockery, Mother U left, creating death, accelerated by drought & famine, so that people could rejoin her in *Shipop*[u]. After the second mockery, fatal battle ensued so all decided that Katsina & Kopishtaiya now inhabit special masks. Since Keresans initiate into these masked cults during the summer, while the Momentum rites occurred during the winter, seasonal activity probably increased in Chaco canyon during the cold period.

Though never stated, it is important to realize that Katsina & other masks exist in two varieties, ordinary ones reassembled & repainted for each use & priest masks which remain intact between uses, although refurbished when necessary. Thus, even among deities, priestly leaders preceded other members. It is likely, therefore, that Keresan deities of great antiquity, older than the Mexican inspired Katsina cult, survive among these priestly masked beings. Not all Keresans agreed to initiation. These dissenters left White House & went south, presumably into Mexico, at least according to legend.

In this way the carefully managed centralized unity of Keresans began to crumble. Since everyone no longer "shared the same mind," priesthoods had to be on their guard to enforce general goodwill. But this very concentration & centralization doomed White House because it exposed everyone to the epidemic that scattered the survivors. This final disease, its cause unstated, disorganized White House & forced everyone to resume their migrations in search of the center of their world, where each town now resides.

The last of the special orders ~ priesthoods to be established was also the most human since *Opi* earned the right to be initiated by slaying an enemy. For it was then, at the end of their separate development as Keresans, that the former Chacoans had frequent & unregulated contact with other humans. Admittedly Chaco was the center of a vast trade system, but goods & services were exchanged on Keresan terms. Now, with the collapse of Chaco, Keresans met other Southwestern communities on a variety of terms.

During the early 1100s, part of the Chacoan theocracy seems to have shifted north to the vicinity of the Aztec ruin complex along the north side of the San Juan

River, the trunk into which Chaco Canyon drains. What is intriguing about this relocation is that it probably involved the manly towns & so represents another aspect of the split between men & women. Since this authority probably moved on to Tyuonyi in Frijoles Canyon, this prosperity & unity of the manly towns stands in marked contrast to the lesser coherence among the womanly towns.

While David Shaul (ms.) noted evidence of word borrowings by Hopi, Zuni & Pimans from Keresans, those terms referred to trade items & religious concepts, such as the Keresic term 'Katsina'. After Chaco, such contacts became more polymorphous, extending beyond the possible hostilities.

Moving out of their extensive homeland, Keresans moved east into the Rio Grande where Tanoans had long been resident. Complex interactions took place, not all of them peaceful. In other instances, however, Keres towns simply limited their movements to their outlying domain, abandoning their seasonal pattern of visits to or residence in a Chaco greathouse.

As with the various classes of masks, fascinating complexities in seasonal residence diversity are taken for granted by Keres & therefore remain oblivious to outsiders. During P II, at least, the number of "fieldhouses" increased, implying "a shift to a pattern of dual residence, with families occupying fieldside huts for part of the agricultural year & rejoining the rest of the family group at larger, more substantial house sites for the rest of the year" (Sebastian 92: 29). While this pattern continues, additional winter occupation or pilgrimaging to a greathouse in Chaco was unique to the time of the Chacoan phenomenon, providing an overarching unity for the Keres.

Indeed, while Sebastian argued inappropriately for either/or situations, the Keres genius did her one better by using all of the options. Thus, while she argued that mobility & flexibility were better adaptations to the arid Southwest than the social complexity developed at Chaco, Keresans were probably using both strategies. Moving among fieldhouses, small houses, outliers & greathouses – seasonally & spatially, the Keres remained mobile while integrating themselves into an overarching theological framework that offered practical solutions to their economic & political difficulties during environmental stresses.

Similarly, these multiple residences allowed Keresans to take advantage of two watering strategies to increase production, either land extensive or labor intensive. The former mode involves "planting in numerous physiographic settings to take advantage of natural water collection, water retention & frost-protection features," while the later utilized "construction, maintenance, monitoring & manipulation of facilities designed to capture & distribute runoff" (Sebastian 92: 100). This labor intensive system, more centralized & providing more surplus, dominated in Chaco, while both systems were used among the outliers, themselves positioned to be land extensive & provide supplies into the canyon towns.

Lastly, by keeping their population moving throughout their domain, with some people resident at each locale all year long, the Keres asserted ownership & control of their extensive territory, fostering their further unity because Keresans interacted almost exclusively with each other.

This is not to imply that there were no external contacts, far from it. While, however, the extent of Mesoamerican influence remains contested for Southwest prehistory, much indirect evidence indicates Mexican trade played an important role at Chaco, where chocolate was drunk from special beakers. Although the Kelleys (1975) overstated the case by suggesting that the population concentrations of Basketmaker III & Pueblo III were encouraged by resident *pochteca* (trading specialists), LeBlanc (1983: 161) correlated the demise of the Mimbres & Chaco with the 1130-50 rise of Casas Grandes, the trading center in northern Chihuahua.

Indeed, such far flung connections were well within the context played by Chaco as Keresan cosmological center & it is to their ritual requirement for keeping the universe moving, particularly, the Sun, that receives attention.

Turning the Sun

While the annual cycle marking the growth & harvesting of corn plays a central role in Puebloan religion, the esoteric rites of the priesthoods always took precedence. Of all these rituals & retreats, the most important ones were celebrated to turn the sun in November & February, before sunrise reached the extremes along the horizon. Presumably these solar momentum rites were once at the heart of the Chacoan system even as they remain the most crucial in modern Keresan towns.

These rites occur at two levels: esoteric involving all of the priesthoods in seclusion at the same time & public for all townspeople.

While these rites have been treated in general for each town, the most detailed account comes from Santo Domingo, as summarized by Leslie White (1935: 132-141). Unlike the other versions, however, Domingo all but ignores the central role played by the Tiamunyi & "her" office (_hotcanitsa_) in the planning & performance of these events. Later, the Acoma version, along with other rites, will expand discussion.

The timing for celebrations is based on solar observations, usually made by the cacique, to trace the movement of the sunrise along the horizon to the far "corners" of the eastern edge, according to Keresan view of the world as a cube. Goldfrank (1927: 60) best described these observations in terms of the cacique at Cochiti, who watched Nipple Mountain (presumably Tetilla Peak near Santa Fe).[19]

---

[19] Curiously, Lange (1968: 249) reported only that the cacique made "her" observations using holes

The associations of cardinal directions with sides of the body, defined when the sisters were first named (facing east), is confirmed by her report that the sun reached the right side of the peak before summer & the left side before winter. Since south is to the right & north to the left, the image of a human facing east provided the model for this association.

The November rite, the most elaborate, is called Southeast Corner (Keresic: *Haniko* = *hani-* = east, *-ko* = south; *Shuk'o* = corner) to move the sun from its southern limit at the December 21 solstice, sending it northward. The February version is called Northeast Corner (*Hanikikya* = *hani* = east, *kikya* = north; *Shuk'o*) & pulls the sun northward toward the solstice extreme of June 21. Since the role of humans is to keep the world functioning smoothly, these rites occur before the actual solstices so that the sun can have time to respond properly to these human petitions.

November at the Southeast Corner

The greater emphasis given to the Southeast Corner probably relates to its role as the empty cell (with the sisters U & N in the north squares & T in the southwest one) that was filled with all the life forms at creation. A Sia priest revealed that at the time of the Southeast rite, the sisters (called Mothers) & all their creations were meeting together at *mawakana gashdiyats kai* (underground(?) rainbow house), a giant cave at the southeastern corner of the world, which some elders equate, not surprisingly, with Carlsbad Caverns. Interestingly, this rite can not be held until the harvest is done & stored away, implying a connection between underground caves, storehouses & the special chambers of each priesthood.

At Domingo, the heads of the four priesthoods (Flint, Shikame, Boyakya, Giant) meet to coordinate their activities. In other towns, the head priests meet with the Tiamunyi in his office to schedule the event & to receive from "her" pieces of fresh deer meat, provided by the war captains, to be cooked for the feast held in each chamber. To prepare, the doctors must purify daily with emetics. Meeting in their separate chambers, for four mornings, all members vomit. Non-members also come to the chamber to purge, but they only stay briefly. At Cochiti, two fasting women assisted each priesthood during its retreat, foaming water to represent rain clouds.

After the fourth morning, each head priest (*nawai*) made the priesthood's dry painting in the middle rear of the chamber. During the afternoon, purging non-members brought turkey feathers to the chamber. All the priests were busy making

---

through the wall of the free standing *hotcanitsa*. When sunbeams touched certain places on the opposite wall or floor, rituals were scheduled.

miniature items to offer to the Sun. Weapons, animals, plants, crops & other wished-for items were carved of wood & placed in front of the sand painting. Each carving was a prayer for that item & its welfare. Anything could be represented. For example, a silversmith made a tiny hammer so he would produce attractive jewelry & have good sales. Lots of prayer feathers were also made, incorporating turkey plumes provided.

When the area in front of the painting was filled with miniatures, priests began assembling the **bundle** called Sun (*oshatsh*). A big Navaho rug was placed on the floor, a large buckskin was spread over it & covered with a fluffy layer of native unspun cotton. All of the tiny offerings were arranged on this cotton cloud, itself a prayer for rain. This cotton was shaped into a bag, wrapped with cord, a prayerstick was stuck into the top opening & the entire Sun was placed at the end of the line of cornmeal connecting the painting to the doorway. Then the priests swept up all the refuse, placed it in a basket & gave it to a girl to put into the river.

Women auxiliaries of priesthoods brought in food & all feasted. Non-member women went directly home & men bathed in the river along the way.

When only priests were present, each chamber set up its slat altar & identifying sand painting. That evening, non-members returned to the chamber to find a large cloth sheet or animal hide blocking the view of the altar. Women sat behind this sheet, out of view. Men brought bows & arrows to the doctors, who placed them in piles on each side of the painting. Food was brought in for feasting.

Then the priests sat in a line behind the altar & the head priest, in the middle, talked about the importance of what they were doing to move the sun. Then the priests sang, as *nawai* divided men & boys into two groups on either side of the meal road & allowed them to sing along. After several songs, men & boys retrieved their bows & arrows to dance standing up. Girls came from behind the sheet to dance with the Sun, holding it like a baby. Jokes kept the Sun happy.

After songs & dancing, two priests took the Sun outside & deposited it as an offering. Though unreported, it seems likely that each of the four Suns was placed in a shrine at the cardinal directions. Like a prayerstick, it was probably "planted", sanctifying the entire world. After the two doctors returned, *nawai* talked about benefits in the coming year before everyone was sent home.

To prepare for the duplicate rite performed by the "raw" ~ ordinary men of the town, war captain Masewi called a meeting in one of the kivas, scheduling the rite for the next evening. After men left, he met with the priesthoods.

All the next day, Turquoise men gathered in one house, Squash men in another, to practice songs, while the priests met in the *hotcanitsa*. In the afternoon, Masewi went to the practice houses to select "raw" men to play the parts of eight priests & four officers. These appointments had the added advantage of trying out a man in an office to which he might actually be selected a month later.

Something of a burlesque, as well as recalling the status inversions that were such an aspect of the Medieval Feast of Fools, the raw version also served as an exorcism of the town.

A separate house was used by the impersonators to "dress up" for their roles, using substitute materials such as corn husks for bear claws & rags for fur. At the same time, the real priests were dressing in the *hotcanitsa*.

About 8pm, everyone gathered in one of the kivas. Turquoise & Squash members sat separately with an open central aisle for dancers; Turquoise on east, Squash on west, with men & women sitting apart. The substitute Masewi talked about what the ceremony enabled. Turquoise members sang a song or two, followed by Squash doing the same.

Then Turquoise sang at the entrance of the procession of "real" priests, summoning the animal patrons of the six directions: Bear, Cougar, Wolf, Wild Cat, Eagle & Shrew. These men formed two lines down the aisle, one led by Masewi & the head Shikame, the other by Oyoyewi & the Flint *nawai*. They all growled like bears & wore a breech clout, an *Opi* kilt painted with a horned serpent, bear paws on their forearms & black face paint.[20] They danced while Squash sang for them. Using eagle wing feathers, they brushed away harmful influences, sometimes slashing the feathers around like sabers. Squash sang again as the priests filed outside, moved around the plaza to purify it, then returned to the cacique's office, changed clothes & returned to the kiva for all to sing & pray.

By this time, special dancers, under a lifetime vow, had entered the kiva, surrounded by "raw" teenagers serving as their attendants. These *Shpinyinyi* (referring to popped corn) wore pointed wooden (*tablita*) frames atop the head, black woven shirts with an elaborate "butterfly" made of flapping sticks & yarn on the back, a dancing kilt & white moccasins.[21] Each kiva had a set of these dancers, sung for, in alternation, until midnight.

At that time, together as one, the kivas sang in the priest impersonators, who danced down the aisle in two lines. The "raw" *nawai* ~ head priest made a speech about the intent of the ceremony, followed by a similar talk from the "raw" Masewi. Then the Squash sang these men out so they could change clothes.

Though unstated, the appearance of these impersonating priests & officers, after the real priests had exorcised the town, suggests that they were a kind of decoy to lure any lingering malevolence into the open so that the community could be made truly clean.

In the kiva, after these "raw" priests had left, Turquoise & Squash alternated singing while their dancers had the floor. They used only ancient songs described

---

[20] The warrior aspects of their dress added strength to their efforts while exorcising the town.

[21] Cf drawings (White 1935: 131, 137).

as simple, monotonous & filled with archaic (esoteric) words. At sunrise, two drums used by the kivas were brought together at the middle of the kiva while ten songs were sung.

Tiamunyi gave a final address about the good they had all done, then the head Shikame & Masewi repeated the same message. Led by the dancers & drummers, everyone left the kiva, washed in the river, went home & ate lunch since it was now about noon.

February at the Northeast Corner

For the Northeast ceremony, four priesthoods again held simultaneous retreats in their chambers, after four mornings of purging. Sand paintings, prayersticks & prayer feather bunches were made, but no tiny images. No "Sun" was assembled. Members & interested non-members feasted together at noon. The *nawai* never left his chamber, but everyone else washed in the river. Women washed their hair at home. That evening, people gathered in the four chambers to sing & dance until midnight. Then two priests took the prayer offerings outside & deposited them. After they returned to the chamber, everyone was given a drink of water from a pottery medicine bowl & priests drank last. The *nawai* gave a final speech & everyone went home, except the doctors who had to clean & tidy the up chamber before they could leave.

For the "raw" Northeast rite, Masewi called a meeting of all the men in one of the kivas to schedule the ceremony either for the next night or for four days hence. Immediately afterward, Masewi met with the priests in the same kiva to ask their participation. The next day, the priests assembled in the hotcanitsa to make offerings & the wife of Masewi brought them food.

In the evening, priests went into the kiva first & sat, as was their privilege, with their backs against the front of the "fog bench".[22] Then everyone else entered, Turquoise on east & Squash on west, men & women sitting separately.

Turquoise sang first, then Squash. When Turquoise sang again, the priests stood & danced in place. While Squash sang, priests sat down. When Turquoise sang, their special dancers entered, dancing back & forth down the aisle. Then Squash sang for their dancers. Kivas alternated singing & dancing for some time. At midnight, while Turquoise sang, everyone stood & danced in place. Then Squash sang while everyone continued dancing. Finally, the two drums came together in the center while everyone sang the same song.

---

[22] Sitting on the bench with back against the murals-painted wall allows *iyaanyi* to be absorbed; ordinarily only ritual vessels & sacra items reside on this bench, not humans.

At sunrise, dancing ended. Masewi talked about the sun & its motions & what they had done to keep these in balanced movement. Led out by the dancers, then drummers, everyone washed hands & faces in the river & went home.

Implications for Chaco

These double (quadruple) rites to turn the Sun can suggest the cosmological role played by Chaco Canyon for Keresan unity. As both private & public rites perpetuating world order, every Keresan would have been vitally concerned in their success. Since the four original greathouses began during a time of environmental stress, challenging both religion & economy because of the key role of maize & farming in Pueblo cosmology, these public monuments, like Gothic cathedrals, concentrated wishes, hopes & prayers of the Keres at locales where the theocracy could better control their own efforts & sincere public responses.

This religious fervor was greeted by succeeding years of better than average moisture, leading to the renovation of the older greathouses & of addition of others to the canyon & outliers to the hinterland. Roads, directing the flow of power and teams, enhanced these improvements.

The solemn retreats of the priesthoods in the small kivas ~ chambers would have consecrated the greathouses anew before the public "raw" rites drew everyone into the canyon & the greathouses brimmed with people dancing, feasting, praying & renewing the world as they knew it. The joking to please the Sun at priestly rites broadened into burlesque of priestly actions during the public rite. Humor must balance solemnity in the Pueblo view, much as sacred clowns of today will sometimes buffoon the Catholic mass, not in mockery but from a concern about preventing monolithic attitudes.

Purging, washing & drinking medicine water aided this renewal, from the person outward to the limits of the cosmos. Commonly known in native religions as "going to water," as in Creek Busks, these acts both flushed the system & sustained it for regrowth, like watering crops.

Coming just after the harvest, the November rite was the more important & drew the largest crowd of pilgrims. The February one, with the weather more uncertain, was more modest & probably less well attended, although many men may have wintered over in the greathouses, fasting & praying. While summer became the time for farming rites & masked dances, the winter, then as now, was a time for more quiet but intense reflection & planning to keep the Sun on track & the world in order. Yet, then as now, each town accomplished these feats in its own particular way, as illustrated by these elaborations at Acoma.

Periodic Rituals at Acoma

Estimates of 250 smashed pots per person every year for 60 years at Pueblo Alto bespeak the enormous size of "consumption events" in Chaco Canyon. Clearly, solar Momentum rituals, even held from 2 ~ 4 times a year, may not explain all of these broken vessels. Yet, looking again at the record adds to the complexity of these events, particularly at Acoma where elaborate & dramatic rites (White 1932a: 84-96) accompanied the Southeast solar rite, the battle with the Katsina & the fire & water pilgrimage.

Southeast Corner

Eight days before the Southeast turning, the Acoma Tiamunyi announced the rite & everyone purged during the initial four days. On the fifth day, all made prayersticks, while abstaining from salt, meat & sex, as priesthoods went into a four day retreat. On the sixth day, men planted their prayersticks in the fields & women threw theirs off the east edge of the mesa. Newly made moccasins, seeds, shrubs & live rabbits were collected. The seventh day, men who were to wear the masks of the Kopishtaiya made "bravery" prayersticks to strengthen themselves.

Boys, particularly if sickly, who had already been initiated into the secret of Katsina, prepared to take part in the coming ceremony. A father signaled this intention by taking a handful of corn meal to the head of his kiva, asking that a man be selected to "look out" for his son during the next morning. The boy visited that man, soon to wear a Kopishtaiya mask, to be instructed.

During the pre-dawn hours of the next day, these boys were taken outside & hidden in depressions & cracks along the east edge of the mesa. Boys were nude except for a flap of rabbit skin around the genitals & some feathers glued to the body. In the dark, each waited on a sheep pelt wrapped in a blanket.

When boys were settled, men who became Kopishtaiya painted their bodies & carried their masks away from the town to the east. As a group, they prayed, planted their prayersticks & put on the masks before scattering in pairs, singing war songs. Just before dawn, they turned & headed west toward Acoma.

Meanwhile, the Outside Priest roused the town to gather on the eastern edge to greet the visitors, who could be seen coming in two lines. By the time they were atop the mesa, each figure had a small fox skin bag filled with seeds, cattail fuzz, tiny trees, shrubs, cacti & other natural objects. Along the edge, each man passed the spot where the boy he looked after was hidden. With a flourish, the man cast tule fluff at the ground & reached down to extract a naked boy. Sometimes, they threw fluff & had live rabbits bound off from that spot. People who were sick, old, or weak came to the dancers to be fortified by having the afflicted place touched with the tip of a lightning stick.[23]

At dawn, all faced east & made a prayer offering of corn meal. *Kopishtaiya* wedged shrubs & plants into rock cracks & passed out seeds to be added by the family to those planted in the spring. When the east side was transformed into a bountiful land, dancers went to their own kivas, one of five, where they unmasked. *Tiamunyi* invited all the dancers to the main ~ East kiva for a breakfast of rabbit stew. Then everyone went back to the other kivas, staying for four nights & days.

On the morning of the arrival, the cacique, captains & priests gathered at the place on the mesa called Sun's House which marked the southernmost limit of the sunrise along the horizon. The priests were fully dressed in bear paws, carrying flint blades & eagle plumes. *Tiamunyi* buried a tiny suit of clothes (shirt, pantaloons, moccasins) for the Sun at this shrine.[24]

During the four day visit, masks rested on the kiva floor, where they were fed & smoked three times a day. Every night, masked men danced in the main kiva, sometimes also visiting the chambers of the priesthoods. Occasionally, kiva groups danced in the plaza, joined by other masked figures.

After four nights, the Outside Priest reminded the dancers that it was time to go home. Dancers gathered at the eastern edge of the mesa, wearing the raised masks slanted along the top of the head, above the face. All plants left standing along the edge were thrown over the side, clearing the area. Masks were removed, held in both hands & pushed upward & forward four times, releasing the spirit. All of the food fed to the masks, twelve times in five kivas, was also thrown away over the cliff. Each man drew four lines on the ground with a flint knife between the mask & himself, sealing off that spirit's passage.

Masks went back into the kivas, where each headman put them in a tiny room & plastered over the door for another year. The men who wore masks slept apart from their wives for the next 18 days. By then, routines returned to normal.

---

[23]   A lightning stick stretches & collapses like an accordion. One of these important items was found at Chetro Ketl (Vivian, Dodgen & Hartmann 1978: 110).

[24]   At Sia, the Sun's clothing was deerskin shirt, leggings & kilt, decorated with a painted snake & moccasins embroidered with yellow, red & turquoise beads. He held a bow, arrows, cougar skin quiver & a huge mask that hid his body (Stevenson 1894: 35).

As a low estimate, ten bowls of food at each meal (10 bowls x 3 meals x 4 days x 5 kivas) would produce 600 broken vessels, three each for 100 people at Pueblo Alto & that was just one phase of a major ceremony. Assuming several hundred pilgrims at the greathouse, the concentrated ceramic scatter can be accounted for by a single ritual of major importance lasting several days. In addition, other rites occurred at longer intervals.[25]

Katsina Battle

Every five years or so, usually early in the Spring, Acoma was ritually defended by the Antelope clan from an attack by Katsina, supposedly as a reminder of the fight between humans & Katsina at White House. Unlike that battle, however, at Acoma it was only Katsina who were killed, not humans. Presumably, this blood letting was another prayer for rain, saturating the ground. Conducted with great solemnity & ritual, the drama was dangerous because of the abundant weapons & anonymity of masked participants sometimes provided an arena for covert murder & personal revenge (White 1932a: 88-94).

Of note, the ceremony of the Antelope clan contrasts with another periodic event sponsored by the Corn clan. Also held every five years, this ceremony of lighting signal fires by *Shuratsha* (below), compliments the Katsina fight. In addition to the contrasting emphasis on meat or crops, these rituals emphasize the protective role of men or the nurturing tasks of women. Both involve set stops within the town, at barricade or bonfire, with Katsina present to threaten or entertain. As a result of both, Acoma is renewed & fortified.

Before the ritual attack, Inside & Outside priests met with kiva heads in the town kiva, announcing the enactment & asking each kiva to provide participants. Each kiva then met with its own members to recruit young men to personify Katsinas. Meanwhile Antelopes expanded their ranks by recruiting young men & women whom they had sponsored at Katsina initiations, acting as ritual godfathers for these young initiates. Some men must choose whether they will be Katsinas or Antelopes during the rite.[26]

The next morning, Outside ~ War priest announced a Katsina dance in eight days. Only those already recruited knew that this would not be typical.

---

[25] Comparison with other Pueblos also suggests dramatic incidents attractive to Chacoan pilgrims. At the Isleta solstice rite in December, the sun itself – described as round, white & blindingly bright while opening & closing – was twice "pulled down" into the kiva (Parsons 1932: 292), Cf Painting 41 (Parsons 1962: 95).

[26] By implication, a host clan could therefore recruit widely to perform its rituals, thus explaining how Chacoan greathouses "owned" by a clan could attract many diverse pilgrims.

During the preparations, intended Katsinas practiced running & jumping early in the morning & late in the evening, vomiting before each exercise. The fifth morning, each man made eight prayersticks in his own kiva. Meanwhile, one at a time, each intended Katsina entered a side room where the leader selected the mask to be worn. The man put it to the side & covered it with an identifying cloth so no one would know what mask he would wear.

The sixth day, every Katsina killed a sheep (anciently, a deer), saving the blood in a bowl, mixing it with tallow & corn meal & boiling it with the head to be eaten the next day. The blood from the heart sack was put into a length of intestines, to be worn under his mask around the neck. The mutton was used for the final feast.

Opi warriors prayed every morning & night to the directions & at each kiva niche. Antelopes prepared the defenses of the town. The governor appointed eight men to keep outsiders away from Acoma during the rite, a pair guarding the road in each direction.

At midnight leading into the eighth day, Katsinas left the town, bidding good-bye to their wives & mothers in case they never returned. Every man stopped at his own kiva to retrieve his own covered mask & went down the mesa toward the west, carrying a pair of new moccasins to wear with the mask, further obscuring his identity except, by mutual agreement, to brothers ~ trusted friends. Three miles from Acoma, they awaited daylight.

First to visit Acoma were two red Gomaiyawish & several friendly Katsina, who warned the war priest of the coming attack. Masewi & Oyoyewi, personified by Flint priests, also arrived in anticipation of the battle. The Twins met with officials in the town kiva. Then each brother, with a flint blade in the right hand & a bow in the left one, pressed these against the house corners to fortify the walls. Some Katsina did the same, while others gave children a calming herbal drink.

Two white Gomaiyawish scouts arrived to pretend that a normal dance would begin. Red & white scouts argued & scuffled about what really would happen until white scouts fled, putting the town on full alert.

Soon, these white Gomaiyawish returned again as spies, but were run off. Meanwhile, six men with this hereditary duty passed from father to son, set up a barricade, fourteen feet long & twelve feet high, on the west edge of the mesa. This barricade was called by the same term as the wooden slat altar of a priesthood.

White scouts came for the third time & red ones reported their threatening message that every Acoman would be killed. Red Gomaiyawish attacked the white ones & took away their moccasins. Fleeing back to _Wenimatsa_ (Katsina home), they hurled many dire threats.

Now all Acomans prepared for battle. Antelopes painted their bodies pink & faces reddish brown with micaceous highlights. Women painted their bodies & faces with yellow corn pollen. _Opi_ painted their faces like Masewi, white below the mouth & black over the face & took up flint knives.

Away from the mesa, the third return of white scouts signaled final preparations among the attacking Katsinas. Every man went off alone or with trusted companions to uncover his mask & put it on, along with different moccasins. The former moccasins were wrapped in cloth & hung from the belt holding up a breechcloth. Masked, all the Katsina came together & rushed toward Acoma. Coming to a deep chasm, they jumped across one at a time. Sometimes, a Katsina would fall & die, to be left until secret burial later.

Near the town, Katsina pulled up shrubs & brandished them, yelling the war cry. At the base of the mesa, Tiamunyi & other officers met them & replaced their heavy clubs with light, less dangerous weapons. While officials held the others off with prayer feathers, two Katsina went up the trail to the barricade, leaned their forearms & heads against it & prayed. After some time, officials returned to the mesa top & Katsinas rushed after them. Pausing once at the top of the trail, each Katsina then went to the barricade, prayed & struck it four times with his weapon. When all the Katsinas had done this, the six men & _Opi_ dismantled the barricade, moved it to the next station of seven & set it up again. Though the Katsinas were yelling & gesticulating, this movement of the barricade was solemn & stately.

At the third station, _Opi_ came around in front & cut the throats of some Katsinas, who bled from an intestine filled with sheep heart blood worn around his neck. (Four days before each intended Katsina had gone to a particular Opi member with a feather offering & stated the time & place for this blood letting, along with some means of recognition. That Katsina fell face down so the blood drained into the ground as a sacrifice to the earth & a prayer for saturating rain. After the blood drained, the war Twins came to each one & placed flints & bows at the head, shoulders, back & legs to revive him.

More throats were cut at the fourth station. At the seventh, white Gomaiyawish were bound & castrated. Blood flowed from a filled intestine in their breech cloth. Twins relieved some of their pain, but these scouts sat for some time rocking back & forth as the battle ended.

Boys came from the Antelope clan house with baskets filled with prayersticks. Also inside each basket was a cotton ball filled with beads. Every Antelope found his or her own bundle of four prayersticks tied into corn husks holding corn meal, gave it to a Katsina & they prayed together. A smudge fire was built on the west side of the mesa to call back the watchmen. All Katsina left, hostiles to the west & friendly ones to the other three directions. They did not return to store the masks until nightfall. The barricade was finally taken down &

each man took some of its parts home for storage until the next use. *Opi* went into the town kiva. Antelopes returned to their clan house to wash & dress.

Ritual chastity was an obligation for eight days before & after the fight. Acoma was quiet & sad for days while the bloody patches remained on the ground, but, in time, stains faded away.

Signal Fires

Every five years at midsummer, at the end of July, the Corn clan hosted a ceremony called "Shuratsha Lights The Fires" (White 1932a: 94-96) which emphasized the modalities of fire & water symbolism among the Keresans.

The rite was announced eight days before by the Corn clan headman at a meeting of members in their clan house. Then Outside Priest informed the town the next morning. The first four days everyone purged & prepared prayersticks & regalia. Corn members recruited boys & girls they had sponsored at Katsina initiations & practiced songs & dances every night in the clan house. Meat, salt & coitus were forbidden to the clanspeople. The day before the rite, masks & clothing were prepared. Some Corn men hunted rabbits to serve at the feast.

At midnight leading into the final day, sponsored boys went to nearby mountains & mesas, making wood piles. A pair waited in each direction, ready with a firedrill. Within Acoma, similar piles were also built, including one in front of the Corn clan house. During the eighth day, only small children could drink water, which was forbidden to everyone else.

Meanwhile seven Katsina personifiers, carrying masks, walked toward a spring some miles west of Acoma, led by *Shuratsha*, a naked ten year old boy.[27] Others were two other pairs of men & a blind son & his mother (though a man wore the mask). The head of the clan & other Corn men & women also went along. Half way to the spring, they built a camp where women & masks remained as men continued to the spring.

At dawn, two boys in the north ignited their fire. Then they moved west, building six fires along the way. When the west fire was lit, the other boys ignited their fires, as did the Katsinas at the spring. Then all converged on Acoma, building small fires along the way.

Before Katsinas left the spring, Shuratsha filled a pottery canteen with fresh water, lit the end of a cedarbark firebrand & carried it with a piece of charcoal. The canteen hung around his neck & down his back. When they reached the camp,

---

[27] Cf. <u>Shulawitsi</u>, the virgin boy Fire god of the Zuni, who appears at the world renewing Shalako ceremony where he leads the Council of the Gods in a re-creation of the Zuni emergence from their sacred salt lake.

Katsina put on masks & went to Acoma. Shuratsha also hung some dead rabbits on his back.

As they came into town, adult Katsinas danced at the foot of the mesa, at the top & at a series of stations. *Shuratsha* did not dance, but instead lit each wood pile until they reached the Corn house, where women came out & took inside the canteen, rabbits & charcoal. The dancers also entered to bathe, unmask & feast.

Outside Priest met with the Corn leader to receive the canteen & take it to the cacique. From "her," at the center, a few drops of this water were taken to every household & town reservoir & sprinkling prayers were made to each of the directions. Finally, Corn women took bits of the charcoal to every fireplace in Acoma. In this manner, fire & water, balanced elements of life, were sanctified & renewed for the pueblo & its world.

Since there are strong Zuni parallels to this rite, it might be suspected that Acoma borrowed the idea for the rite & made it their own. On the other hand, the Great North Road (Sofaer, Marshall & Sinclair 1989) into Chaco Canyon included a mound & elaborate stairway at Kutz Canyon & a signal fire station at El Faro & more than 20 other features "located on pinnacles, mesa tops & steep ridge slopes" (89: 370). Moreover, many of the roads lead not to ruins but to "pinnacles, springs, or lakes." The *Ashlislepah* Road from Peñasco Blanco to the northwest ends at a group of cisterns & now-evaporated Black Lake.

Chaco therefore was the likely source for both Acoma & Zuni versions.

Chaco, Kashkachrutya, Katsinas & Beyond

If Chaco Canyon is White House, emphasis on roads to the north, rather than west or another direction, confirms Keresan belief in emergence from *Shipop*[u] & subsequent migrations to the south & then, after several disasters, to other directions, particularly of late, to the east & Rio Grande.

Indeed, as this examination began with admiration of the Keresan Pueblos but disappointment with academic, specifically archaeological, theories as depersonalized, abstracted & reified, this speculation into Keres culture history serves, yet again, as a reminder that Pueblos, both ancient & modern, have much to teach about the meaning of culture, history & meaningful existence.

Recently, as a result of oil & gas exploiting on the Colorado Plateau, intensive archaeological efforts have been devoted to the surveying, mapping & testing of sites throughout the region. In particular, archaeologists have walked the terrain to inspect the roads & the ruins associated with the rise & demise of the Chaco. As an east-west canyon in the center of Keresan distribution, its location is symbolic, rather than economic or political, although archaeologists remain baffled about why Chaco is located where it is (Doyel 1992: 3). Nevertheless, interesting reevaluations of "Chaco phenomenon" have emerged.

First, the roads were not what they seemed. In fact, they may not even be roads because most could not have been used to transport logs & other bulky items very far.[28] PreChaco, in the 800s, roads linked huge Basketmaker III sites in southeast Utah (Gabriel 1991: 71, Windes & Ford 1992: 75).

Second, the ruins are much more complexly planned & constructed than had been suspected. Each greathouse was part of an entire "built ritual landscape" of mounds, stairways, processional paths & rings, shrines, ramps & earthen platforms. Chaco Canyon alone had 45 stairways (Gabriel 91: 185) &, to the south, Llave de la Mano, which may have begun about AD 450, had a massive earth & rubble temple-like platform, over twelve feet high, set against a cliff edge.

The amount of time & labor involved was enormous, adding further support to my supposition that all of these construction projects were a vital aspect of the religious training of young men (and women?) being initiated into the complex cult that supported Chaco Canyon & outliers. Clansmen who finished & received their "degree," before undertaking another session of training for a higher order, were entitled to build a clan greathouse in their own homelands.

In this sense, greathouses were every bit as significant as the "houses" (as in the House of Windsor, House of David & House of Medici) that dominate European feudal estates & empires. The difference with the Chaco "houses," however, was that they were "religious houses" rather than political ones. The motivation that encouraged people to undertake the labor & fulfill the roles was that of a postulant working to become a bishop, where material wealth followed from spiritual preparation, rather than the reverse. In this regard, membership in the Chaco system required more of a personal, physical, emotional & spiritual commitment than just working for compensation or building a home.

Among the important mechanisms for forging Keresan solidarity during the initiation of newer members into the Chaco phenomenon, the moving of logs to roof the buildings probably played a considerable role. While the ordeal of moving these trunks has not been detailed, a possible parallel for this activity may be the "log races" held by the Sherente in Brazil (Maybury-Lewis 1965: 85-88, photos 5, 13). Teams of men race to carry 200 pound palm logs into the village, shifting the burden from one runner's shoulder to the next to accomplish the task. The race was not competitive, but instead a gesture of fellowship & stamina very

---

[28] Among the Maya, the causeway (_sakbe_, "white road") "functioned principally as pathways for ceremonial processions & pilgrimages among related nobles. Such rituals were, in all the cases we have come across, political statements of obligation & responsibility" (Schele & Freidel 1990: 498, note 12). Cf #43

much in keeping with Pueblo ethos of serenity. Moreover, kickstick races between teams of young men would have benefited from available roadways.

The sequencing of greathouses in one place has been superbly studied in Manuelito Canyon (Fowler & Stein 1992), where the unbroken succession – before, during & after Chaco – consisted of *Kin Hocho'i* (AD 700-1150), *Ats'ee Nitass* (AD 1150-1250) & Big House ~ *Naat'a'ani Bikin* (AD 1250-1300). A "long row of slab houses & great kiva" occurred in the 800s, affirming the Keresan & slab link. Indeed, the hatchure designs so distinctive of Chacoan ceramics (Toll, Blinman & Wilson 1992: 151) also express this banding ~ layering so important in the Keresan cosmology of the underworlds. In Manuelito, some roads link to ancient ruins, suggesting a "time bridge" between present & past, facilitating the ritual pilgrim's return to ancestral sites still made by Keresan priests. Equally important, later sites seem to collapse the symbolism of localized elaborately built ruins into a single unity of place & time (Fowler & Stein 1992: 111).

Because so much was involved, elderly clan & priestly leaders probably lived in the greathouses & hosted the influxes of pilgrims attending public rituals. That the greathouses were occupied by married couples & families is indicated both by household artifacts & by continued use of kiva chambers to separate men from women. While Bc smallhouses were an organic outgrowths of the Southwest landscape, located wherever farming & resources were practical; established elders dwelt in the greathouses, where they were maintained by a regional community who cared for them physically in return for spiritual support. All of these people came together for scheduled rituals when flows of power were directed from Chaco to their own communities. That is why most roads are not continuous, but are best defined near a greathouse or shrine. Indeed, these avenues are not roads, but landing strips for this transmission of *iyaanyi* and athletic energies.

Yet power also had material manifestations, inhabiting either fetishes, effigies, images, shrines, emblems, or priests. Some of these probably followed along the route marked by roads at each end. Examples include tally sticks or knotted strings sent to each greathouse to count the days until the next major rite. During the spring, special sproutings of beans, as at the modern Hopi Puwamuya, could have been carried by runners from Chaco great kivas to local ones to sanctify spring plantings. Furthermore, snakes were probably carried over these roads & left in the rugged terrain where the roads noticeably fade out into the landscape. Since Hopi attribute their own Snake priesthoods to the Keres, as these song words support & several modern Keresan towns such as Sia, have active Snake priesthoods, a snake cult in the Chaco seems a strong possibility. In fact, personally running a handful of consecrated rattlesnakes beyond plazas into the countryside seems strong incentive for roads that are straight & smooth.

Like other communities throughout the Native Americas, Keres culture was & is based on intimate relationships with the landscape, particularly of men with animals & of women with plants. Clans took their names & identities from beings & places where ancestors had lived & interacted with the land. Similarly, priesthoods evolved from personal bonds between an ancestor & a spirit at a particular locale. Since the spirit was immortal but the human was not, the bond was passed on through later generations of males. The Pueblos, however, as a communal society, institutionalized this bond into a priesthood whose officials belonged to a patriline. With the shift from pithouse to kiva chamber during Late Basketmaker, many priesthoods were established in families. Presumably, men who married into a community also set up their own chambers to function as curers, rain makers, solar observers, star charters, crop enhancers, war magicians, spirit go-betweens, ritual managers & many other specialties. Over time, the most successful of these family cults coalesced into leading priesthoods among other elite families to create internal degrees, grades, or orders within the priesthood as a way of complicating the initiation process & expanding membership. These intermeshed priesthoods then & now oversaw Keresan social arrangements, eventually centering themselves in Chaco Canyon at the heart of Keresan distribution.

As a total cosmological system the "Chaco phenomenon" would have had seven levels based on relations with more & more of the land. At present, these full seven compass points are the four horizontal directions, two vertical ones & the center; that is, North, South, East, West, Up, Down & Center. During the apogee of Chaco, however, these seven levels became increasingly more inclusive. As modern Keres still provide labor, supplies & food for the Tiamunyi of their town, working & harvesting fields set aside for "her" family, so all Keresans probably once supplied food & other necessities to the priestly elite living in the Chaco greathouses. In return, the priests saw & see to the spiritual wellbeing of the town & its members.

As an approximation, from smallest to grandest, these territorial levels would have been a) the shrines & farmsteads at the fields, b) smallhouses of kin & in-laws c) chamber kivas of the local priesthood, d) great kivas of the local communities, e) Chacoan greathouse outliers where the ranking district clan & priests lived, f) Chaco Canyon greathouses community of clan & priestly elite & g) Chaco Core (particularly Pueblo Bonito & Chetro Ketl) where everything came together, including international relations with elites & traders from as far away as the Valley of Mexico & the Maya.[29]

---

[29] Keres-Mayan connections are suggested by the remarkable parallels between Kokopelli & Ek Chuah, the Maya god of merchants (Miller 1975).

This Keres system, thus, ranged from the local to the global under the management of priests who kept the calendar & arranged the flow of *puwah*, both along its natural course & by periodic ritual renewals & redirections. For example, Chaco may have observed the 52-year renewals of the world dictated by the Mesoamerican ritual calendar when the different timing systems coincided. Two 52-year cycles (104 years) would match various phrases seem to cover a century in the canyon. Some Chaco involvement in Mesoamerica (Weigand 1992) is suggested by the distribution of Cerrillos turquoise (found as manufacturing debris in many of the Chaco Canyon smallhouses) throughout Mexico, such as the sites (and states) of Guasave (Sinaloa), Las Cuevas & Zacoalco (Jalisco), Ixtlan del Rio (Nayarit), Casas Grandes (Chihuahua) & Maya sites (Yucatan).

By the time of Chaco, priests had formed an overall theology with a distribution of ranked spirits arranged over the landscape. Some remained local patrons, represented by stone & other images kept by clan households & priesthoods, while others had pan-Keresan significance, such as the Koshari who had primary responsibility for all the winter ceremonials. Overarching & interlinking all of these was Consciousness Deity (Thought Woman), who must have been directly linked with Bonito if not the downtown Core.[30]

The other paramount deity was the Sun, also linked with the Core. In its heyday, the core consisted of Bonito, Chetro Ketl & Pueblo del Arroyo. In terms of their shapes on the land, Bonito was a north half & Chetro Ketl a south half. Of particular note, based on its straight west wall, Arroyo was an east half, located west of the other two ruins. Presumably, there was no pueblo ruin on the east side so as not to obstruct the direct rays of the rising sun. As holy allies, Core towns probably relied on these new daily rays to empower their purposes.

As cosmic center, Chaco would have influenced all of the Anasazi & most particularly, Keresans. All avenues to power would have been welcomed so ancestors of other Pueblos probably acted within the Chacoan system & even maintained a smallhouse in the Canyon. Ethnographic evidence from modern Pueblos indicates the profound impact that Keresan priesthoods have had on all others, presumably during the Chacoan period.

What does seem to be limited to Keresans, however, was the great kiva, the Keres badge of community solidarity & membership, now as in the past. Since their modern-day equivalent is the paired town kiva wings, ancestral great kivas

---

[30] Bonito was so crucial to the overall global system that, after people left the canyon, Aztec West & Salmon have been described a "Bonito clones" at the center of the northern system (Stein & Lekson 1992: 91, Fowler & Stein 1992: 119). Moreover, "The La Plata, Animas & San Juan each have four great houses" (McKenna & Toll 1992: 134), suggestive of later San Felipe, Santo Domingo & Cochiti, along with a missing fourth manly town.

must have had seasonal associations based on winter use linked with the Chacoan global system or local summer congregations.

In the aftermath of Chaco, the global system unglued & drew inward, if not collapsed, into an arrangement of regional towns, each with two kivas & a population moving seasonally into farming colonies & farmsteads. Overall linkages provided by Chaco apparently now only exist among the priestly elites of these modern towns. Indeed, such priesthoods have always been involved in aspects of international cooperation. For example, during his visit to Zuni, the medicine maker of the Ant Priesthood exchanged sacred breaths with Edward Tylor, British founder of modern anthropology (Stevenson 1904: 211, note a).

In lieu of Chacoan integration for all Pueblos, another organization arose with wider popular appeal. This new integrator was the Katsina cult, which began to spread about AD 1300 from the Upper Little Colorado Valley, a border area between Anasazi & Mogollon that had also been on the edge of the "Chacoan phenomenon." Located between the Zuni, Keres, Hopi & Pimans, the Little Colorado was a fertile region for such a new cultural synthesis.

Charles Adams (1991), who has examined the archaeological evidence for Katsina cult, which he viewed as a replacement for the great kiva (91: 153), noted that like Puebloan society generally, Katsina are divided into priestly & ordinary grades, but priestly leaders appear only at the major rites &, presumably, their masks are worn by the priests themselves or with their sanction, thus enhancing ranks of both human & spirit elites.

The cult emerged along the Upper Little Colorado between 1275 & 1325, marked by the joint occurrence of Fourmile (glaze polychrome) pottery, open plazas separated by houseblocks, rectangular kivas & depictions of masks (1991: 83). Each of these traits began in other traditions. Thus, the enclosed plazas can be traced to the Salado of southern Arizona & the square kiva to the Mogollon. Secondary associations are duck (slipper) pot, piki (wafer bread) griddle, square medicine bowls with terraced sides & more trade of obsidian (91: 79).

Masks themselves had a long prehistory in the Southwest & Mexico. Body disguises with paint & costume are even older, as shown by the painted flayed human head skin found by Kidder & Guernsey (1919: 190-192) in Northeastern Arizona in a Basketmaker context. Modern Koshare painted in bands of black & white harken back to this practice. Basketry half masks, such as those worn by modern Katsina line dancers, are about a thousand years old. Only the cask helmet masks worn by modern Katsina & made of bison hide may originate in the cult.

The impetus for the rise of the cult was a 1275 population displacement of Anasazi from the Four Corners area of the Colorado Plateau moving south of the Mogollon Rim. To integrate these migrants into existing communities, the cult provided a common focus for cooperation between old & new villagers.

Over time, two other versions developed among the Hopi, about 1400 & among the Jornada Mogollon of the Lower Rio Grande, about 1450. The Hopi aspect emphasized rain making & spread to areas where moisture was precarious (1991: 142). The Jornada version had warfare ~ protective overtones.

Thus, at a time when populations were shifting & aggregating because of climate change or Ute & Athapaskan enemies moving into the region (91: 160), the Katsina cult provided a mechanism for integration. Of note, it arose in a former Chacoan area & received input from the Hopi region, where Keres lived on Antelope Mesa. Moreover, the very word Katsina is Keresic, strongly suggesting Keres were in the forefront of revitalizing Pueblos in the post-Chaco period.

By means of this cult, huge towns were formed of disparate peoples, allowing orderly transmission of land ownership & usage, safety in numbers, intermarriages & on-going stability (91: 149). In addition, while most Pueblos adopted the cult, except along the upper Rio Grande, town specializations were helped not hurt by this inter-town system (91: 159). Mutually interdependent towns, each with its own specialty, shared this common cult bond. Then as now, pueblo-specific types of pottery (bowls, jars, mugs), weavings, baskets, jewelry & ritual items were traded among far flung members.

The modern cult is distinguished by masks, group performance, plazas surrounded by occupied roomblocks, square kivas, line dances, rectangular designs, cloud terrace forms, depictions in rock art & kiva murals & general membership by all men (and sometimes also women) (91: 14). It fulfills a variety of community functions, like priesthoods, but on a more democratic basis. In particular, the cult is associated with clouds & rain, as well as curing, fertility, military strength & ancestors. Most importantly, while cult & priesthoods overlap in function to some extent, Katsina priests & leaders still reinforce Puebloan theocracies, defended by *Opi* warriors.

The other major work to suggest a link between Chaco & Animas (Aztec complex) is Stephen Lekson's The Chaco Meridian (1999: 71, 137, 160; 2015: 74, 131, 154), tracing transfer of regional authority from Chaco ~ AD 800-1125 (300y +) to Animas ~ AD 1110-1275 (165y), both in New Mexico, to Paquime Casas Grandes ~ AD 1250-1450 (200y) in Chihuahua, northern Mexico. Among their similarities are "colonnades, room-wide platforms, stone disk post foundations, platform mounds & tri-walls" in these "ceremonial cities," consisting of dispersed, distinctive building blocks & geoforms made of dirt, adobe & layered stone walls.

Thus, positioned along the same meridian are the complexes of Chaco, of Animas just to the north & of Paquime (Casas Grandes) far to the south. These relocations allowed for improved farming, from Chaco dry waffle field farming to Animas ditches to Paquime irrigation canals, as "The political prestige economy of Chaco & Aztec exploded into a mercantile economy at Paquime," especially in breeding & trading macaws. As Lekson (99: 50, 158) quips, it is a "case of macaws & effects," after "Aztec fell, like Chaco, because rainfall didn't."

Yet it is easier to observe the priesthood's proliferation of small kivas & *kihus* (chambers) at Chaco & Animas than at Paquime, where mounds, rooms, ballcourts & plazas nonetheless indicate important roles of priests & shamanic curers (Di Peso 1974 1: 223, 2: 574).

While the 1980s Chaco Project began with the hypothesis that apartment-like greathouses served as food banks for storing crops in a desert region of fluctuating rainfall & harsh weather conditions, excavations proved otherwise. Greathouses had only a few hearths indicating dwelling rooms & middens showed distinct thick layers of smashed pottery, marking huge periodic gatherings. Plazas had huge kitchens & cooking pits, presumably roasting maize, to feed periodic seasonal influxes of many pilgrims.

At Pueblo Bonito in downtown core Chaco, beautiful but problematic tall cylindrical jars with lugs were found in a single room cache of 192 (of 210 known) & Lekson (99: 97, 98) dubiously compares them to open ended hand drums at Paquime, assuming a dry hide drum when a "water drum", like that used in the Woodlands, is a better percussion analogy. That these jars were special containers seems assured, but of what? *Chayainyi* wear a left bear paw during cures & use more easily handheld rattles but not drums. The most likely jar contents, therefore, are dry herbs & other remedies sanctified by Chaco clergy. Anyone who has taken sacred soil from the shrine at Chimayo, New Mexico, or holy water from a Catholic church font understands the need for a closed container that remains spotless after use, though their wide mouths precludes long-term storage of liquids in this desert. Such speculations proved to be in error when a chemical residue analysis was finally done of these jars & chocolate was found, substantiating direct links with Mexico.

But these movers & shakers remain mute in Lekson's analysis, language locales & speech communities are ignored. Paquime is in a Uto-Aztecan region. Pilgrims were multilingual. Yet Chaco greathouses were Keresan, as Paris is French, despite a mix of worldwide peoples. In Great Kivas their priests conducted periodic, seasonal, astronomical, public rituals which, then as now, "keep the world moving" (Nabokov 2015: 476 #2; Aztecs famously fed it with sacrificial blood). Other Puebloans probably attended such rites hosted by Keres, especially renewing the world which all shared. At Chaco's heart, though, were private kivas of the priesthoods, caring for the dis-ease of patients & the cosmos.

Over time, Chacoan priesthoods entered other Pueblos via successful cures because, then as now, to be healed by a priesthood was to be initiated into it. Patients in need might be inlaws ~ pilgrims ~ desperate, yet once healed they received further instruction in songs & prayers in Keresic & formed the core of a new priesthood in another Pueblo. Such chains of initiation insured revivals, as needs arose, after a town's priesthood lapsed.

Surrounded by branches of Uto-Aztecan, along with the remarkable migration of Tanoans from south to north along the Rio Grande, Keres held their own because of respect (and fear) of their priesthoods (and enforcers). Indeed, the shift of the theocracy tradition that "perpetuated their power through architectural & landscape symbolism" (99: 141), but not population shifts, from Animas to Paquime may have been motivated by this Tanoan influx into the north, leading to Tewa climax at Mesa Verde. The sightline for the meridian was probably less on the ground & more in the sky, using some astronomical fixture overhead. To his credit, Lekson (99: 145) disagrees with Florence Hawley Ellis, my own revered professor, that the mythic _Kashkachrutiya_ ~ Keresic White House was not Mesa Verde or the Four Corners, but indeed Chaco itself & I concur.

Lekson & Cameron (1995) are particularly insightful on the reoccupations of the greathouses that changed them from monastic centers into today's all too familiar Pueblo-style apartments, repurposing instead of reoccupying

Most remarkable of all are the Pueblo I sites along the Dolores River, abandoned over a thousand years ago after sacrificing obviously engendered couples. This coherent Keresan population occupied secular villages on the east, while "four western villages – McPhee, Cline Crest, Windy Ruin & 5 MT10-12 – are consistently horseshoe shaped to enclose plazas on three sides" & enable public ceremonies for priesthoods (Wilshusen & Ortman 1999: 383, 386-7).

> McPhee had several group burials with evidence of violent death, as well as a striking pattern in the abandonment of pit structures. Three distinct classes of pit [387] structures have been identified at McPhee on the basis of associated ritual features & pit structures at each level of this hierarchy were abandoned in different ways. The most ritually important community pit structures were intentionally burned, secondary ritual pit structures were abandoned with their roofs intentionally collapsed on paired (male & female) adult burials on the pit structure floor & pit structures that exhibit little evidence of use in community ritual were left to fall down on their own.

Abandoning Dolores villages coincided with regrowth of villages in Chaco, strengthening its rise as the premier religious center of its time, with echoings that continue to this very day.

While lines are balanced by curves, circles seem to be ideal for towns since it allows free flow of _puwah_, since corners can trap both good & evil. Chaco town plans are quadrant arcs & half circles, using its direction to help define its role in the culture.

World Renewal, especially corn ceremonialism, probably brought people into Chaco because these rites are public & celebratory, featuring lines of dancing families under the waving of long pole wrapped in men's clothing. Roadways served as race courses, particularly for kickstick games between teams, one kicking a male billet & the other a female one. Other games, perhaps log running, also used these routes.

Of more serious concern, moreover, were priestly Momentum rites to assure continued motion ~ movement of the world, alternating "raw" public & "ripe" private sessions. Examples reviewed herein are Domingo's Turning the Sun: 1) at Southeast Corner in November with its bundled cotton cloud filled with wishful effigies & alternating Turquoise ~ Squash moieties; 2) at Northeast Corner in February with feasts, dry paintings, prayer feathers & alternating singing by moieties.

More dramatic are Acoma rites, also at the Southeast & Northeast. Most inspired by Chaco echos are Signal Fires, sponsored by Corn clan & Katsina Battle, sponsored by Antelope clan, with it blood drenched aftermath. *Opi*, especially fierce priestly warriors ~ hunters, enforced order. Special poles, stone knives, masks & crystals all feature as near universal aspects of human ritual.

Today, post Chaco Katsinas dominate public ceremonies among Pueblos & priestly guilds, with tiny memberships, continue to meet, pray, cure & "keep the world moving".

Since religion was~is the dominant institution of the Pueblos, Keresans could have had no greater impact than they clearly did because their contribution to Anasazi tradition was esoteric priesthoods with internal degrees ~ ranks ~ grades, the most crucial of all Puebloan – & Keresan – institutions.

Cahokia & Mississippians

Across the Americas, a major reason for earth moving was the construction of mounds (inversely, of ubiquitous storage ~ cache pits). Best known as the abodes for Adena burials & Mississippian temples, related monuments include Anasazi Pueblo gateways, Tsimshian fort emplacements & shaped effigies throughout the upper Midwest. Regardless of intent, congruent form was always a significant consideration. The difference between Adena cones, Hopewell ramparts & Mississippian sloping blocks probably reflects beliefs about geometries of their worlds.[31] Moreover, throughout the East, mounds were believed to be chambered & occupied by spirits & the dead. Artificially constructed, mounds were built equivalents of a "holy home" inside hollow (hallowed) hills where a particular infrahuman species lived or met, as with the Pawnee animal lodges.[32]

A Timeline for the East, in terms of years ago for Early, Middle & Late periods, follows:

Historic 300 >
Mississippian 1200 > 270
Woodland E >2,000 M > 1,500 L > 500
Archaic E > 7,000 M > 5,000 L > 3,500
PaleoIndien ? > 9,000

Once thought to arise (literally) a thousand years ago, earliest dating of square mounds has now doubled into the Early Archaic. "Platforms imply hierarchy" both in the labor needed to construct them & in the disparity between those a step above or below.[33] They also imply deliberate planting, but not because fields have to be square. Rather, once people were no longer commuting among distant camps & regenerating plant parts in the ground, they placed them in lines or rows for convenience of caretaking. In the Southwest, Pueblo farmers spiral their rows out from the center of a field, to boundaries marked by stones buried at the corners. In the Southeast, however, where water was more abundant, these rows stretched along river & stream terraces, creating squarish plots. Unlike European

---

[31] There is also a sense that mounds mimic body parts, with domes suggesting a skull & blocks suggesting a torso or chest.

[32] Vernon Knight, Symbolism of Mississippian Mounds 1989.

[33] Roger Kennedy, Hidden Cities ~ The Discovery & Loss of Ancient North American Civilization 1994: 67.

broadcasting of seeds, natives treated each one respectfully. The result was separated hillocks of corn, beans & squash, in even numbers since they were equated with the breasts of Corn Mother. Such doubling of twos & fours also produced squares by basic principles of geometry.[34] Similarly, because plants "rest" in the ground until they sprout, these fields are like beds, evoking both the English term "flower beds" & the Creek term (*topv* 'bed')[35] for the arbors set around the sides of a square ground.

All these mounds, domed or platform, served as centering tysics ~ time space centers for dispersed populations. Indeed, since the dead were the only fixed & sure residents of a district, burial mounds provided claim deeds passed through ancestral bloodlines. Though many of these genetic links did not survive European epidemics, likely ethnic continuities can be traced between archaeological sites & modern day entities. While archaeologists have been reluctant to do so in much of the continent, given huge regional displacements; those in the Southeast do so enthusiastically. Their advantage, of course, was that many desperate people took refuge among a few historic native confederacies which coalesced after the collapse of chiefdoms & traumas of disease & slavers.

Thus, HoChunks ~ Winnebagos, whose Chiwere Siouan ancestors were among those who built Effigy mounds, were at the northern limit of the Mississippian tradition of chiefdoms & cult of the dead, while others, like Osage & Caddo, were mainstays in the US heartland. In the aftermath of the Mississippian collapse, other confederacies, such as those of the Huron & Iroquois of the Northeast or Creeks of the Southeast, represent regroupings of survivors who had lived around the former intertribal borders.

While Mississippians were obviously multitribal ~ multiethnic, Cahokia as paramount nerve center seems to have been more centralized, hierarchical & given to human ~ retainer sacrifice, with militarized enforcers, as vividly depicted by the sculpture of an armed ~ armored warrior in the act of decapitating a naked foe ~ rival.[36] Probably facilitated by shared Mobilian Jargon among Southeast Mississippians, Cahokia most probably relied on its own specific languages, most likely Dhegiha Siouian, though related Mandan with their spectacularly cosmic Okipa (See last section) renewal initiation would have made a significant contribution too.

---

[34] While there are many small sites with only a single mound, there is a sense that a ceremonial center had three mounds – consisting of a big & a small platform along with a rounded conical – identified, by tradition, as A, B & C.

[35] Varied, less technical spellings for 'bed' include *dubba*.

[36] Osage war imagry of knife "cutting" emphasized decapitation (LaFleshe 1939: 16, Bailey 1995: 137).

After Mississippian chiefdoms, radical changes were devised. Previously, the heads of clans probably met inside temples atop mounds. After severe depopulation, beginning with Spanish-introduced diseases & British slaving to supply Caribbean plantations, communal labor force became difficult to muster. Mounds could no longer be built according to complex ritual requirements & few leading families survived to direct work & worship, yet their obvious surviving bulk provided reassuring ballast, hoped-for blessings & reserves of vitality during tumultuous times.

Ritual came down from the heights, onto the ground of the town & focused around the town fire. The open, public plaza replaced the private temple atop the mound, though some councils & elites retreated into rotunda ("hothouses"). Instead of ranked seats in the temple, men sat according to their clans in sunshades on the four sides of a town square. Senior men were in front & youngsters at the back of each 'bed'. Images depicting each clan were painted over the front of its section. Town treasures were kept in a small room behind the west arbor where the town chief sat, facing the sunrise. The sacred fire burned at the plaza center, an intense symbol of the "purity" & vigor of the town & an avatar of the Sun. In large multi-clan towns, these four seating areas were built like stepped bleachers. Sometimes, covered walkways & arbors formed a stadium around the plaza, with passages at the corners.

Ceremonies honoring ancestral elite & ceremonial (enforcing not defensive) war ended & sequential rites marking the stages of the agricultural year became more important. In the past, six month names were doubled to fill out one year, once in summer & then repeated again for winter. These months were duplicated in each half, making up the entire year, just as each town had two moieties to make the whole. This duality lapsed when European calendars of twelve continuous months was imposed by church & state.

Four times during the summer, gatherings celebrated stages of ripening crops, culminating with the Busk ~ Green Corn ceremony just before the harvest to mark the New Year, dividing the twin (half) month year. Towns gathered to fast, pray & dance while the corn was yet alive in their fields. The final rite was held in the fall (around Halloween) when animal-masked dancers consecrated the economic shift from farming to hunting.[37] During the winter half, some towns met in a huge domed rotunda, often called a hothouse, for indoor gatherings & ceremonies, until these too became too difficult to repair or build by survivors (Miller 2015: 94), though memory of them survives among today's Creek

---

[37] John Swanton, Religious Beliefs & Medical Practices of the Creek Indians 1928b: 556 {old men's dance}.

ceremonialists, especially whenever they participate in Cherokee outdoor winter dances.

Cahokia Hub

Coinciding with a rare supernova that appeared brightly on 4 July 1054, then continued day & night for weeks, the homes & yards of Old Cahokia were removed & replaced by prefabricated houses & a 50-acre plaza, specially leveled & drained. The result was a "new city of black-earth pyramids, red cedar walls, cypress uprights, yellow thatched roofs & fragrantly burning tobacco along the Mississippi River in the heart of North America".[38] After this "Big Bang", New Cahokia became the hub of a religious network fostering trade, gifts (tribute?) & sports, especially the competition known as chunkey.[39] It became the capitol of "Mississippian culture … based on beliefs about ancestors, the stars, maize agriculture & powerful male & female characters [such as] earth & sky gods, including the Morning & Evening stars".[40]

Like the Keres AD 900 priestly power shift from Dolores back to Chaco, Cahokia blossomed as Toltec (below p74, Toltec Module) in Arkansas faded about AD 1050, after they had pioneered the use of mound tops for public rituals & feasts, thereby opening a way for leaders to build their homes atop such elevations to insert themselves between earth, sky & congregations.

Mounds, built of alternating layers of light or dark clay, were covered by light-colored sand & a final topping of dark (brownish black) clay. Excavations into the mounds at Emerald, Kunnemann, Horseshoe Lake, Red (#49) & East St. Louis also indicate alternating light & dark, sandy & clayey fills, some of which appear "engineered".[41] Mound numbers varied with the importance of the location, one for a minor shrine, many for a center. These pyramids served as "elevated stages for special community ceremonies, ritual performances & feasts probably hosted but not 'owned' by high-ranked leaders".[42] Diplomacy was

---

[38] Timothy Pauketat, <u>Cahokia</u> 2009: 9.

[39] Chunkey stones are polished disks with concave sides, distinguished by width & depth of these depressions as Jersey Bluff, Salt River, Prairie Du Point, Cahokia & Bradley, which is more like a hockey puck (DeBoer 1993: 88). They were owned by towns not by players.

[40] Timothy Pauketat, <u>Cahokia</u> 2009: 8.

[41] Timothy Pauketat & Susan Alt, Mounds, Memory & Contested Mississippian History 2003: 165.

[42] Timothy Pauketat, <u>Cahokia</u> 2009: 18, 22.

enhanced by these feasts, as well as gifts such as male effigies[43] sent far away, in contrast to female ones kept in local temples to encourage local crops.

Building projects, renovations & adjustments only ceased at the 1450 CE demise of this city, leaving an empty quarter along the entire middle Mississippi River. At its height, elites were mobilized by fine-tuning mounds, meetings & manufacturing, especially art works; while growing maize & other crops occupied the daily life of most other families. Diplomatic gifts featured reddish flintclay figurines, special flint Ramey knives, long-nosed human faces fashioned in shell or copper to be worn as earrings & Cahokia style slim chunkey rollers made of stone quarried at Thebes Gap, 130 miles downriver on the Mississippi, where a petroglyph map indicated a Falcon city upriver.

Chunkey spread with the expansion of Cahokia's influence, keeping its soldier ~ enforcers fit. Javelins were thrown at this disk as it rolled along a prepared runway marked by tiny mounds at each end. In the genesis epic known as Earth Diver, a speck of dirt expands to become tribal homeland, stretching outward by magical means, varying from special songs to propulsion devices like chunkey rollers & javelins to pin down earth's outer limits. Furthermore, the insertion of rod into hoop & post into ground are universally regarded as sexual consummations, with symbolic & practical consequences in terms of fertility.

Farming & specialized towns filled surrounding bottomlands, with mortuary zones along the bluffs where scaffolds exposed burials that, with decomposition, were successively bundled & retained in charnel temples until buried in an eventual mound. Some settlements were composed of migrants from far away, living more like peasants on meager diets of too much maize & dogs, "small lizards, frogs, snakes, turtles & rodents" than those rich diets of the lords resident at the downtown core.

All communities had a center post at their heart, serving as their integrative axis & focus. The post & its shadows served to mark the vital passage of time & seasons, while also representing key personages for that locality. A likely parallel is the Northwest totem pole, where this column, along with the spine (backbone) of the acknowledged leader, serves as the conduit for bringing life-force into the community, clan & its lands.[44]

More important neighborhoods also included at least one mound. But, in contrast to the clay core mounds of downtown Cahokia, "other mounds clearly

---

[43] Thomas Emerson, Mississippian Stone Images in Illinois, Illinois Archaeological Survey, Circular 6 1982.

[44] The symbolic importance of the spinal column as a channel of vitality in human ritual & belief has been slighted, though it is a nod to our biological status as vertebrates. It appears for the San in Africa to Tsimshian & other First Nations of the Northwest Coast.

began as mere lenses of fill beneath important buildings ... the earliest "stages" of a particular platform were sometimes only a few centimeters high. These blanket mantles probably would not have been visible from a distance ... several blanket mantles or stage enlargements later, the shape of a platform may have finally become evident. However, it seems reasonable that in these cases, an imposing mound was not the goal of mound construction. Possibly, the goal of construction in these cases was continuous construction itself (and all that this entailed). Presumably, the greater the frequency of communal construction, the greater the integrative effects on a disparate population".[45] Indeed, such continued activity translated into increased vitality for the mound.

At Cahokia & its allied mound centers, mound shapes served many functions. Those with ridgetops along boundaries were repositories of offerings, honored families (royalty) & carnage that included dozens of sacrificed people, mostly young women. At the center of Mound 72, a pair of reversed males bracketed a huge cape shaped like a falcon & covered in 20,000 shell beads. The top man faced up, while the lower one, reversed & off 10 degrees, had his feet under the skull above, faced down onto a layer of animal skins. Nearby were almost 200 skeletons arrayed in separate pits, one including splayed men & chunkey equipment. At the Wilson ~ Junkyard ridgetop mound, filled with females, the central burials were three women – pregnant, with newborn & with child & dog. Though also serving as boundary markers for the town core, these ridgetops emphasized both gender & generation, since they were built every twenty years over a span of 150 years.

Binding these congregations together was a communion in the form of massive meals, especially at the main plaza, where "feasts that took place over the course of a few days would have involved killing, butchering & carting in as many as thirty-nine hundred deer, the use of up to seventy-nine hundred pots & enough smoking tobacco to produce more than a million charred tobacco seeds".[46]

For Cahokia, political "theater [enhancing legitimacy & authority] seemed to take the form of a grand & repetitive retelling of the age-old story of human creation through festivals, chunkey matches & mortuary rites".[47]

Above all, Cahokia & other Mississippians relied on communal expressions, with priesthoods both instructing & intimidating the faithful toward the proper route into the afterlife. Humans were sacrificed for the greater good of all. For the elite, mortality led to a long complicated process involving upland scaffolds,

---

[45] Timothy Pauketat & Susan Alt, Mounds, Memory & Contested Mississippian History 2003: 165.

[46] Timothy Pauketat, Cahokia 2009: 109.

[47] Timothy Pauketat, Cahokia 2009: 111.

cleaning of flesh & bone, burnings & bundlings, communal storage & final rest within an earthen mound in the company of certain others. If the 1054 supernova pointed a new way to the afterlife, priesthoods at Cahokia directed its pan-tribal response across ranks, statuses & distances for centuries, while their espousal of chunkey, now replaced by stickball with its simpler gear & other continuing traditions are only now being fully appreciated.

Downtown Core

Cahokia is an enormous, upstart, planned community, no doubt stimulated by anxieties brought on by Big Bang bright sky events like the Crab Supernova AD 1054 = 962 years ago & Halley's Comet AD 1066 = 950 years ago (Young & Fowler 2000: 275). Archaeologists worked out these CE~AD phases for Cahokia:

> Lohmann 1050-1100
> Stirling 11-1200
> Moorehead 1200-1275
> Sand Prairie 1275-1350
> Oneonta 1350-1650

Downtown Cahokia was outlined by palisades surrounding enormous Monks Mound, carefully leveled Grand Plaza & paired dome & square mounds around the edges. Nearby were outer & inner mound clusters. Outer ringers (clockwise, with cardinal direction) are called Kunneman N, East E, South, Rattlesnake S, Rouch & Powell W (Fowler 1997: Chapter 10, 193-200; 1989: 198-205). Inner ones (clockwise) are Creek Bottom, Ramey, Tippetts, Barrow Pit, Merrell W, Mounds 44. A causeway[48] runs from Rattlesnake to the south edge of the Grand Plaza between Barrow & Tippetts, aiming at a small mound ~ tysic on the front top east corner of Mounds Mound. This alignment physically confirms that the plan for the entire site is 5° E of N, which esoterically is the flip mirror image of Moon maximum south rise at 130° (Romain 2015: 34).

A thousand years ago, at today's St Louis, on either side of American Bottom, the wide meander plain of the Mississippi, ritual activities featured 200 mounds of various sizes & numbers. On the west, St Louis, once known as Mound City, leveled dozens as it grew into the gateway to the West & hub of industrial Fur Trade. On the east, they dotted over 10 miles along Cahokia Creek, with a cluster on the Big Muddy & more removed concentration at "downtown" Cahokia,

---

[48] It recalls the Mayan *sacbe* (*sacbeob* = plural) "white way" linking past & present times & sites as an elongated tysic. Cf #25

with 100 plus mounds, several woodhenges & bastion towered palisade. Fields grew crops & lowlands provided nutritious seeds & nuts (Hall 2004: 96).

For Hall (2004: 102), the quick diaspora from Cahokia was merely a moving up the Missouri into the bison-rich Plains, where 8-row Northern Flint better withstood drought with its shorter growing season. Their guide was the North Star Polaris in the Big Dipper, the model for "Seven Council Fires & 7 tribes in Sioux origins, 7 bands in Teton (Western Sioux) social organization, a Council of 7 Chiefs &/or Seven Pipes among the Omahas, Iowas & Otos & the Hidatsa association of their Dog Soldier societies with the 7 stars of the Big Dipper."

Monks Mound

Named for refugee French Trappists led by Dom Urban Guillet, after seeking refuges in Switzerland, Hungary, Russia, Belgium & England, landed in Kentucky in 1802 with 34: 7 priest, 18 brothers, 9 students. When fire destroyed that monastery, they moved to American Bottoms in 1808 to begin Our Lady of Good Hope atop various mounds, then called Cantine ~ Canteen. Cahokia's main mound, now named for these monks, was reserved for an eventual church, though its first terrace had a 1735-52 French Catholic chapel & cemetery for Cahokias, a tribe within the Algonkian-speaking Illiniwek confederacy. In addition to gardens, orchards & bred livestock, monks incongruously traded watchworks, silverwork & prize horses for local crops to support their austere lives, though periodic agues were mortal to many workers. Compensating for past neglect, several of the monks served as parish priests, which cut the work force & delayed building projects until everything crumbled during the prolonged New Madrid earthquake of 1812. Fr Guillet tried anew at Pittsburg, then Philadelphia, but finally, after the defeat of Napoleon, returned to France where he died at the renewed Trappist community.

Over a century later, federal highway expansions, especially around the continental hub of St Louis, sent archaeologists into the field to survey, record, salvage & watch the obliteration of Cahokia's tangible remains under projects such as that of FAI 270, which ended up as Federal Alignment Interstate 255.

Earlier called the Great Knob, Monks Mound was built in 14 construction

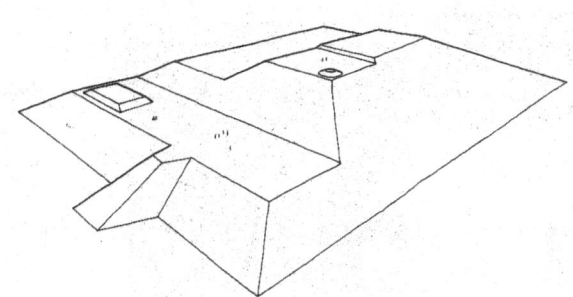

phases within 8 stages, alternating between a single remantle over the whole & then one that included an added second ~ double layer under what became the highest 4th terrace, which eventually held a huge hall with a line of six massive support posts down its middle (Skele 1988: 79, 81, 89).

Beside it was a 20-foot post associated with copper bits (sheathing ?), whose reconstruction proved to be a lightning rod (Pauketat & Alt 2015: 20). Occasional mounds & fences on fresh inner surfaces to act as eventual internal buttresses became incorporated into the finished construction, with stairs between a front ramp & 3rd terrace eventually covered by the 1st terrace that buttressed the finished mound. Monk started about 900 & stood about 20 feet high before major additions raised it to a hundred feet during a hundred years after 1050, when the annual New Fire ~ Busk ceremony also began to celebrate the new focus on maize (Brown 2004: 119A).[49] The four tiers were probably involved in successive initiations or life passages into increasingly higher degrees of priestly knowledge & authority.

Once relocated in the 1800s, locals worked for & against Monks. Dentist John JR Patrick undertook a careful survey map of the city & a cast-iron model of Monks in 1876 (88: 41). For thirty years (1831-59) until he was buried on the 4th terrace, mechanic (aptly named) Ames Hill owned Monks & lived there, building a house on the 3rd tier that destroyed the small axial mound on that corner & sinking a well on the 2nd terrace (88: 21, 28). The Ramey family then held Monks, 1864-1923, when they sold it to become a small state park.

In 1998, boring sideways into Monks for drainage to halt further slumping, a $5,000 smart drill broke against a rock layer that is at least 32 feet long, 30 ft below 2nd terrace & 140 ft into this mound (Young & Fowler 2000: 285), confounding its status as the largest "entirely" earthen mound in several countries.

All of this effort & publicity inspired a novel, named Cricket Sings (King 1983) for a lame woman herbalist & featuring literary use of datura ~ jimsonweed seeds, a dangerous hallucinogenic herb, found during bio sample floatation.

Her story begins as Cahokia prepares for Solstice rites, involving all social ranks of Suns, Warriors, Honoreds & Ordinary drudges, who work in return for food from haughty priests. The old kingly Sun lingers near death, soothed by datura. Cricket Sings, an old herbalist with crippled leg, is summoned by Eagle, son & heir & old Moon, the Sun's wife. Cricket's father had been a priest & her mother sacrificially buried with the last Sun. They switch the body of a recently dead man to the Sun's lodge & move the old man into her lodge, hidden under robes the night before the Sun Celebration, when Eagle dons the yellow feather cape & mask to greet the Sun from atop a pole in the center of a woodhenge. Bear in the Sky, brother of Sun, intrigues in favor of his newborn son, but all goes well for the public feast. Atop the Holy Hill (Monks Mound), priests feast on roasted humans. The old Sun dies during the night, so Eagle has legitimately fulfilled the vital greeting role.

---

[49] Today Creeks & others say the Busk originated with Yuchi (Jackson 2003), suggesting they joined & shared with Mississippians a thousand years ago.

Later the death of the old Sun is announced in public & priests pick out young women to accompany him in the grave, including Cricket's two nieces. Plans are made to rescue them & escape while everyone takes datura seeds to receive visions on the night before the funeral. Cricket & her sister Running Water take fine robes up to the two "brides" atop the mound, then wrap the girls up & roll them down its backside to waiting family in canoes. Cricket goes back for her sister-in-law Soon To Be Winter, who has overdosed, so Cricket takes a handful of seeds & stays. At dawn all the brides are led out to kneel beside the grave with old Sun's body & masked new Sun has them drink poison from a black sticky pot to die quickly & enter Night. Cricket, last in line, asks Eagle Sun to be buried with her own kin. Then, in the last sentence, she wakes from this dream, alive.

Azimuths ~ *Sky Alignments*

At Toltec Mounds, near Little Rock, Arkansas, which suspiciously ended as New Cahokia began, 18 mounds with complex geometry surround two plazas, with an embankment & ditch on three sides & a river oxbow on the fourth. From the middle of mound C, all other mounds are intersected by lines radiating out at 60° intervals. Moreover, overall layout suggests a standard unit of measurement, called the Toltec Module, of 47.5 (46~49) meters, which more commonly appears doubled as 95 meters. The projected original height of Mound A is 1/3 of the module & that of B is ¼, suggesting consistent proportions.

This standard unit may be based on a more human one, with an increment of 1.67 meters (5'6"), the height of a healthy male member of the elite ("a ruler"). Half of this measure is about the span of a stride, so 57 paces would equal 47.5 meters. A cubit, measured from elbow to tip of middle finger, would be ½ of a meter, repeated 95 times for the standard unit.

Excavation of some mounds indicates their different usages. Mound C holds burials, while B, D, E, S & G had a succession of priestly homes. Of note, a line from the center of A to B has an angle of 61.5°, "precisely the azimuth of the rising summer solstice sun for the latitude of the site (34°18'15") at AD 700".[50] A sight line from A through G & H marks the 90° equinox sunrise. From H to B is summer solstice sunset, from H to A is equinox sunset & from H to S is winter solstice sunset. A to R angles the southern-most setting in moon's 18.6 year cycle.

Though stellar alignments are problematical, a line from E to A sees Polaris, the North Star, a steady & important celestial guide throughout the cultural world. It often served as the model for a steady, sure human leader (chief). The star Vega,

---

[50] Clay Sherrod & Martha Ann Rolingson, Surveyors of the Ancient Mississippi Valley ~ Modules & Alignments in Prehistoric Mound Sites 1987: 5, 26, 30, 41, 65, 84, 98, 134.

prominent during the farming season, can be tracked via the mounds beside the oxbow along the northwestern side of the site.

Comparative studies on either side of the lower Mississippi, in the eastern Yazoo Basin & in western Red River Caddoan sites, confirmed solstice & equinox alignments. The Insley Site in Louisiana includes fascinating sight lines from its Mound A through an arc of seven mounds, each aligned with a different bright star that sets in winter. Strangely, lunar correlations were not attempted for the Caddoan sites, despite the obvious ethnographic fact that the Caddo priestly head was known by the title of Mr. Moon.[51]

Surveys at Cahokia add further confirmation. Cahokia, occupied for 400 years, includes over 100 mounds within 15 square kilometers. The entire city was laid out with great precision. Mapping indicates axis lines that are confirmed by excavations. Key spots on the earth involved intense human activity, though the visible outcome seems deceptive. Precise engineering was serious business.

The most spectacular of these thus far is Mound 72 (below), a low mound at the location of a projected main axis intersection. This nexus was proven by the remains of a huge marker post, placed about CE/AD 950. Nearby, Twin VIPs rest above & below a falcon-shaped cloak of beads, with hundreds of human sacrifices & grave goods from thousands of miles away.

Given the complexity of all the earth, sky & human relationships that seem to have been expressed at Cahokia, it is not surprising that specialized engineering transect devices have been proposed. Now called woodhenges, these were four or more circles (or perhaps arcs) of standing posts, another reflection of the human orientation to the sky also seen at Stonehenge in England. While they were probably used as calendars, solar markers, sacred enclosures & a place to watch gnomon shadows shift in rotation, they could have also been used as surveyor instruments. Set up in a populous neighborhood of Cahokia, with posts that stayed in place for hundreds of years, sighting between a central & standing post provides obvious alignments for half of the mounds at the site. More are possible but the tangible data are not at hand. Another factor for consideration was a consistent spacing of 1045 meters (22 times the Toltec module) among the mounds.

In all, mound spacings & alignments convey a profound redundancy or overlapping of relationships. The same unit of measurement is simultaneous multiples & proportions of the length of a human stride, human height, dimensions of a plaza, aspects of the sky & one or more of its phenomena in orbit. A mound, therefore, is not a single entity but instead the nexus of many, many concerns ~ concepts. Always, mounds obviously steady the earth, allowing reuse of a vital plot, rising steadily upward.

---

[51] Jay Miller, Changing Moons 1996. Kolomoki in Georgia also used the Toltec Module.

Mound 72

Cahokia provides the stellar example of a practical as well as symbolic community with at least four administrative tiers decreasing from 1) the downtown of six square miles, 2) multimound clusters, 3) one mound villages & 4) moundless farmsteads or hamlets. Melvin Fowler, the archaeologist who devoted his career to systematic work, proposed the use of a basic measuring unit of 1.055 meters or 3.46 feet (comparable to the Toltec module of 47.5 (46~49) meters). His careful mapping & confirming excavations have shown that this Mississippian capital was impressively planned, aligned & engineered.[52]

The ramp on two-tiered Monk's Mound indicates that it faces south, with the tysic of the whole site at its southwest corner, aligned to a north-south axis that intersects the eastern side of Mound 72, as confirmed by evidence of huge post holes at these points. Its role in the master plan, mapping the Sky on the Earth, drew scholarly attention, though what was inside soon dimmed all other considerations for excavators. Four years were spent on this seven-foot high, ridged-top form, revealing six major episodes of burial & building that entombed about 300 people.[53]

The space was first claimed about 950 AD by a woodhenge of 48 posts set in a circle, serving as a celestial calculator, solar marker & surveying station. Of notable significance, Cahokia is positioned at the latitude where solstice sight lines form a triangle of exactly 30 degrees per side (summer is 30° N of E, winter is 30° S of E). Given the Mississippian link between rulers & Sun, it is significant that two mounds were constructed opposite each other at the post marking the summer solstice sunrise (SSR at 72Sub1) & at the winter solstice sunset post (WSS at Mound 96). From atop Monk's Mound, therefore, the far south horizon showed a ring of standing posts with paired low mounds, each pierced by a solar marker.

Near the SSR post, mound 2Sub1 began as a black earthen platform arraying three groups of impressive burials. Twin central burials, resting against a cloak covered with shell disk beads outlining a bird much like a falcon, was composed of men lying back-to-back, head-to-feet, offset by 10 degrees. Atop, the full skeleton

---

[52] Biloine Whiting Young & Melvin Fowler, Cahokia ~ The Great American Metropolis 2000: 155, 183, 277.

[53] Young & Fowler, Cahokia 2000: 139-145, 155, 183, 238, 250, 277; Fowler, The Cahokia Atlas, Studies in Illinois Archaeology 6 1989 [1997]; Melvin Fowler, Jerome Rose, Barbara Vander Leest & Steven Ahler, The Mound 72 Area: Dedicated & Sacred Space in Early Cahokia 1999. Under pressure from AIM activists & waning funds, Features 107 & 356 were not excavated, clouding final body count.

was face-up, while the man below was exactly reversed, face down with feet under the skull above. Accompanying this pair were a range of human remains in various stages of curation, including a full skeleton, wearing a necklace of 700 shell disk beads, with a flexed right leg suggesting activity or burial alive. In two nearby pits, aligned to other posts in the woodhenge, were bone bundles & elaborate grave goods, including copper tubes, mica sheets (2 bushelfuls), hundreds of foreign arrows with stone points sorted by specimen type (to the delight of all classifiers) & two stacks of chunkey stones (10, 5 in each). All three of these burials were then covered by three feet of a north-south roundish mound (72sub1) with extensions to the east & west, giving it a lumpy cross (cruciform) shape. Its blue-black consistency was capped with dense off-white plaster that effectively sealed & preserved it for a thousand years.

The flat rectangular top of the mound, approached by a ramp on the west side, was directly over the beaded burial. Later, the SSR post on its east side was replaced twice & new burials, aligned to other posts, were positioned above earlier ones, indicating that adepts in charge of this mound had full knowledge of its contents. An altar basin was then added & then a final dark soil triangle.

Across the henge from the SSR post, another cruciform mound (#96) was built at the WSS post. Since it never had a plaster cap, it so deteriorated that it was identified as a mound only recently. Unexcavated, it is presumed to hold burials associated with the Earth, in balance with the Sky associations of Mound 72. Both include ramps leading toward the post that once protruded over its upper level.

Near 72Sub1, construction began on a companion mound (72Sub2) over the wall-trenches of a building that had probably been a charnel house where bodies were curated for defleshing, resorting, bundling & burial. It was dismantled & replaced by a low platform to display the remains of 13 humans sorted by bone size into three piles, along with four distinct bundle burials. Paired burials, two face-down men & a paired face-up woman & face-down man, were set along the wall lines of the prior building. All of these remains were then covered by a two-terraced square mound (72sub2), to which were added a new post & two pit burials of females (numbering 22, 19), both in two layers. Later, a pit was dug to leave offerings of pottery, 36,000 shell beads & 450 unhafted stone points. In the southeast corner, 24 females were buried in two layers, divided by mats & cloth & covered with a ramp.

In three construction phases, space between the two small mounds was filled in by unusual burials covered by small mounds. Eventually, a tiny ridge mound (72sub3) consolidated these & was topped by four men, with arms interlinked but missing their heads & hands, covered by a conical mound of alternating layers of light & dark sands. In a downslope pit, 50 young women (average age 21) were placed in two layers. Both burials were then buried under another mound of black soil (72Sub3A).

For a century, as 72Sub3 grew to include 72Sub2, 72Sub1 stood alone as the focus for offerings & sacrifices. Eventually, an overall ridgetop mound was planned, aligned to the solstices & the diagonal of the diamond-shaped border of Cahokia "downtown". The axis ran parallel to Feature 229, where humans on the bottom, which was lined with white sand, were a jumbled cross-section of 40 people & the top level, separated by mats (shown by their remains), held 15 bodies that had been wrapped & placed on litters whose cedar poles provided a date of AD 1030. These sacrifices (of genetic kin) had lined up along the southern side of the pit, struck at the back of the neck with a heavy weapon (perhaps a mace) & sprawled into the pit, where finger gouges convey their final agony. Other oval pits held extended burials.

Lastly, henge posts were removed & ridged-top mound was capped with a hard surface of plaster, with triangular altars at each end enabling solar observations. Periodically, burials continued to be placed along the south side of the mound, indicating continued vitality of these rulers.

In all, Mound 72 represented a thoroughly-engineered master plan that began with the 48 post woodhenge, followed by two roundish mounds (72Sub1, 96) at solstice points. Then 72 added a squarish one (72Sub2), built around another post. Intervening space was filled with a sacrificial ridge mound that expanded in tribute to free-standing 72Sub1. Together, these three mounds represent the full triple range of dome, platform & ridge shapes occurring throughout Cahokia, repeatedly emphasizing two levels (& moieties) as both terraced mounds & layered burials. Periodic burials were made, including elite bodies, bundled bones, offerings & sacrifices. Finally, all 72 mounds were capped & sealed, though some offerings & burials continued to be made into pits dug along the south edge.

Mound 96 faced east at the winter solstice sunrise (WSR) in mirror image as 72Sub1 faced west at the summer solstice sunset (SSS). Cahokia has other mounds paired as round / long, as well as other buried pairs (dorsal/ventral males & females), reflecting ancient twining.[54] Within Mound 72 the twin birdmen burial, reversed (head to foot, face up & face-down) conjoined Earth & Sky (as moieties), while marker posts & solstice axis of the finished mound allowed the living to stay aligned to their ancestors of the past & world of the future.[55]

Its contents have been much discussed. The degree of human sacrifice has been argued to be evidence of an early state – in political terms, while the burials

---

[54] Young &Fowler, <u>Cahokia</u> 2000: 250.

[55] Fowler, Rose, Leest & Ahler, <u>The Mound 72 Area</u> 1999: 167-185.

around the beaded cloak have been given a mythological interpretation based on the ballgame epic. Yet many of these remains had clearly been curated for some time, so a highly cosmological interpretation conjoining space & time seems the most likely explanation, reinforcing a sense of overall community rather than just elite rank, as was initially proposed.[56]

Byers 2006

After brooding on earthworks during a long career at a small Toronto college, in his 80s, Martin Byers (2006) crafted a terminological morass of great precision for a "rigorous formal analysis in critical realist symbolic pragmatic persepective". Focusing on Cahokia after former forays into Ohio prehistory, his archaeology is minimally informed by plausible ethnography (Hall 2007). A key Cahokian innovation was moving terminal mortuary rites onto the floodplain, while retaining upland exposure scaffolds, opposing floodplain-female-underworld to upland-male-heavens concerned with male fertility world renewal cults (06: 389,402).

His most plausible assertion, therefore, is that this native city was organized around a mutually autonomous duality of clan & cult ~ female fecundity & male fertility ~ ♀ rounds & ♂ squares (06: 27, 89, 288, 295, 423, 470) without any single rigid authority apex. Age grades are proposed for cults, with much of the manual labor done by younger junior age-sets & some larger buildings as possible men's lodges (06: 498, 508).

While major Cahokianists, such as Hall, Pauketat, Emerson, argue "Cahokia … was about agriculture & appropriation, production & power, ideology & authority & monuments & mobilization" (B06: 20) under, in his mind numbing terms, a preferred hierarchical monistic modular polity, Byers (06: 26) argues for a

---

[56] Patricia O'Brien, Cahokia: The Political Capital of the "Ramey" State 1989; James Brown, The Cahokia Mound 72-Sub 1 Burials as Collective Representation 2003. While O'Brien argued that the many sacrifices indicate a sanctioned "legitimate" authority over life & death typical of early states, Brown saw the complexity of the "beaded burial" as portraying the founding epic of the ballgame in terms of antihero & hero. I concur with Fowler & other excavators, however, that the falcon cloak more likely joins embodiments of Earth & Sky moieties so typical of historic Siouans. More importantly, Mound 72 represents public political theater, as well as religious cosmology.

Goldstein correctly noted that the burials in 72 are a collective statement, covering a long time span of curated remains, not the status burial of an elite leader (or two); Cf Lynne Goldstein, Mississippian Ritual as Viewed Through the Practice of Secondary Disposal of the Dead, Mounds, Modoc & Mesoamerica: Papers in Honor of Melvin L. Fowler, Illinois State Museum Scientific Papers 18: 193-205 2000.

heterarchical polyistic locale-centric order based in kinship or companionship, of clan or cult. Its setting is a <u>deonic</u> ecology to "constitute the ethical, moral, legal & constitutive dimension of social life {of} Interrelated entitlements, rights, duties, obligations, responsibilities & privilege {distinguishing} poaching, pilfering & squatting from hunting, gathering & dwelling … " (B06: 29, 33).[57]

In a world of immanent sacredness, communities are concerned with survival, reputation &, especially, world renewal through pragmatic collective understanding that monument building is "participating in & thereby presencing the essential powers" of the cosmos (B06: 52, 55, 58, 79).

Crediting the efforts of Bob Hall, AFC Wallace, Karl Marx, Liz Brumfield, he builds his case through details, arguing that the appearance of Z-twist cordage markings on pottery marked a specific reverence for maize in the special storage of these kernels when newly extensive ~ intensive farming signaled that maize had become staple food. At the same time; prior use of S twist cordage continued for mundane foods. Ramey Incised became a pottery type with a religious intent, marking Cahokia's outreach (B06: 142, 496).

Reviewing site reports, though rephrasing cemetery as = collective burial locale ~ CBL), he easily locates clans in houses, but seeks cults first in hearthless keyhole buildings with long ramps with obstructed doorways, allowing spirits but not mortals that entry, then, about AD 900, keyholes were replaced by plazas with a center post surrounded by four side caches & nearby platform mounds as "icons of the earth & sky, while plazas & large water filled borrow pits might be icons of the middle world & underworld" (B06: 119, 176, 197, 222, 302).[58] In addition, many mounds were sealed with black gumbo as an expression of the Earth Diver genesis that brought muddy land up from the universal sea bottom.

"Earthworks would be important symbolic warrants of the postulated male-based fertility & female-based fecundity world renewal ritual spheres … focused on regrowing-the-earth rites tied up with the fertility of rains & floods by which the comic powers of fecundity were revitalized … monumental constructions usually derive their symbolic pragmatic meanings (their action-constitutive powers) from perceived real, expressively mediated connection with cosmic elements {of} form (circle, square, platform, ridge top, size, layout (plaza-platform pattern, orientation (celestial turning points or mythical directions), spacing from

---

[57] In arguing that urban natives thought they were countering their own polluting of the earth by growing sacred maize, Byers echoes earlier arguments by Clark Mallam (1976) that mounds were a native way of atoning for their abuse of the earth.

[58] Strangely missing is likely use of sweatlodges by men & their cults. Pauketat (2004: 53, 60) saw keyholes as winter homes & Z-twist a result of brief use of shard spindle whorls.

each other or from some central focus & even material constituents (surface or deep soil, black gumbo/brown loam, limestone/sand & so on" (B06: 498, 470).

Growing out of shamanism, Woodhenges were under the care of custodial priests concerned with spirit release rites, who progressively formed an academy to share knowledge, shifting among reorganizations analogous to Congregationalist ↔ Presbyterian ↔ Episcopal frameworks (B06: 355, 465, 467, 484).

For massive communal graves, he (B06: 561 #7) distinguishes lethal from postmortem sacrifices, noting further symbolic associations in terms of a paired burial in Mound 72 such that a male (#118) to the east was face down on his front (♂ E prone dorsal) with face to the West & right hand near his neck, while a female (#117) to the west was face up on her back (♀ W supine ventral) with flexed hands near neck & a pot at her left elbow; Both had feet to the north & head to the south (B06: 363 #118); Thus, equating male right east :: female left west. Further, some paired mounds had a waterway barrier between them (B06: 455).

Seeking whether Cahokia solar alignments were equinoctial or solstitial, evidence suggests both equinoxes & the polar star, along with use of Toltec Module (TM = 47.5 meters), but a misdating of the 15A Woodhenges wrongly ignores potential solstice alignments (B06: 474, 476, 485).

Warfare increasingly interfered. While the initial palisade around downtown had only 3 sides for ritual reasons, it soon closed up, adding bastions & other defenses, whose need is substantiated by attacks that left stone points scattered along the outside of these walls (B06: 254). Overpowering raids by Cahokia warriors probably captured distant prisoners for public sacrifices. Vital trade in hoes, spades & shells then had to be facilitated by neutrals away from the fray.

Byer's ethnographic parallels are drawn to Osages & rich texts left by Francis LaFleshe, particularly complexities of their village plan based on 24 patriclans with 9 of the Sky moiety (7 Sky + 2 last) & 15 of the Earth (7 Water + 7 Land + 1 Isolated). Moreover in their own rites, Osage priests reverse these East – West polarities of the ordinary village (B06: 343, 511, 513).

Seeking "best-fit truths" of belief ~ cosmology, desire ~ ethos, perception ~ worldview, intention ~ ideology, Byers explicates Mississippians as relying on their Maize Model, soul release, world renewal rites, "immanentist cosmology, a squatter ethos, the Sacred Earth principle, the essential contradiction of human existence that this implicates, the inclusive territorial & custodial domain perspective, the dual clan-cult structure & so on" (B06: 347, 516).

With typical Mississippian features of shell-tempered pottery, wall trench housing, tri-notched points, internal storage & sweat lodges, he concludes Cahokia became a mutualistic heterachy more like a shopping mall than Vatican before all collapsed about AD 1300 (B06: 229, 292, 516, 517, 527).

Milner 2006 [1998]

By stark contrast to Byer's over elaboration is George Milner's minimalist (nay-saying godless doubting, gruel to others glitz) concern with a broad comparative study of Cahokia's setting within a dozen modern counties on either side of the Mississippi from today's Alton, Illinois to Cape Girardeau, Missouri, with perpetually meandering channels & sloughs (M06: 15, 28-34, 38-43) which "in summer was undeniably a steamy uncomfortable place, rank with smells of decaying vegetation' (M06: 44). Significantly, Cahokia itself is located in the middle of widest expanse of this floodplain (M06: 119, 168).[59]

In addition to fields of 10-14 row maize, people relied on goosefoot, erect knotweed, maygrass & little barley for their starchy seeds & on sunflower & marsh elder for oily seeds (M06: 66). Maygrass, as its name implies, harvests in late spring. Since deer were scare nearby, wetlands were crucial, fish nets were very effective (M06: 68) & marsh life abundant, including waterfowl, such as ducks, geese, swans, cranes, herons, grebes, along with beaver & muskrat (M06: 69). Nuts included thick shell hickory, pecans, black walnuts, butternuts, chestnuts & acorns, with hickory oil a cooking staple (M06: 70). Though there is no evidence of beans,[60] there were grapes, blackberries, persimmon & pawpaw (M06: 71). While venison & other meats, including bison, were gifts, tribute, or offerings, the local larder was more than sufficient for anticipated workload, harvest & reliability & storage potential (M06: 75).

Throughout the Mississippian era, house size increased by six times & shape shifted from square to rectangle wall trench, to larger square. Special building outlines were L, T & keyhole. Sweatlodges, paired hearths & halls (M06: 94), including a huge one atop Monks Mound, speak to communal activities. Pottery included shell tempering, but this has effected preservation since shell dissolves as water percolates through tiny holes subject to winter freeze & summer thaw destroying many sherds (M06: 54). Effigy bowls were modeled as ducks, snapping turtles, beavers & owls. Outside Z twist cord marking became more common in the northern sector of American Bottom around Monks Mound (M06: 57, 60). Flakes were preferred for most purposes, including arrow points. Standardized hoes tended fields & dug house wall trenches. Bead manufacture involved traded-in shells, sandstone saws & microdrills, but most of these beads were not fully rounded, polished, nor finely finished because mostly weathered porous shell reached the end of the line trade (M06: 164). Blatant status signs for "puissant chiefs" included shell, copper, mica & cherts (M06: 130, 131, 156).

---

[59] To distinguish each of these 2006 works, Byers cites are B06, Milner is M06.

[60] Wild beans were staples; farmed beans were added later, with their own style of bean pot.

Calculating the labor for mounds & monuments, Milner determined volume in terms of length, width, height & shape, relying on formulas for "paraboloid of revolution, frusta of a pyramid & cone & a combination of a prism & cone" to arrive at a combined figure of 555,780m^3 for the rest of the Cahokia site & a total of 1,177,701m^3 by adding in Monks Mound itself with 621,921m^3 (21,976,000 ft^3) or about half the entire site. Within the full complex, ridge mounds at St Louis – Big Mound; at East St Louis – Cemetery Mound; & at Cahokia – Powell & Rattlesnake became huge.

In long term, successful sites benefited from slough edges with more reliable productivity. Numbers & sizes of site mounds were influenced by their support population, exalted lineage persistence & continued remantling (M06:155). Most favorable settings were longest occupied & largest with the biggest mounds (M06: 161), so Cahokia at the widest floodplain expanse naturally became the strongest complex chiefdom in this area. Over time, under its protection, nucleated settlements dispersed over favorable ridges (M06: 168).

For the region, Milner (M06: 174-6) traces productive slough edges into prosperous communities with social ranks. Maize is grown from AD 200 for ceremonial purposes while other plants provide staples. Bow & arrow arrive a couple centuries later to increase conflict & tensions as territorial claims tighten & maize predominates. By AD 1000, people aggregate in palisaded villages at favorable pockets within land & water scapes. With standardized hoes & specialized homes, pottery & art; Mississippians emerge as chiefdoms relying on arranged marriages, fear of retribution & rewards for cooperation. Imbalances, such as deforestation, produced catastrophic runoff & flooding damaging to crops & other resources. By 1450, the central Mississippi became an "empty quarter" as people dispersed among uplands, away from river traffic & climate chilled by the Little Ice Age. In all, Cahokia was not unique: like its neighbors only bigger.

Emerson

Thomas Emerson (1997) expounds on Cahokia suburbs, convincingly tracing administrative nodes & hamlets during the rise & fall of this elite driven hierarchical chiefdom cum semi-state (97: 251) & drawing plausible ethnographic parallels, especially in terms of today's Busk ~ Green Corn Ceremonialism within an Upper & Under World cosmos (97: 256), mediated by Mother Earth in various guises. Relying heavily on both his excavation dirt experience with Illinois DOT & academic symbolic theory, phrased as post processual, he unabashedly looks at culture & context expressed through "structuration" by an individual actor. In his view, the elite arose by insidiously co-opting existing fertility ideology to insert themselves as crucial mediators in the cosmology, leading to their sanctification ~

deification at their brief apogee. Distinguishing recursive, integral *"power to"* from controlling *"power over"*, their built environment, including mounds, is "a means where power is operationalized in space" (97: 20) within their hegemony.

By the Lohmann phase, countryside homes had been resettled as pockets at strategic locales, with specialized buildings such as meeting halls, sweatlodges & storage caches indicating 4 tiers of control from Monks Mound down to local officials. Of note, after Cahokia dispersed, this scattered rural pattern reemerged, showing its stability, even as regional violence & war resumed after the *pan pax* ended with the dispersal of Cahokia & its thuggish soldiers.

Architecture & special artifacts express layers in either direct or sequential hierarchy, including "sacred fires; world-renewal features with ceremonially killed artifacts & plants; extensive use of red cedar for purification; presence of hallucinogenic & emetic drugs such as tobacco & jimsonweed; red color symbolism; plaza/courtyard organization & the four-side world [as iconic platform mound]; manufacture of ceremonial Ramey pottery; Corn Mother mythology; & directional symbolism" (97: 261).

"Luxuries as weapons of exclusion" by the elite included materials of "hematite, galena, shell objects, crystals, limonite, mice & copper" & manufactured "earspools, shell & galena beads, pendants, Ramey knives, projectile point caches, or discoidals" & flint clay effigies (97: 266).

In all, Emerson's conclusions ally with Pauketat, who came to the fore by proposing the 1050 Big Bang that motivated vast prophetic world renewal at New Cahokia & throughout the Mississippian world.

Because Cahokia is so complex, repeopling it with ethnographic analogs must seek far-ranging soures, beginning with locally eponymous Cahokias themselves, moving to Southeast Busk participants such as Creek as well a mound-building Iroquoian Cherokee & Caddoan Pawnee before looking northward to likely Cahokian Siouians now farther away up the Missouri River, still sustaining their focus on blood & bundles on the High Plains.

GREAT LAKES

Central Algonkian
  Ojibwa(Chippewa)-Ottawa-Potawatomi
  Menomini
  Sauk-Fox-Kickapoo-(Mascouten ?)
  Myaami--Illiniwek
  Shawnee
Siouian ~ Chiwere
  Ho-Chunk ~ Hochungara ~ Winnebago

Iroquoian
  Huron ~ Wendat ~ Wyandot
  Erie
  Neutral
  Petun ~ Tobacco

Cahokia Illiniwek

Cahokias themselves were Central Algonkian Illini-Myaami speakers loosely affiliated with others collectively known to French as Illiniwek, living along the Illinois River flowing into the Mississippi & ultimately bludgeoned & diseased into five surviving tribes: upriver Peoria ~ backpacker, Kaskaskia ~ katydid, Michigamea (with a line of chiefs named Chicago) & downriver Tamaroa ~ cut tail & Cahokia. Jesuit priests worked among upper river tribes with limited success, while parish priests had better luck near Metis ~ mixed French Indien communities.

In the 1600s, Jesuits reported 60 villages until Iroquois terrorizing during the 1650s Beaver Wars, left 5 big villages in 1670 that famously repelled Iroquois in 1677, only to suffer utter defeat in 1680. Kaskaskias found refuge at Starved Rock, Lake Peoria & American Bottom. Others moved across the Mississippi to join Osage, only to battle them in 1689. In 1682, Onondaga captured 700 prisoners, then roasted & ate 600. A final Iroquois raid came in 1715.

In 1698 Chickasaw & Shawnee slavers carried off 100 Cahokias (Temple 1966: 33) & by 1700, during Sioux hostiles Tamaroa & Cahokia again moved across the river among Missouria, themselves devastated in *??. Hostilities now came from Fox until French allies massacred them in 1730. In 1725, to strengthen ties, six Illini chiefs went to France (66: 41), recruited before a disastrous to French attack on Chickasaws in 1739. Internal bickering was rife, with Cahokia & Peoria disputing over Sauk prisoners in 1741. In 1752, Cahokias burned to death six Fox hunters; one escaped still tied to a pole to plead for all-out vengeance, charging that Illini killed both male & female beavers in Wisconsin, a horrific crime.

When British took over Ft Chartes, renaming it Ft Cavendish, in 1763, Peorias moved south & welcomed defeated rebel Pontiac until he was murdered at Cahokia in 1769. In 1773, Illini sold these lands & crossed the Mississippi, then a treaty with the US at Vincennes 13 Aug 1803 ceded Illinois, supplemented by a treaty in 1818 to include Peoria. The last Kaskaskia left on 27 Oct 1832.

Cahokias had allied with Tamaroa at East St Louis, then with Peoria, before settling in Kansas, where all surviving tribes, including Myaami Piankashaw, consolidating in 1830s as Peoria under Baptise Peoria. Forced to Oklahoma, they were terminated on 2 Aug 1956, then restored on 15 May 1978. Their headquarters is now on 8 Tribes Trail in Miami, Oklahoma (with Miami, Ottawa, Modoc, Peoria, Shawnee, Eastern Shawnee, Quapaw, Mingo Seneca Cayuga, Huron Wyandotte).

Long before these ethnographic & historical tribes, a deep archaeological record along the Illinois River traces mounds & funerary rites back 7000 years.[61] The Lower Illinois River, above its confluence with the Missouri & Mississippi, has three loci of interments at bluff crest knolls, at flood plain sand ridges & at villages beside slackwater lakes. Accretional mounds begin about seven thousand years ago, atop bluffs, with "sequential additions of bodies [of young & middle-aged adults, tools, offerings] & enclosing sediments". On the floodplain, dotted later by huge platform mounds, at lakeside dwellings, young & infirm were buried in middens without offerings, while sand ridges were used for reburials with dense & varied offerings. In all, size & location serve to distinguish an exclusive ancestral ~ political cult focused on knolls from an inclusive earth ~ fertility one based on floodplain platforms. The former separated out kin units, while the latter integrated whole communities, sustained by these vital mounds.[62]

Bluff crests are double liminal zones (between the earth / sky & valley / uplands), where these Middle Archaic monuments provided an overview of the living by ancestors: "Thus began the mound-building tradition." During mortuary rites, carrying bodily remains across these pitched surfaces, including raised scaffolding, provided both a reintegrative cosmological tour for the living & a route for souls to reach the afterworld. Orchestrated reburials in the sand ridges clearly show the expected reversal between living & dead because pottery decorated with raptors is always stacked below that showing spoonbills, inverting the natural habitats of these birds.

In terms of overall built environment, moreover, these large & small Middle Woodland monuments re-created the cosmos, both vertically & horizontally, as well as provided a forum for intensely negotiated power relations among the living.

Busk

Bound up in the beginnings of Cahokia is the Green Corn ~ New Fire ritual now known to Oklahoma Creeks as *poskita łako* great fast ~ Busk, where women wear turtle-shell leg rattles.[63] The following review of this extensive literature augments contextual understandings of Cahokia, Maize & manpower.

---

[61] Jane Buikstra & Douglas Charles, Centering the Ancestors: Cemeteries, Mounds & Sacred Landscapes of the Ancient North American Midcontinent 1999: 208, 212, 216, 218. Dr. Robert Walls kindly provided a timely pdf of this chapter.

[62] Burial 8 in Yokum Mound 4 buried with four sets of age-graded antlers was probably not a shaman. Throughout the East, deer antlers are badges of political office, as they still are for Iroquois royaner or league chiefs.

[63] A Cahokia woman was buried with 2 turtle shell rattles at her right leg (Perino 1967: 540).

SOUTHEAST

Algic	/ Gulf	Iroquoian	/ MacroSiouian
Powhatan		Cherokee	
Pamlico		Tuscarora (pre 1712)	
	/ Muskogean	Nottaway	
	Choctaw-Chickasaw	Meherrin	
	Koasati-Alabama		/ Tutelo
	Hitchiti-Mikasuki		Catawba
	Creek-Seminole		Biloxi
	Atakapan		Ofo
	Tunican		Saponi
	Natchezan	Isolate	
	Timucuan	Yuchi	
	Chitimachan	Calusa ?	

Creeks have profound respect for the orderly motions of their world, which they believed was pervaded by an all-embracing energy (*boea fikcha* ~ *puyvfekca* literally 'inner heart'; also meaning soul, spirit, ghost). Because pulsing, quivering movement is a fundamental manifestation of this active energy, the link between right living & world order means that "When people lose their moral path, the earth will tremble."[64] Increasing tensions, resistance & uncertainties − often between culture & nature, humans & others − are its cause. Hence, while a slow, steady pulsing was the ideal state of this world, any disruption resulted in its intensification toward violent trembling. At fault were humans disrupting the world & like geologic faults, causing earthly distress.

Ibofvnga, deified mental energy (cosmic Mind), willed the conjoining of four elements at creation. Two were male (Fire, Wind) & two were female (Earth, Water). Within each pair, one is definite & specific (Fire, Earth) while the other is indefinite & diffuse (Wind, Water). As breath, wind animates all life. Winds individuate by direction, indicated by the crossed logs at the sacred fire. From sky, Grandfather Sun & Grandmother Moon provide moderating heat & light & communicate with Earth through Fire. Today the Christian God is known to Creeks as Breath Holder (*Hesagedamese*), addressed at local churches in prayers & hymns in both Mvskoki & English.

Benjamin Hawkins, federal agent to Creeks in 1800, summarized 8 full days of "Boos-ke-tau" at Kashita, White Mother Town of Lower Creeks.

---

[64] Jean Hill Chaudhuri & Joyotpaul Chaudhuri, <u>A Sacred Path</u> ~ The Way of the Muscogee Creeks 2001: 106.

1ˢᵗ day "… warriors clean the yard of the square & sprinkle white sand, when the a-cee (*assi* = decoction of cassine yupon holly leaf[65]) is made." The Fire maker kindles the new flame as early as he can, while warriors cut & bring in four logs, each as long as a span of both extended arms.[66] Shaped into a cross by these logs, the new fire at the center of the square will burn with these logs for four days.

"They collect old corn cobs & pine burrs, put them into a pot & burn them to ashes. Four virgins who have never had their menses, bring ashes from their houses, put them in the pot & stir all together [before dividing them into two pots].[67] The men take white clay & mix it with water in two pans. One pan of the clay & one of the ashes are carried to the cabin of the Mic-co [*mikko*] & the other two to that of the warriors. They then rub themselves with the clay & ashes. Two men appointed to that office, bring some flowers of tobacco of a small kind, (*Itch-au-chu-le-puc-pug-gee,*) or, as the name imports, the old man's tobacco, which was prepared on the first day & put in a pan on the cabin of the *Mic-co* & they give a little of it to every one present.

"The Micco & counselors then go four times round the fire & every time they face the east, they throw some of the flowers into the fire. They then go & stand to the west. The warriors then repeat the same ceremony …

"The *pin-e-bun-gau*, (turkey dance,) is danced by the women of the turkey tribe [clan]; & while they are dancing, the *possau* is brewed. This is a powerful emetic. The *possau* is drank from twelve o'clock to the middle of the afternoon. After this, the *Toc-co-yule-gau*, (tadpole,) is danced by four men & four women. (In the evening, the men dance *E-ne-hou-bun-gau*, the dance of the people [*hiniha*] second in command.) This they dance till daylight." …

2ⁿᵈ day "… about ten o'clock, the women dance *Its-ho-bun-gau*, (gun dance.) After twelve, the men go to the new fire, take some of the ashes, rub them on the chin, neck & belly & jump head foremost into the river & they return to the square. The women having prepared the new corn for the feast, the men take some of it & rub it between their hands, then on their faces & breasts & then they feast."

---

[65] *Assi* literally means 'leaf' in Mvskoki, expanding to refer to 'medicine' by part for whole metonym.

[66] The length of the logs determined how long a fire burns & it was an art to make sure, even with periodic feedings of firewood, that the last bit of four foundation logs burned up at the end of a rite.

[67] Hawkins mentions only one pot of ashes here, but there clearly have to be two to account for the four containers mentioned immediately afterward.

3rd day "The men sit in the square."

4th day Women, early in day, get [glowing] coals from the new fire, clean out their own hearths, sprinkle them with sand & remake their home fires. The initial four logs burn out at the central fire. Men put ashes on their chin, neck & belly, then go to water. "This day they eat salt & they dance *Obungauchapco*, (the long dance.)"

5th day Four new logs were set at the fire. Men drink *a-cee*.

6th day "They remain in the square.

7th day "Is spent in like manner as the sixth.

8th day Two large pots filled with water & fourteen of "their physic plants"[68] are beaten by chemists (*E-lic-chul-gee*), who "blow in it through a small reed & then it is drank by the men & rubbed over their joints until the afternoon."

"A cane is stuck up at the cabin of the *Mic-co* with two white feathers in the end of it. One of the Fish [78s] tribe, (*Thlot-lo-ul-gee*,) takes it just as the sun goes down & goes off towards the river, all following him. When he gets half way to the river, he gives the death whoop; this [war] whoop [*yahola*] he repeats four times, between the square & the water's edge. Here they all place themselves as thick as they can stand, near the edge of the water. He sticks up the cane at the water's edge & they all put a grain of the old man's tobacco on their heads & in each ear. Then, at a signal given, four different times, they throw some into the river & every man at a like signal plunges into the river & picks up four stones from the bottom. With these they cross themselves on their breasts four times, each time throwing a stone into the river & giving the death whoop; they then wash themselves, take up the cane & feathers, return & stick it up in the squares & visit through the town.[69] At night they dance *O-bun-gau Haujo*, ([crazed] mad dance,) & this finishes the ceremony.

"This happy institution of the *Boos-ke-tuh*, restores man to himself, to his family & to his nation. It is a general amnesty, which not only absolves the

---

[68] Specifically numbered & named as 1) *mic-co-ho-yon-e-juh*, 2) *toloh*, 3) *a-che-nau*, 4) *cup-pau-pos-cau*, 5) *chu-lis-sau* (the roots), 6) *tuck-thlau-lus-te*, 7) *tote-cul-hil-lis-so-wau*, 8) *chofeinsuck-cau-fuk-au*, 9) *cho-fe-mus-see*, 10) *hil-lis-hut-ke*, 11) *to-te-cuh choo-his-see*, 12) *welau-nuh*, 13) *oak-chon-utch-co*, 14) *co-hal-le-wau-gee*.

[69] Stone is emblematic of permanence, if not immortality, combining pebbles with the war cry asserts long life, represented by the feathered cane tube.

Indians from all crimes, murder only excepted, but seems to bury guilt itself in oblivion."

Busk Today

Much of this prior Busk complexity is now gone. One man fills roles that several performed in the past. Fewer numbers are involved & periodic gatherings to camp at the ground & mound now limit & simplify any involvement since the town is no longer a place of full-time residence. Three studies, two dissertations & a book, provide information on recent practices.[70] By combining their insights & details, a more comprehensive understanding emerges on present practices.[71]

In the best treatment of a modern-day Busk,[72] in one of the Seminole Creek towns, Willie Lena & James Howard note that it occurs over a long weekend to accommodate the constraints of wage labor during a work week. Families live in nearby villages & cities, or fly from far away, leaving houses with all the modern conveniences. For their Busk, therefore, members return to a rural place where the women manage camps (*hvpo*) that are roofs held up by support posts, with wood fires for cooking. Since it is often over 100 degrees, heat is intense around these fires, adding to the sacrifice made by women. Propane-run refrigerators & ovens help to feed the crowds who attend as guests.[73]

The scheduling of dances must take into account events at other square grounds, especially those of ancient town allies ("tied up together"), either descended from the same ancestral mother town, such as Coosa, or sharing the same fire by moiety affiliation.[74] Over the years, towns tend to follow the same

---

[70] Lester Robbins, The Persistence of Traditional Religious Practices among Creek Indians, 1976, based on his own "touching medicine" at Greenleaf (*Asilanibi*); Amelia Rector Bell, Creek Ritual, The Path to Peace, 1984, based on Seminole-Eufaula, with visits to all the other towns; James Howard with Willie Lena, Oklahoma Seminoles, Medicines, Magic & Religion 1984, based on New Tulsa (Talisi Little River).

[71] Bell gained some fluency in Mvskoki & recorded many of the relevant terms, which have been updated according to the new dictionary of Muskogee – Jack Martin & Margaret McKane Mauldin, A Dictionary of Creek~Muskogee, with notes on the Florida & Oklahoma Seminole Dialects of Creek 2000.

[72] Howard with Willie Lena, Oklahoma Seminoles 1984: 123-156. Howard's earlier description of the Busk in this town (The Southeastern Ceremonial Complex & Its Interpretation 1968: 103-119) did not have the insights later provided by Lena. His prior diagram also misplaces the main mound.

[73] A duplicate pattern of open buildings periodically or seasonally occupied by families occurs in the "church camps" of Creek & Seminole Christians.

[74] Lester Robbins, The Persistence of Traditional Religious Practices among Creek Indians 1976: 67, 111, 121.

weekend order, especially for their Busk, so everyone can plan ahead. The actual date for that year, however, is announced at the Spring Stomp dance held a few months before the harvest season.

Thursday is the camp-in day, with women readying their outdoor kitchens. A stickball game may be played in the afternoon by men against women around a tall pole. An evening meal is served to all & another pole game may occupy the twilight. Messengers called (night) deacons are sent by the *Mikko* (town chief) four times to the camps to announce a Stomp dance that night. Those attending give money & tobacco (as cigarettes, cigars & plugs)[75] to the *Mikko* for the fasting men to smoke during the coming days & nights. At midnight, a Long Dance ends the stomp & all go to sleep, the men apart from the women.[76]

At Friday dawn about 5:30am, the town crier awakens the men, fasting from food & water after midnight, to assemble in their arbors (*api:ti: ~ topv ~* 'bed') at the sides of the square.[77] Grabbing garden tools, men raked the entire inner surface of the ground (*pasko:fa* = 'swept within', *tvceofv*) bare & clean. Any weeds are pulled out & uneven places are filled in to level the ground for easy dancing. A low circular ridge (*tvce ~ paska tikin* = 'swept to the edge') marks the edge of the ground, made up of all the refuse that was raked out to there. The poles holding up the arbors are inspected & replaced if needed, using young trees cut nearby. These saplings are always kept upright, never laid on the ground, since they hold up the arbors & thence symbolically the sky. Benches are examined for rot or damage to their stump supports & plank seats. Any weakened ones are replaced. Stringers, with some newly replaced, are evenly spaced out across the roof. Brown, dried willows from past dances are removed from the roofs & taken away to a remote area to decompose. At marshes, pickup trucks are filled with fresh-cut willows that are then driven around the outer square, pausing at each arbor. Some of these moist branches are then tossed upon each of the four roofs to provide sunshade & cooling by evaporation. Work moves counterclockwise from the Mikko's arbor in the west, to south, east, north & back to west.

---

[75] Bell (Creek Ritual 1984: 234, note 1) lists tube-like objects closely associated with men as cigarettes, ballsticks, feather canes, long flashlights, etc.

[76] Rules & restraints (*si:yinfayatka ~ sintackita*) are a defining duty of men, while women have their own obligations & both together are well aware that their wrong actions will harm others & the whole town as well as themselves, See Lester Robbins, The Persistence of Traditional Religious Practices among Creek Indians 1976: 153.

[77] Only men sit in the arbors, which are called their "home," assigned by matriclan such that those clans named for land animals are often in the north arbor, those for birds & other sky beings in the south one & amphibians with the Mikko in the west − serving as cosmic mediators. This male Earth / Sky opposition balances female Red / White moieties.

When everything is clean & tidy, all of the men stand outside the ring. Twelve special plants (= wormseed) are used to brush off each of the arbors, posts & benches. Then one plant is placed in the crook of each of the three front posts. Called "killing the greenwood," it propitiates the freshly cut trees, protects the fresh arbors & vivifies the square. If it is too hot & dry, water is sprinkled over the bare ground to keep dust down.

Meanwhile, *Mikko* instructs men to clean off two oversized wooden knives (*atassi*), then coat them with white clay. The same clay is also applied to two coconut shell rattles. Small white crane feathers are tied at the tip of each knife & top of each rattle. At intervals, the "deacons" are sent (four times in all) to the camps to tell the women to get ready to Ribbon dance.

At noon, when the sun is on high, at some grounds, the women begin the Ribbon Dance (*hoktaki o:panka* = 'women's dance'), wearing long colorfully silk strands hanging from their dresses. Theirs is the first public use of the newly cleaned central plaza & they finish its spiritual preparation. Their long patchwork dresses, beribboned blouses & rattles secured on their leg calves are seen, while their diligent work remains unseen. Toward the front of the line, leg rattles are made of whole turtle shells; those behind are made with perforated condensed-milk cans. They are shaken in a distinctive style that sounds like a chugging railroad train. To honor the women, men also dress up, often in new cowboy-style clothes, to sit in the arbors, urge & watch.

A red blanket is spread over a pair of folding chairs in the south arbor for two singers, who are given the coconut rattles. Each now places a long crane feather in his hat band. The *Mikko* gives to each of the two deacons a cane staff topped by a white feather. They then lead the women into the inner square ground, drawing a line in the dirt midway between the empty fireplace & the arbors, etching small circles to the side in front of the north & south arbors. The two women in front carry the wooden knives, with the handles wrapped in cloth so there is no direct contact with the skin. All of them wear or carry wet towels to wipe off their dripping faces during the intense heat of the day.

For the first song, the women tread in place, heel-toe left, heel-toe right. At the second dance, the lead woman, a respected matron, dances out in front, half way around the circuit, to stand inside the north scratched circle. Thereafter she keeps a quarter pace ahead of the line, pausing at each arbor. As the women approach the starting point, they hop, pounding the pellets in leg rattles. Men cry out an encouraging *loja loja* = 'turtle turtle'. Tiny girls at the end of the line are called "the tail" & also thanked loudly.

A second set follows before the drained women are allowed to rest & drink from a bucket & ladle carried among them by the deacons. They are also offered sticks of gum. The final two sets are then danced & dressed-up men file onto the ground to begin a regular Stomp dance, as a line of alternating men & women, which ends this event. Everyone is invited to eat in the camps. A stick ball game may be held in the afternoon, before supper. Another stomp dance is held 9-12PM that night.

The next morning, Saturday, the men, again fasting, gather inside the ring before dawn & begin to use shovels to remove the ashes & mounded earth of the central fireplace (*tvco ~ tvcopaskv*). These are added to a nearby mound, human height, in the southeast.[78] The small fire mound is leveled & inspected for irregularities. Men stand behind each of the middle back posts of the arbors & help to sight on a peg that is pushed into the exact center of the square. New dark soil, often taken from a specific direction, is then brought by wheel barrow to rebuild & bless this low fire mound.

A new fire is laid with fresh logs in a cross [+ plus sign] shape. A tree has been cut into four equal lengths & each is placed to align to a cardinal direction. Each growing tip is pointed away from the fire, as though nourished by it. The medicine man blows [mouthing dicta] along each length to bless & pray before placing it down. They are positioned at the north, south, west & east. The same procedure is done with four ears of corn, which are placed beside each log.

Dry tinder is placed in the center & a pure flame is lit to start the fire. Meanwhile, women have put out the flames in their own camps & cleaned out their fireplaces. The deacons are told to announce when enough glowing coals have been produced so boys can carry new fire to the family camps, usually upon blades of long-handled shovels.

This fire is the earthly parallel of the Sun, buffered from the earth surface itself by being set atop a small raised & flattened mound disk. It & all the fires in the camps must be extinguished yearly in order that it sink into the ground & "forget"[79] (in short term memory) any anger of the past year that could have adverse effects. This forgetting explains why murderers & other offenders gain amnesty if they can safely enter a square during the Busk that is held a year after their crime.[80]

In the square, watched by the new fire, preparations begin for making the medicine. Button snakeroot & red willow were gathered before dawn.[81] These are

---

[78] Bell (Creek Ritual 1984: 100, note 17, 166) said these ashes were scattered in the woods, but this is preposterous. As a woman, she would not have been involved nor well informed about such men's business.

[79] Bell, Creek Ritual 1984: 100.

[80] Many sources insist that a murderer did not gain amnesty by entering the square & only wergild or execution resolved this heinous crime.

[81] Yaupon holly, a key ingredient in the SE, only grows in a tiny spot in Oklahoma.

pounded soft & placed in a tub ~ crock of fresh water.[82] The medicine man then blows into them through his cane tube (*spofkita*), bubbling, blessing & praying while everyone on & near the ground is absolutely silent so only these sounds can enter the medicine. After steeping, one frothy ladleful is sprinkled by a man spiraling around the open plaza & another measure is poured slowly onto the fire. This medicine offering "cools" these places as everyone cries *ma-do* = 'thanks'.

Women & children gather outside the ring. They carry containers to hold medicine, which they drink & wash with. Some is taken back to the camps for immediate use. Women & girls come forward to be scratched with a needle ~ thorn that marks four parallel lines along the arms & legs. The scratcher should be a man of the same clan, to keep the wounds light & "friendly."

Then the men file up, paired by arbor, to drink of & wash with the medicine. Both plants are used only the first time; just willow roots are used for the other three sessions. Each male is given a dipperful, or more by request. Using two fingers, the medicine is first splashed to the four directions, before drinking & washing with it.[83] The crooked left ring finger flicks the medicine because it has "no name" & forgets easily, especially any ill will. Some officials are expected to step off into the field & vomit up a frothy discharge to show that they have indeed fasted. Some are scratched.[84] Each arbor's members proceed in the order of west to south to north.

After the second taking, new members are named, each receiving a plug of tobacco while standing before the west arbor & then running counterclockwise around the fire & whooping. The plug is kept or given to a respected man in hope

---

[82] Only ordinary, everyday items (crocks, sauce pans, lawn chairs, buckets) are now used, though they are dedicated only to this ritual purpose & are carefully stored away from women. As such, their common availability helps disguise & protect the Busk, in lieu of the attention-getting Mississippian art works for which the region is so famous. See Richard Townsend, Hero, Hawk & Open Hand ~ American Indian Art of the Ancient Midwest & South 2004.

[83] Such liquid flicking was once typical of every meal, such as venison soup when eaters would "dip their middle finger in the broth & sprinkle it over the domestic tombs of their dead" under the house floor, James Adair, The History of the American Indians 2005: 159.

[84] Throughout the Southeast, people, especially men, would ritually vomit before hazardous or critical undertakings. Often this was associated with gorging on the caffeinated Black Drink, but this was not an automatic response. Such purging had to be physically or psychologically induced, most often by leaders & officials. Doing so in public proved, by the frothy byproduct, a commitment to fasting, as well as providing a means of divination & a litmus test for any diagnosis of internal conditions. The immediate object was to fill the mouth with saliva & thereby gain the support of the lower world, associated with water & the river as "long man." By contrast, the upper world is associated with fire & with blood, which is purged from the body by scratching to remove impurities, gain strength & win stamina, Cf Charles Hudson, Vomiting for Purity 1975.

of a return blessing. The name is recorded in the town ledger kept by the Mikko as that newly named person takes his place in the arbor of his own mother's clan.

The men then prepare for the Feather Dance (= *ta:fv o:panka*), their complement to the Ribbon Dance. A man of the Bird clan takes a staff topped with a white feather & stands upon a tiny mound in the northeast that was rebuilt at the same time as the fireplace that morning. It is just wide enough for his two feet. Using a low, drawn-out cry, he "calls the birds." Other men of the Bird clan have tied white feathers atop many cut river canes. These are passed out among the men, each holding one.

The men file around the edge of the ground, led by two men shaking coconut rattles & another beating a water drum formed by a wet skin fastened over a ceramic crock partially filled with water. Four circuits are made during each dance, pausing at each arbor. Overall, there are four sets of 16 rounds. If the afternoon is very hot, only two sets may be danced, with the last two done during the cooler evening or next morning. Because they are in the midst of taking & drenching in medicine, the men do not dress up & young men often wear cutoff jeans. The wands are carried upright during the march, but clacked together over the heads of the musicians at the end. The four songs refer in turn to blue crane, snake, buzzard & circling birds preparing to fly south.

After two dance sets, men take medicine a third time. Then the last two Feather sets are often danced. From the moment they began taking medicine, men pair up for the rest of the night. They were never to be alone so as not to be tempted to sleep, eat, womanize, or drink until the proper time. A collection is taken up for the *hilis haya* & given to him with shouts of "*ma-doe.*" Transferred out of the town along with the money is any anger or resentment among members because the medicine man is technically an outsider.[85]

After the Feather Dance & "touching medicine" are finished, a beef (or deer) tongue is placed on the fire "to feed it & give it voice."[86] In some cases, it is first placed on the swept-up rim around the ground until the medicine "touching" is done, then it is picked up between ballsticks & placed on the fire. Usually, however, it is stuck on a carefully peeled forked stick beside the fire to cook before finally buried deep in the flames. Its consumption ends formal fasting.

After the fourth medicine taking, the men "go to water," retiring to a nearby stream or metal tubs to wash off, sometimes counting off so all can hear the exact number of participants. As they march to this location, men whoop back & forth along the line. They return to their arbors for final prayers & instructions. Then

---

[85] Bell, Creek Ritual 1984: 209.
[86] Bell, Creek Ritual 1984: 172, 300.

they go to the camps to eat, but they are forbidden to sleep. A stickball game may occupy the afternoon.

At twilight, nicely dressed, people gather in the square for the Buffalo Dance (= *yanasa panka*), alternating pairs of men & of women along the line. The men hold staffs or ballsticks to represent front legs. This dance begins at the tiny mound where the bird caller stood before the Feather Dance & the drummer now stands. The step is a double pat of left foot followed by two rights. At the end, the deacons gather up the staffs & the dancers form a single file for the twisting, spiraling Long Dance & a final Stomp dance. The camps again feed everyone.

At dusk, the men of the ground gather for a special evocation of their ancestors in the Mothers ~ Ancient Dance. Only members of the ground dance the first four Stomps, each led by a member of one of the arbors. Thereafter, visitors are selected by the deacons to lead stomps all through the night. No medicine taker can sleep, but they can eat & drink tea, coffee, soda (pop) & water.

On Sunday, after the sun appears in the sky, the last dance is held & the men take a final round of medicine before they go to water & are dismissed after a final speech. During the morning, a stickball game is held while everyone waits for the seen fire to burn itself out for another year.

Members of a square ground will gather four times during the year to take medicine, but the Busk is the most elaborate & intense of these. The Stomp dance season is active from the first budding of trees to first frost. Two of these dances are held in the Spring, the Busk in late summer & the fourth in the Fall, according to the Gregorian calendar. For Creeks, however, sequencing begins with the Busk & continues through Fall & Spring to bracket Winter & assure vital regrowth.

Town fires move periodically, so even they are not constant. Over time, dancing feet will wear down a central depression that can threaten the fire in heavy rains. Disputes among members themselves or concerns about continuing on leased land can also move a fire. Few tribal towns have not had occasional gaps in their continuity, though their fires are believed to continue burning underground, endangering unprotected members. Presumably, in ancient times, this vitality resided within the big mound chamber.

Once decided, a town relocated along with ashes from its ancestral "fire," establishing direct continuity with its ancestral past. After holding stomps for four years at the new site, a pole is set up in the center to cast a shadow at sunrise on the solstice to mark the location for the center front post of the Mikko's (west) arbor. As the sun moves through that day, the locations & separating spacing for the central front posts of each arbor are marked to the north & south. Once all the arbors are in place, the pole is pulled up to leave a hole, ashes from the prior fireplace are buried ~ cached by the medicine man (*hilis haya*) at arm's length into the bottom of that hole & the new fire is built atop a small mound placed over the top as the town's *axis mundi* tysic.[87]   At every subsequent Busk, placing the central peg repeats this founding of town & arbors using shadows cast by this pole.

In sum, Creek rituals & culture regard an entity as moving among fixed contexts, rather than blending them together.[88]   All are engendered as male (variously grandfather ~ light ~ sun ~ defended) / female (variously grandmother ~ dark ~ water ~ nurtured). Acting in partnership, men sustain the old, while women create the new. More dynamic though dangerous, further equations are hot / cold, growth / stasis & conflict / peace. Recurrent rituals & well-lived "clean" lives serve to check the extreme growth of superheated tumult because "weeds grow at night" as a sign of danger & chaos.

Firelight & dawn of a clear day bring lives & perspectives to clarity for the wellbeing of world, cosmos & universe in all dimensions & expressions.

Iroquoian Cherokees

The Cherokee world began as a speck brought up from the sea bottom by Water Beetle & expanded as a mushy disk until Buzzard's wings slashed into it to make the rounded ridges & the deep, dark valleys of ancient Appalachia. Thunders put fire into a tree on an island, which Water Spider rescued after many other animals tried & failed. Soon, immortals, ghosts, monsters & big & little people inhabited this world. Cherokee mixed economy of farming & hunting became personified in the epic of the hero twins, whose parents were *Selu* (maize) & *Kanati* (lucky hunter). Fishing was vital – using hooks, nets, weirs & crushed plant poisons to stun & surface a catch hauled in by families.

Society, with 30,000 members at its peak before epidemics struck, was divided between White & Red, civil or martial, duties. The White side was led by the <u>uku</u>, a calm elderly priest & the Red by a younger, aggressive war captain. Each was advised by elders, clan leaders & honored Beloved Women, such as Nancy Ward, the most famous <u>gila</u> because of her warnings to settlers & rescue of a woman already tied to a torture stake. Towns consisted of a central plaza for public dances & events, a rotunda atop a mound for councils & winter rites & numerous households, each with component square arbor, oval home & small domed hot house (<u>oosi</u>) for frigid weather. Their Mother town centered on the mound of Kituwha, near the heart of their territory.

Townhouse rotundas were often built atop much older mounds, attributed to an ancient people who occupied the region before another group moved in & then

---

[87]   Bell, Creek Ritual 1984: 98, 219.
[88]   Bell, Creek Ritual 1984: 54, 77, 136, 218.

were themselves displaced by the Cherokees. For 1762, Lt. Henry Timberlake[89] reported that the townhouse at Chota (*Itsodiyi* 'fire place(d)', "metropolis" ~ capitol ~ sacred fire of the Overhills), held five hundred on its tiered benches. When the Cherokee national government formed in north Georgia, its capitol became New Echota, where they fought against their eventual deportation to Oklahoma. Known as the "Cherokee Cases", their appeals to the US Supreme Court in the 1830s set the course of Indien policy in the face of the Removal Act of 1830 & the racist administration of the SOB, the seventh president (who cannot be named, but appears on the US $20 bill, which some Cherokees will not handle).

The year was divided between summer (*go•ki*) farming & winter (*go•la*) solidarity rites. When grass greened in early March, at the new moon, a rite celebrated the coming fertility of the earth. When roasting corn was ripe in late July, the Green Corn ceremony included drinking an emetic, scratching to release blood flow & all-night dances. At the full harvest, in September, flour corn & other maize was thanked in the same way. In mid-October, each town "went to water", bathing in rivers that had been medicinally-charged by falling leaves. Ten days later, all fires were extinguished, a new one was kindled in each rotunda & shared among all the homes, beginning a new year. At the same time, homes were cleaned, old clothes discarded & wrongs forgiven. In early December, after a huge collective hunt to supply a passenger pigeon feast, people gathered to pray & wave purifying evergreen boughs. During winter, communities gathered in their rotunda for company & warmth, instructed & entertained by bawdy, lewd Booger (begger) maskers & by animal dances, held while the earth was quiet & these animals resting. In time, all Cherokees professed Christianity & abandoned this ritual series, except for a ritual thanking of the life-giving corn crop. Sports retained religious aspects. Two-racquet ballgame continued to include blood-letting scratching, conjuring & traditional prayers.

Driven from the few Out Towns along the eastern frontier, native homesteaders filed, through friendly whites, on private property that became the core of the Qualla Boundary reservation in North Carolina. Redeemed & avenged by the US Army's sacrificial execution of *Tsali* (Charlie) & his sons, Cherokees still remain at Qualla, Snowbird & Murphy. With casino funds, they have repurchased, at a cost of millions of dollars, their mother mound of *Kituhwa* & also Cowee. *Nikwasi*, a crucial mound, is now a tiny park, purchased by local school children, at the industrial edge of Franklin, NC. In 1730, Sir Alexander Cumings forced a council in the rotunda atop *Nikwasi* that "named" a Cherokee "emperor" (however ludicrous) & selected leaders to visit London. During the US Civil War, decades after the Cherokees "drive away", *Nunnehi*, tiny people who live inside

---

[89] Lt Henry Timberlake, Memoirs 2007: 17.

mounds & in these lands, emerged from *Nikwasi* to drive off Federal forces attacking local Confederates.[90]

By historic times, kinship was traced through seven matriclans: Wild Potato ~ *ani•ko•take•wi* ~ *ani•ka•thoke•wi*, Deer ~ *ani•khawi*, Bird ~ *ani•ci•skwa*, Wolf ~ *ani•hwaya* ~ *ani•wahaya*), red Paint ~ *ani•wo•ti*, Blue ~ Panther ~ *anihsaho•ni* & Twister ~ Long Hair ~ *ani•kilohi*. Clan members had to marry into another clan, with the groom (husband) moving to the town of his wife. Conformity was enforced by kin etiquette, joking, gossip, mocking, or ridicule before official public censure was invoked. Acting from the dark side was sorcery & witchcraft that siphoned off life force & led to long, lingering, painful death.

Conjurors had a series of divinatory & healing techniques to restore the patient. Diseases, in general, are caused by animal "bosses ~ masters" avenging disrespect or insult shown to their species, but each, in turn, had a specific plant cure applied by skilled herbalists. Stories also warn about the dangers of the huge Uktena serpent, monster Leeches & predators who are stone-clad, liver-eating, spear-fingered, or razor-elbowed.

In their Appalachian Summit homeland, Cherokees, during historic times, occupied four districts. The Overhill (along the Upper Tennessee) were expanding into former Creek lands & contending with Chickasaw & Choctaw toward the southwest; the Valley (Hiawasee River system) were moving southward toward Creeks; the Middle (Little Tennessee), noted for famous townhouse mounds, were hunting northward in lands drained by the Ohio River & fighting Yuchi & Iroquoians; & the Lower (Upper Savannah) were facing eastward & contending with Catawbans of the Carolinas.

The only surviving southern Iroquoian language, spoken Cherokee has six pitches.[91] Known dialects (with their distinctive sounds & their fates) include Otali (*l*, *m*, *tl*) of the Overhills, now spoken in Oklahoma; Kituwha (*l*, *m*, *ts*) of the Middle Towns still spoken at Qualla (Polly), Valley (close to Otali) spoken at Snowbird (Cheowah) & the extinct Elati (*r*, *w*, *ts*) of the Lower Towns. Ironically, Elati was the source for the tribal name Che<u>R</u>okee, where others have Che<u>L</u>vki.

---

[90] James Mooney, <u>Myths of the Cherokee</u>, Glossary 1982: 515, 542 [Bureau of American Ethnology, <u>Annual Report</u> 19 1900]; Duane King, A Grammar & Dictionary of the Cherokee Language 1975: 183; Durbin Feeling, <u>Cherokee – English Dictionary</u> 1975: 91, 93, 116, 221, Cf *gaduhv'i* = town, *gadugi* = mutual aid co-op. Mooney (1982: 527) lists the famous mound of Nikwasi near *nakwisi* = star, meadow lark, suggesting, like landmarks in Washington State such as geological Grand Mound, it may be a Star who plunged into earth. Oklahoma Cherokees know moundbuilders as Red Eye People ~ *Dinikani*, Fierce People ~ *Aninayegi*; <u>Cherokee Stories of the Turtle Island Liars' Club</u> (Teuton 2012: 61).

[91] These 6 pitch accents (with their graphic codings) are low = 2 \, low fall = 1 \\, low rise = 23 V, high = 3 /, high fall = 32 ^, high rise = 4 //.

The genius of Sequoyah (George Guess), a silversmith, produced a syllabary (86 pairs of consonant-vowel) to make Cherokee a written language by 1821 after decades of experimentation, burning of early attempts by his wife & great suspicion that only a sorcerer would be so involved in mysterious seclusion.

Traditional Cherokees retain the word *gatiyo'i* – from *gada* 'soil, dirt, earth' + *–yi* locative for 'place(d)', once meaning septagonal townhouse & substructure mound – for their modern stomp grounds. These are the result of a deliberate reform by Redbird Smith, who studied with Natchez Creek religious leaders before reviving a Cherokee ground & receiving venerated wampum belts (M 354) from the Ross family. Every summer, Cherokees host a birthday dance on the weekend nearest July 20 at his grounds.

Keen to get to the source of Europeans power & to play their kings off against each other, Cherokees at Tellico welcomed the enigmatic Christian Priber in 1736, who is sometimes called a Jesuit & French agent, though he was German. During his many years of wise council & advice for assuring proper weightings by traders, he died uncharged in a British prison in the Carolinas.

Cherokees (including Major Ridge, John Ross & Sequoya), assuming support for their loyalty, fought with US forces under the SOB at Horseshoe Bend, devastating hostile Red Sticks during that Creek civil war. Afterward all Creeks, including US allies, were punished with the loss of their Alabama homelands. In Georgia, Cherokees had moved south to occupy former Creek lands, founding New Echota. Key families built mansions at river fords & ran ferries & stores, such as the Ridges at Rome, the Vanns at Chatsworth &, especially, the Rosses at Chattanooga. After his father was murdered, Rich Joe Vann prospered until he & his prized thoroughbred died in a steamboat explosion.

Cherokees welcomed missionaries for their schools, including Presbyterians at Brainard near Chattanooga in 1817, Moravians, after 1734 overtures, at Springplace, Georgia, in 1801 &, especially successful, Baptists in 1820 (Mooney (1982: 107). Also in 1820, Dwight Mission was founded among Arkansas Cherokees by Congregationalist Cephas Washburn & survives to this day in Oklahoma under Presbyterian auspices.

In North Carolina, Cherokees held on to land through the aide of *wilusti* ~ "little will" ~ Major Will Thomas, adopted son of chief Junaluska, as well as lawyer, officer of Cherokee Confederates & periodic asylum inmate.

Today, Cherokees comprise three federally recognized nations, Eastern Cherokees in North Carolina &, in Oklahoma, either Western or Kituwah Cherokees, both headquartered in Tahlequah. Western Cherokee citizenship is traced through a person named on the 1906 Dawes enrollment list & includes a quarter million members. Official government was so shadowy that once a year the US President, acting through the head of the BIA, appointed at Cherokee principal chief for one day to sign all necessary documents. The Kituwah, growing out of the "pins" (Unionists during the Civil War) are more traditional, generally darker & more fluent in the language. In the 1860s, in punishment for their support of the South, Western Cherokees, with many acres but little money, sold adopted citizenship to Delawares & Shawnees in exchange for lands in Oklahoma. Today, ongoing legal battles in federal courts are trying to unravel jurisdictional & sovereignty issues in the 16 counties that were Cherokee reservation before Oklahoma unilaterally imposed statehood in 1907.

Pawnee of Nebraska

Pawnee consisted of four tribes: three South Bands along the Platte River of *Chawi* ~ Grand, *Pitahawirat* ~ Tappage, *Kitkshahki* ~ Republican & along the Loup River, the *Skiri* ~ *Skidi* ~ Wolves, who occupied about fifteen villages. Within the Plains Caddoan languages, Skiri, Arikara & South Band Pawnee (which preserved more archaic forms), diverged about the same time. *Chawi* seems to have been the parent of both *Kitkshahki* & then *Pitahawirat*.[92]

Historically, all but two of the Skiri villages belonged to a confederacy organized around a hierarchy of mystic bundles in several classes, variously associated with an individual, a village & the whole confederacy. Every visionary assembled a bundle to confirm his own spiritual partnership. When merited by prestige, warriors could also request a special war bundle to take along.

A village was defined in terms of its own mystic bundle in such a way that the hereditary chief – expected to be wise yet humble, strong yet not aggressive & generous yet reserved – was supposed to descend from its original owner, a Star who decided to come to earth. Each village (of about 20) was a basic unit with its own ancestral Star, chiefly founder, bundle, fields & cemetery. Lodges of the same town might be scattered among those of other villages because allegiance came through matrilines rather then location & marriage was limited to other members of the town in order to in-focus the bundle & its <u>*wa•ruksti•*</u> ~ *puwah*.

Pawnee economy combined bison, hunted by men from tent (tipi) camps, with crops, farmed by women at mudlodge villages, especially maize (15 varieties), beans (8 varieties), squash (7 varieties), melons & sunflowers. Seasonal bison hunts took place after the Spring planting & after Fall harvest, with families returning in Summer to their "mudlodge" in town so women could store dried meat & work their fields. These homes looked like big grass-covered mounds, with long entry ways to keep out cold, that had to be cleaned & fumigated before families moved in for the Nebraska winter. Thick inner layers of poles & outer sod

---

[92] Roger Grange, An Archaeological View of Pawnee Origins 1979: 136.

provided insulation. At the village & along the trail, Pawnee women gathered berries, fruits, seeds, nuts & tubers, particularly prairie turnip, groundnut, sunroot, plums, riverbank grapes & chokecherries.

When willows sprouted, heightened rituals conducted by men & female work parties ("bees") greeted the farming season. Fields were hilled, planted, hoed, weeded & harvested. Three ceremonies marked this bounty – Green Corn, Ripe Corn & Four Pole, when an earthen ring & tiny mound were formed by bundle priests. Crops were processed & dried for storage in enormous cache pits, both inside the lodge for easy access & hidden outside for emergencies. Farming beliefs & rituals centered on maize, which (who) was specifically identified as a symbolic Woman. Therefore, every cornfield was planted with an even number of hillocks to represent her breasts.[93]

In the sea of grass that was the Plains, just like open ocean, people relied on the stars to guide them at night. One of the Pawnee bundles included a star chart painted on antelope hide that fascinates modern astronomers because it is so accurate for the 1200s night sky.

Each bundle safeguarded its own village, strongly encouraging ties of internal solidarity & endogamy as well as its own cornfields & burial grounds. Bundles of Wonderful Skull & of North Star represented all the Skiri confederated villages. Directly below these in *puwah* were four bundles associated with the semi-cardinal directions, each with a leading chief who held authority over everyone for six months within an overall two year sequence. These were Yellow Tent Bundle of the Northwest, Red Star of the Southwest, Big Black Star of the Northeast & White Star of the Southeast. Accordingly, North bundles led during the winter & South ones in summer.

Complementing this sky-based system of priests & bundles were the earth-based shamanic doctor cults, including the Medicine Lodge that was unique to Pawnee (Cf Omaha). The landscape of all Plains tribes was dotted with buttes & hills which were "holy homes" of spirits of particular species – such a bison, bear, elk, deer & antelope. Those blessed by each species formed a separate guild & presumably recognized a hill as "holy home" of that particular species. Twice a year, in the spring & the fall, each lodge met to sing & dance.

Named *rahurahwaarukstii'u* ~ "holy grounds", fourteen of these animal lodges have recorded names & most correlate with specific geographical places that looked in profile much like earth mudlodges of ancient Pawnee towns. The

---

[93] Gene Weltfish, The Lost Universe 1964: 124, 144. To vivify crops & earth, Morning Star sacrifice of a young captive ~ enemy girl also took place in the Spring, See Douglas Parks, Pawnee, Part 1 2001: 515-547.

insides of both were arranged in the same way, with spirits & humans sitting on the north or south sides of a central fire & an east-facing entryway.

The most famous of these places, shared with other Plains tribes, was Spring Mound ~ Waconda Spring in north central Kansas, developed into a health spa about 1884 by local whites, who also bottled & sold its water. As an artesian spring atop a low mound, the site became famous for spiritual & medicinal help.

In addition, Pawnee recognized a special set of animal lodges where spirits of many species gathered &, in special cases, had instructed a human in the conduct of an all-encompassing tribal Medicine Lodge. This Medicine ~ Doctoring Lodge featured in each of the four bands, made up of leading doctors of other cults. Each Medicine Lodge met in spring & summer to sing & dance before holding their major rite in the fall to display their amazing curative *puwahs*. That of the Skiri lasted a month.[94] During each one, offerings of smoke, corn & meat were given to animal lodges dotting the landscape.

Pawnee society was organized around a series of overlapping triads, defining social classes & polity, with pervaded by symbolic Man & Woman, reflected in economics, ritual & cosmology. Classes consisted of elite "high" born, ordinary ("good") & poor, sometimes with captives beyond the pale (outside the system). Included in elite were families noted for generations of chiefs, priests & shamans. At lesser rank were the families of warriors & other ambitious individuals, lacking pedigree or ancestors of distinction. Chiefs benefited both from Star ancestry & their own life-long training & personal prestige.

In general, all these triplets reflected a basic one of leader / executive / commoner.[95] Society as a whole consisted of hereditary families / ambitious families / ordinary families, including "boys" – aimless young & old men. Cross-sectioning these threefold segments was the duality of gender reflected in hunting by men & farming by women. Genders had different roles, functions & responsibilities within the overall whole. For example, while society was matrilineal, succession to office was generally patrilineal.

In all, this duality expressed a profound belief in the creative conjoining of opposites, epitomized in sexual unions such as male lightning fertilizing female earth, male fire kindling flames on a female hearth board & ubiquity of chiefly *puwah*, which was represented by lances in its coercive aspect & by cobs of Maize Mother in its nurturing mode.

[94.] Douglas Parks & Waldo Wedel, Pawnee Geography, Historical & Sacred 1985.

[95] Specifically, these triplets ranged from leaders as chiefs/ priests/ doctors, to subsets of chiefs/ attendants/ members, or leading shamans/ cult shamans/ ordinary doctors, to domestic roles organized as grandmaternal leader/ senior wives/ junior wives.

This belief in Man & Woman creative union was a privilege known only to the elite, basic to their store of esoteric knowledge, together with titles & badges, bundle custody & generosity. On its basis, Pawnees recognized that death & destruction were more apparent than real. Time ran in cycles, so life transmuted. Thus, death of plant crops at harvest allowed people to live, until they too died & returned to the soil to nurture plants.

The Skiri universe consisted of many metaphoric engenderings, particularly represented in mythology & ritual by Morningstar Man & Eveningstar Woman:

MAN =	red	day	light	fire	dry	warfare	sky	sun	winter	north	east
WOMAN =	white	night	dark	rain	wet	farming	earth	Moon	summer	south	west

Siouans

lodges   *tipis*
Mandan
Hidatsa   Crow
Chiwere = Ioway Oto Missouria
     HoChunk
Dhegiha = Omaha Ponca Osage Kansa ↑
     Quapaw ↓
Dakota~Santee~E (4 fires)   Nakota~Yankton (2 fires)
                                 Nakoda~Assiniboin~Stony
                                 Lakota~Teton~W (1 fire)

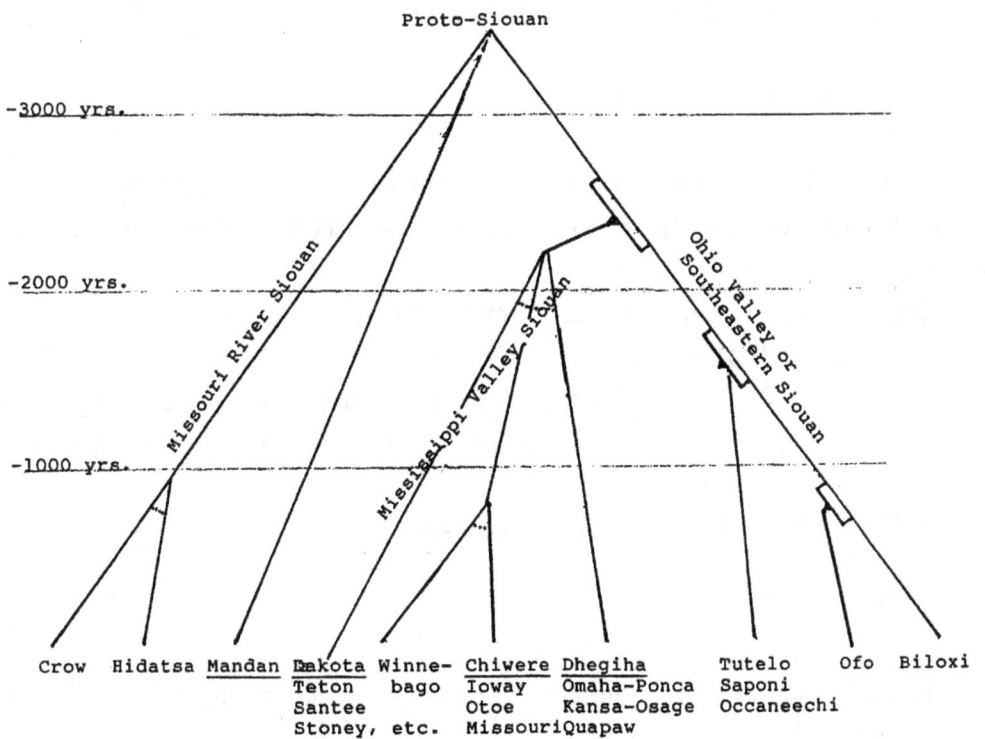

Epidemics, battles & dislocations took a heavy toll so only a comparative study of Midwest & Plains Siouians, both earth lodge & hide tipi, can present a satisfactory glimpse into antiquity. Ohio Valley Siouians (Ofo, Tutelo, Saponi, Biloxi) & Catawba were long involved but less is now known of their pre-devastation societies & cultures. Tribes have distinguishing features. Chiwere Oto stand out by reversing usual sunwise circuits.

Thus, Siouians "rang the changes" on themes of kin, clans, cults & clubs. Sky / Earth moieties, composed of gens ~ patriclans, variously by tribe emphasized usual linkages with gender (man / woman), economy (hunting / farming) & seasons (winter / summer) so that some were unnamed even / odd while those of the Kansa were termed Right / Left ~ *ištóge / yátta*.[96] All groups were sanctified by special bundles ~ power packs composed of appropriate items of clothing, animals, plants & tools. Poles & piles remained important among each & all.

Omaha

Tribal palladia were engendered. Among Omaha (Fletcher & LaFlesche 1972 < 1911), the foremost Dhegiha, their sacred pole set at an angle pointing to the North Star Polaris was male in contrast to the white bison cow hide that was female & kept in a tipi decorated with painted maize stalks. A more ancient Cedar pole was kept in the Tent of War. Though maize remained the staple crop, complex religious rites sustaining Maize within the community lapsed (11: 457).

Aside from gens, members joined clubs ~ cults ~ groups devoted either to social activities or to sacred one, termed mysteries.

Omaha social clubs included

Hethushka = extolling a heroic spirit, valor, thunder & lightning. Its two pipes were kept by leaders of the Kansa gens, other tribes adopted it as the Grass ~ Omaha dance (11: 459).

Kikunethe = leading men met around a fire (11: 485).

T'e Gaxe = stimulated death & recovery (11: 486).

Mo^nwadathi^n ~ Mandan & Tokalo = adopted from Mandan & Dakota by men of good repute, promenading through a town on horseback in finery (11: 486).

Omaha Secret Sodalities included

---

[96] Robert Rankin, 14 December 1981, noted these words mean both the hand & the moiety.

Mo^{n}chu Ithaethe ~ Bear Compassioned for those who envisioned bear healings (11: 486).

Te Ithaethe ~ Bison Compassioned who cured wounds (11: 487).

Wano^{n}xe Ithaethe ~ Ghost Compassioned foretold events (11: 489).

I^{n}gthu^n Ithaethe ~ Thunder Compassioned were gifted with weather control, bringing rain & deflecting storms (11: 490).

Ho^{n}hewachi ~ honorary chiefs who had provided 100 honor tallies as gifts & were privileged to have their daughters tattooed with the Morning Star at the base of the neck (11: 493, 503).

Washiska Ahi^n ~ Shell Having, Omaha variant of Great Lakes Mide Shamans Academy, features *Megis* cowry shells, earth & sky internal grades & final death rites changing a soul into a star for later reincarnation (11: 509, 553).

I^{n}kugthi Athi^n ~ Crystal Having relied on water symbolism & minimal clothing (11: 565).

Of note, maize & mounds are always mentioned together in Omaha cultural history & stories (Will & Hyde 1964: 229, 251).

Hidatsa

Hidatsa (Bowers 1965) featured named age-grades for both men or women between the ages of twelve & about sixty (65: 174). For males ♂, boys began as Little Dog (Crazy Dog, Dog, Old Dog), Notched Stick (65: 176), then bought out Stone Hammer (65: 180), next Kit Fox when unmarried (65: 181), Lumpwood when married (65: 183), Half-shaved Heads in their 30s (65: 183), became tribal police as Black Mouth (65: 184), were released from enforcement as Real Dogs (based on the dog husband story, 65: 194) & became Bulls (65: 198) before they entirely retired from the whole system.

Women ♀ age grades were Skunk, aged 15-20 (65: 200), Enemy when married (65: 200), Goose as mature mothers tending crops & corn bundles (65: 200) & finally White Bison Cow attracting bison as winter food (65: 204). Of note, Hidatsa attributed their farming & associated rituals to nearby Mandans.

Of great significance for understanding pottery production across the Americas, Hidatsa pottery was sanctioned by bundle ownership, since "making of a pot was a contest between the big [Thunder] birds & the snakes" (65: 374). As placation, designs represented snakes, lightning, clouds, water birds & rain", such that herringbone is wading bird tracks, while curved rims evoked clouds & rainbows. Production is also engendered since clay & firewood was provided by men, pot & designs by women (65: 166, 374). Before beginning the process, word is spread is to be left alone & the lodge door is barred.

Crows

Crow, who loosened from Hidatsa, had weak matriclans,[97] moieties in the afterworld & bundles (Wildschut 1975)[98] that channeled *maxpé ~ puwah* specifically of & for Sun Dance (75: 20), War (75: 34), Hoop (75: 43), Arrow (75: 48), Shield (75: 65), Skulls (75: 76), Rock (75: 90), Pipes (75: 114), Love (75: 123), Sorcery (75: 133), Healing (75: 136) & Hunting (75: 146).

HoChungara ~ Winnebago of the Great Lakes

Among nations of the Midwest, the mythic traditions of Ho-chunk (called Winnebago by Algonkians) are particularly well known. Their homeland was Wisconsin, although half later found refuge in Nebraska. There, Paul Radin undertook 1908-13 research, followed by a lifetime of friendship & writing. Hochungara distinguish two types of literature: *Waikan* {= what is sacred, mythic} is set in the fixed past & noted for happy endings; *Worak* {= what is recounted, experienced, historic} occurs in a time that is subject to memory, often with tragic outcomes.

Sacred epic describes creation by Earthmaker, in an oral text once known only to initiates of the Medicine or Mystic Lodge. This is a guild of shamans like the Mide of the Ojibwa. Interestingly, the story of how Rabbit (Hare) founded the Medicine Lodge is regarded as historical, not sacred, because it directly relates to humans, like the origin accounts for various clans.

Through amazing circumstances, Jasper Blowsnake provided this epic of the Mystic lodge, whose ritual initiation of new members enacted creation of the world & was also retold during memorials for deceased members. Blowsnake gave his account only with the greatest reluctance because compelled by a series of startling events. By 1908, the peyote religion, brought to the Ho-chunk by John Rave, had achieved a core of strong converts, including men who had formerly belonged to the Medicine lodge. In their zeal to convert others, three old men were convinced to give Radin an account of Ho-chunk creation, though they had to leave Nebraska before doing so to avoid revenge from local spirits.

Thus, in the top floor of a small hotel in Sioux City, Iowa, precisely at midnight, these men began the saga & finished it five hours later. By the next afternoon, every Ho-chunk knew what had happened & many pressed for a public

---

[97] Ironically, Crow is the technical label for the matrilineal clan kinship system, though transitioning toward bilaterality among Crows themselves.

[98] Sadly, hardships were such that Wildschut collected 260 Crow bundles for the Museum of the American Indian, then in New York City & now in DC.

reading of the text. Previously, only elite members of the lodge knew & told its details. After quick agreement; Radin read his transcription to a stunned audience. Much anger focused on the old men, but John Rave gave firm support until Radin left for New York at the end of the summer, taking along untranslated native text.

The following year saw more converts, including Jasper Blowsnake, who was regarded as the most knowledgeable member of the Mystic lodge. As a test of his change of faith, peyote leaders urged Jasper to dictate the fullest account & he agreed to recite the Ho-chunk words, though he warned that someone would die from this forced telling. Radin wrote out the text in longhand (no tape recorders yet), working six hours a day for two months.

As recitation ended, Radin received a telegram that his own father was gravely ill, dying a few days later. More grievously, Radin was distressed that while he had a native text of unusual significance, never to be repeated, he lacked a proper translation because Jasper blamed himself for the death of Radin's father.

Later, in Washington, DC, Radin gained a literal translation of the rite from a visiting Ho-chunk. But that speaker was not a member of the lodge & could not understand the many esoteric, poetic & metaphoric usages.

After great effort, Radin returned to Nebraska Ho-chunk, but Jasper avoided Paul until he took ill & remained at the home of a friend. There, feeling compelled, he decided that recording the rite was indeed "his mission in life".

For the first month, Jasper corrected prior dictation. Translation to English took six hours a day for another two & a half months. Initiates remained bitter at Jasper for half a year, but peyote believers continually extolled his courage for performing this dangerous & heroic act.

Four other mythic cycles appeared later. After creation by Earthmaker, various protagonists engaged in complex activities to make the world as it is today. For Radin, these different cycles – named for Trickster, Hare, Red Horn & Twins – formed a temporal series of psychological growth for individual & tribe. Each of the four, in turn, progressively gained & gave future virtues of character.

Trickster lived during a primordial, unformed cosmos of vague beings. Many of his traits were (or foreshadowed) human ones, but his total being was never specified. From the beginning, although he is a chief, all of his actions were contrary to modern ideals. Some of his adventures were prophetic, others were parodies, yet all contributed to an increasing orderliness of the world.

Hare ~ Rabbit, born of a spirit father & human mother, was raised by his grandmother, Earth. In his cycle, humans made their initial appearance & gained advantages as he matured & learned about parts of his body through a series of misadventures. Through his actions, few of them laudatory, various customs & institutions began. These included the use of tobacco, slain bear thanking rituals & menstruation observances, along with the special creation of the Mystic rite.

Red Horn was heroic, living in a well-differentiated world with a wide range of defined characters – including humans, monsters & giants. A majestic figure, his death was avenged by his sons, who revived him, then rid the earth of giants. They received war bundles from Thunderbirds, a great benefit for human beings, who now came into their own.

Twins (Flesh & Stump) behaved as bravado juveniles, with a promise of new beginnings. Their contrasting temperaments caused trouble, until a final lesson from Earthmaker curbed their unbridled enthusiasms. After killing one of the four animals (Snakes) holding up the earth, they were terrorized by a giant Turkey to learn fear & restraint. Thus, the Twins benefited from prior characters to mature as full individuals. Since they had at least one adventure with Red Horn, they were doubly tied into the Hochungara mythic past.

By the end of all these cycles, this world included four underworlds led, from bottom to top, by Turtle, Trickster, Earthmaker & Rabbit. The sky was supported by four island weights as anchors ("island quiet makers"), located at its corners. One was near Effigy Mounds National Park, along the Iowa shore of the Mississippi. There, in addition to a collapsed Longtail mural on a cliff face & earthen mounds shaped like lines & dots, a row of heaped hummocks in the shape of bears & birds march up the hillside. At Gottschall Cave in southern Wisconsin, some of their images were painted on the walls of this shrine, in continuous use for 1700 years after AD 350.

Osage of Missouri

Any coherent understanding of the religious & symbolic use of mounds within an integrated cultural system was burst apart by epidemics, slaving & trauma. Indeed, vital aboriginal transmissions became quite fragile. Throughout the Americas, knowledge, especially esoteric information, is synonymous with healthy long life, but, to be valued, is always rare, contested & protected. Transmission of linchpin information was supposed to be given only at the last gasp of a mentor released from life. Among Omaha, this final offering of vital knowledge had a tinge of patricide. Among Osage, special knives were dedicated to "cutting off the heads of enemies", gaining a war honor in defense of the lives of women & children rather than outright aggression & killings (LaFlesche 1939: 16).

Indeed, our best example of a living Mississippian priesthood, though historically located on the Plains, is the Siouan Osage as studied by Francis LaFlesche, himself a chief's son & native speaker of related Omaha. The Osage word for "mound" = *hpá* means "bulge, head, snout" (Quintero 2009: 76, 299) as a poking up ~ leading forth. Osage, with a population of 4000 largely spared devastations from epidemics until the 1880s, were governed by priesthoods relying on patriclans ~ gens, sacred pipes & the tribe as a whole. Led by Eagle, people descended from the Sky as Water, Land & Sky grouping to form patriclans divided between Earth or Sky halves ~ moieties, further divided into Land & Water for Earth & into Day & Night for Sky to dominate daily life. Thus, those of the Land slept on their right side & put on their right moccasin first; those of Sky slept on the left side & donned left shoe first.

Concentrating on clan & tribal initiation rituals, which both prayed for blessings from the Creator ~ _Wakonda_ & explained the universe in progressively learned stages, La Flesche deduced there were 170 such rites.[99] Clan priest initiations generally filled four days, most of the time spent in alerting all the universe for the finale.[100] After pledging to be inducted & submitting to threat from "penalty verses", a candidate had seven years to gather necessary gifts & food for his graduation feast. Both tribal priest inductions took only a single day, because the unseen universe hung in the balance until both of the great bundles were owned ~ secured by priests belonging to Earth & Sky halves. The other 168 initiations concerned the visible world, inducting a member into a clan priesthood, with each of the 24 clans having seven degrees that culminated in the ultimate "Sayings of the Ancients".

Osages equated rituals with books since they preserved & transmitted knowledge through a complex interaction of words, actions, images & objects, intended to puzzle the serious, intrigue the curious & impress the literal minded. Each ritual combined songs ~ _wathon_, actions ~ _we'gaxe_ & recitations ~ _wi'gie_, repeating many of the same poetic verses, except that the main image of each stanza derived from that specific clan & degree within its moiety.

A vital identifying phrase specifies "I am a person who has made of X his body" to indicate the clan's "life symbol" through which they approach the Creator. The list of life symbols fills five pages, with examples of X varying from

---

[99] Garrick Bailey (1995: 284, 305) took on the herculean task of synthesizing the cosmology of the Osage, one of the last & most populous Siouan nations to sustain priesthoods directly out of the core Mississippian area, if not from the urban center of Cahokia itself. Of note, this cosmology was articulated in elaborate initiation rituals into Osage priesthoods, as recorded by Francis La Flesche, son of an Omaha high chief, law school graduate & ethnographer, both on his own & in collaboration with Alice Fletcher, his adoptive mother. His Osage research, of much greater complexity compared to Omahas, was marked by tragedy since Black Dog, former high chief & source for comparative materials, died a month after Frank began interviews in 1910 & Saucy Calf, the Buffalo Clan priest whose early dictation to Frank filled 140 pages, suspiciously burned to death in his cabin in 1912. Within a decade, many Osages were brutally murdered by their grasping white husbands in order to inherit headrights to huge fortunes from oil pumped from their unique underground reservation.

[100] Garrick Bailey, The Osage & the Invisible World ~ Works of Francis La Flesche 1995.

immensities such as Sun, Water & Stars to specific animals, plants, objects, weather conditions, colors & abstractions, whose intent is to announce "I am a specific embodiment of my clan". For instance, in the Earth half, Crawfish clan's life symbols are this crustacean & clay that is colored blue, red, yellow & black; while, in the Sky half, Wolf clan's images are Dog Star, Sun & Bison tail.

The special embodiment of each clan & priesthood was its sacred bundle. That of a clan, called a "hawk," held a hawk skin, woven mat bag, deerskin bag, buffalo hair bag, buffalo hide rope, eagle leg, human scalp & buffalo-hide hanging strap. All clan "life symbols" were _waxo'be_ ~ sacred. Hawk, especially as falcon eye emblem, pervaded Mississippian art, indicating martial contexts.[101]

Though Kehoe (2007) traces close parallels between Cahokia archaeological remains and Osage ritual texts, she overlooked a major instance involving the twin burials in opposite directions sharing the bead bird cloak and the slaying of an enemy to provide a ghostly attendant for an Osage soul making its way to the afterworld.

The twin burials had shrouds because large disc "bone beads were found near the bones of the burials indicating that the burials were bound before their placement" (Fowler 1999: 132b). Similarly, while a war party is out to kill an enemy so his ghost can serve the deceased,

> two men wrap the corpse in a robe and wind around it, from the head to the feet, a long lariat. A pole is passed through the loops of the lariat and each of the two men grasp an end of the pole, lift the corpse & slowly march toward the house of the Ceremonial Mourner, followed by the Non-hon-zhin-ga [clan priests] in single fire, all wailing as they go. Arriving at the house of the Ceremonial Mourner, where had assembled the of the Hon-ga [Earth moiety] division, the men carrying the corpse enter & lay it in the middle of the house. The Non-hon-zhin-ga of the Ṭsi-zhu [Sky moiety] division follow & take their accustomed places by gentes at the north side of the lodge. With the corpse a fine horse was brought & tethered near the house for the services of the Ceremonial Mourner (LaFlesche 1939: 88).

A temple ~ House of Mystery held tribal ceremonies and initiations.

---

[101] James Brown explores Osage political economy in his quest for "The Identity of the Birdman" image & Alice Kehoe cites remarkable parallels between Cahokia artifacts & Osage sacred texts for key rituals, both in Kent Reilly & James Garber, <u>Ancient Objects & Sacred Realms</u>: Interpretations of Mississippian Iconography 2007: 56-106, 246-261.

TEMPLE[102]

	OUTSIDE	INSIDE
SEEN	24 clan priests	moiety priests
	war, hunt, weather	namings
	life rites	all 24 clan priests
		war
UNSEEN	2 great bundle priests	2 pipe priests
	tatooing	peace
	New Year	(Bailey 1995: 46)

Moreover, two clans referred to as Men of Mystery & Buffalo Bulls were the symbolic keepers of all clan bundles. For the entire tribe, by moiety, the great bundle's keeper belonged to Gentle Ponka clan, while that of great medicine bundle was Gentle Sky. Osage unity rested on these two tribal great bundle priests ~ *wawathon*. Elder Water clan was symbolic keeper of the peace pipes expressing tribal unity. Among secondary sacra were war standards, rattles, war clubs, sacred bows & arrows, charcoal & more. Known only to adepts, unconsecrated symbols, called "those carried to excite enthusiasm" ~ *wazhawa athinbikshe* & therefore "not real",[103] might be substituted in some rituals, involving all degrees of faith & commitment, both credulous & not.

Each initiation involved officials with formal, functional roles.[104] Typically, these were candidate & his wife, sponsor, assisting sponsor, priests of all 24 clans sitting at fixed seats, holy warrior with all 13 possible military honors, messenger, widows of former priests & singers. Candidate & sponsor were entitled to formal claims to that clan & degree, but it was the assisting sponsor who thoroughly knew this involved ritual in all of its intricacy & precision. Songs – expressing beauty, order & purpose – especially brought the universe "to life", with special verses extolling human ancestor's ability to think – to search with mind & thereby learn ~ *wathi'gethon* "to bring things to pass". Songs & texts described a body from head to feet to convey birth & new beginnings, from feet to head for growth & maturity.

As all of life, original Osages came from the sky (called father) to the earth (called mother), where they met one clan surrounded by death which had always been there & so became known as the Isolated Earth. Between sky & underworld,

---

[102] Most often conceptual, this temple became the House of Mystery when built as a house frame covered with an elk hide on the east, black bear skin on one side, puma hide on the other & white swan pelt spread out on top (LaFlesche 1939: 44).

[103] Bailey, The Osage & the Invisible World 1995: 47.

[104] Bailey, The Osage & the Invisible World 1995: 76.

along the surface of the earth, is the "snare of life", belonging to a sacred spider,[105] holding everything together between birth & death. On this vital snare, clans divide into Sky, split into Day & Night or Earth, split into Land & Water.

Symbolic oppositions between these moieties include

Sky =	♂ male	left	6	morning star	father
Earth =	♀ female	right	7	evening star	mother

Other associations are

East	sun	birth	life	red	male	♂
West	moon	death	harm	black	female	♀

After uniting the two moieties on Earth, Osage priests reorganized their society three times, each a "move to a new country". First came an internal reordering begun by Water people of the Earth half. Isolated Earth priests became responsible for the symbolic "house" where all Osage children were named. Land (particularly Bear & Puma) priests were charged with the "house" where war ceremonies were held. War or hunt leadership was assigned to the Bear, Water, Sky & Isolated Earth clan priests.

Prompt action, however, was impossible because of very excessive ceremonialism, so another reordering improved military tactics, though each expedition remained led by a war priest. This second "move to a new country" organized three types of war parties – men from all the clans, from a few clans within one moiety, or from a single clan.

The third move instituted civil government by two chiefs ~ *gahi'ge*, from Ponka clan of the Earth half & Sky clan of the Sky moiety. To distinguish these as the source of chiefs, they added "gentle" to their name because that was a defining characteristic of such leaders. Each man held vigil until a spirit revealed to him the contents of a "great bundle", either for "medicines" (symbolized by the cormorant & by man & woman roots) or "long life" (symbolized by the pelican & tattoos). The other great bundle priests had the pipes, particularly one with a human face carved into its black pipebowl & hanging from the stem, seven shell beads for the Earth & six copper beads for the Sky. Such emphasis on shell & copper is distinctly Mississippian.

---

[105] Bailey, The Osage & the Invisible World 1995: 241, line 13.

While clan houses were arranged in order around the edges of the town, the two houses of these tribal chiefs were set across the central east to west path of the sun.[106] While each ordinary house had a door facing north or south across this plaza, these chiefly homes had two doors, one on either of the east & west ends.

The goal of all this complexity was an unbroken line of descendants, especially sons, stretching far into the future since the strongest belief of all was that nothing in the universe ever moved backwards. Today, having deliberately set down ~ "unloaded" these arduous religious burdens, Osage seek the same intent through Big Moon peyote rituals of the Native American Church, as well as a strong tradition of Catholic rituals.[107]

Mandan

Among Mandan (Bowers 1950) whose unique far upriver location among other Siouans bespeaks ancestral links to Cahokia, their spectacular Okeepa (below) ceremony saved & renewed the world & was arduously continued by those few survivors of the 1837 smallpox epidemic that obliterated the entire tribe (50: 111). Many Okeepa participants wore costumes from bundles sanctioning their roles with *xópini*, Mandan power ~ *puwah* ~ energy ~ force (50: 335).[108]

Mandan Maize rites provided blessings to assure a good corn crop via a complex of sacred epics, songs, pipes & bundles, including two large pots that served food in one rite & served as drums in another version of rain making feasts when their patron spirit, Grandmother Old Woman Who Never Dies, was represented by a dressed pole with attached pack basket

APPROXIMATE TIME AND PURPOSE OF PRINCIPAL TRIBAL CEREMONIES

Approximate Month	Ceremony	Purpose of Ceremony
June to August	Okipa	General tribal welfare Buffalo fertility rites
May	Corn Fertility	To insure good gardens
March to October	Goose Society	Rains and good growing conditions for crops
August to October	Harvest festival	Thanksgiving rites for crops
March to October	Old Woman Who Never Dies	Rain and good growing conditions to insure good gardens
January to January	Old Woman Who Never Dies	Doctoring and warfare
March to October	Corn Pipe	Fertility
September to November	Eagle-trapping rites	To capture eagles
July to September	Eagle-trapping rites	To trap fish
January to January	Eagle-trapping rites	To corral buffaloes
April	Eagle-trapping rites	Success in hunting or warfare
April and November	Big Bird	Warfare Rain
January to January	Small Hawk	Warfare
June to August	Small Hawk	To call buffaloes
December to March	Snow Owl	To call winter buffaloes
January to January	Snow Owl	Warfare
March to October	Snow Owl	Rain
January to January	People Above	Warfare Doctoring
January to January	Shell Robe	Warfare Doctoring
December to March	Red Stick	To call winter buffaloes
December to March	White Buffalo Cow	To call winter buffaloes
January to January	Bear	Doctoring and warfare
March to November	Snake	Rain Doctoring Warfare

---

[106]   Recall that this is also how Onondaga longhouses, where the Iroquois League met formally, were distinguished from those of the other Five Nations, See Edmund Wilson, Apologies to the Iroquois 1960: 64.

[107]   John Joseph Mathews, The Osages 1961: 627.

[108]   In written Mandan, a murderous sister allied with Women Above crafts the Shell Robe shawl (Parks, Jones & Hollow 1978: 107).

ready to harvest maize. The oldest Maize bundle came up out of the underground world with emergent Mandans, when maize was a man, but once above ground maize could take the form of women (50: 183, 191, 196).

Snare power bundles included those for eagle trapping, when men in lodges with ash pole pillows representing snakes (♂ on left, ♀ on right) camped apart from their families in the hills (50: 206, 234) & for catfish trapping (50: 255). These bundles were best used in alternate years for eagles or fish, as well as providing success with a bison corral.

Thunderbird bundles evoked hawks, ravens, crows & eagles, sanctioning a fall feast & sweat before these birds migrated south (50: 260, 269).

Kite Hawk was a two part bundle devoted to fidelity, with that of the husband ♂ including a "hawk, sage, hide rattle, pipe, bison skull" & that of the wife ♀ a "sacred robe, gourd rattle, sage, magpie" (50: 270) within a world composed of four layers of earth & four of sky. Of note, this bundle also included male transvestism (50: 272).

The Snow Owl bundle involved feasting, arrow making, bison calling & the Holy Woman (50: 282).

With some dread, People Above ~ Day Boat bundles served to avert misfortune & ill will. One includes a copper ring representing Old Woman Above, copper ring for Sun, copper crescent for Moon, large gourd rattle, six magpie tail feathers, twelve owl tail feathers (linked to Moon & night), human scalp, grizzly bear left arm, grizzly bear skull, bison bull lower jaw hair tuft, bison calf head hide strip, bison foreleg long hair, bison left horn, bison skull & stuffed jackrabbit as Sun's scout. Danger is involved because the Sun is a cannibal, urging warfare to feasting on slain warriors. Grizzlies are pets & firewood carriers for Women Above. Effigies of these women are set atop poles upon small mounds, which then attracted fasters & rings of human skulls (50: 296, 298, 302 #5, 305).

Shell Robe held an elk hide with a painted Morning Star & rows of clam shells dangling scalp hairs & magpie tail feathers, sweet grass braid, ash digging stick, buffalo bull skull & plain wooden pipe (50: 308), for hosting war feasts.

Red Stick bundle – featuring 12 tapered boards, "large wooden pipe, an owl, two hide rattles, a painted robe & sage" (50: 315) – sponsored four nights when "wives walked with buffalo", calling bison closer during coldest days of winter.

White Bison Cow, highest women's age-grade, celebrated bison coming into river bottoms for winter, while Goose ♀ sang for maize & for spring & fall bird migrations (50: 324), with the Corn Priest drumming (Will & Hyde 1964: 268).

Widespread Calumet Adoption Pipe, derived from Arikara & Caddoan Hako, extended kin ties to honored children & their families (50: 329).

Until Moves Slowly died in 1905, Mandans sustained a line of 34 Corn Priests, who also kept one of the 3 (4) tribal turtle drums, recorded in pictographs

& listed by Scattercorn (Curtis 1909 V: 17). As just noted, he drummed as Geese sang for crops & birds when "The wild goose signifies maize; the swan, the gourd; the duck, the beans." While singing, two girls wore duckbill headbands, chins of left side women were painted black & those on the right side were painted blue (64: 248, 263, 267, 268, 273).

The measure of Mandan fields is a *nupka* (*naxu* in Hidatsa) of 7 rows of maize interspersed with 5 rows of beans for the equivalent of a US ¼ acre. Planted on small hills, with squash leaves giving shade, harvests were systematically stored in huge cache pits, both in house floors & sealed outside, entered by ladder.

At the spring corn blessing, this priest wore a fox skin turban, sage sprigs & moccasins, with blue paint on his upper face & red paint covering his body. Stretched between his house posts was "a map of the world, drawn on skins". Fall harvest featured a robe offered by a woman & a pole. An entire maize plant, 5 roots to tip, was outlined three ways on the robe, a fresh cut cottonwood was wrapped with this robe by the priest, all feasted in his lodge & then the wrapped tree was erected in that woman's field, where harvested ears were piled up to the bottom edge of the robe to show bounty. The robe then belonged to the first to touch it.

Mandan Okeepa

Along the Upper Missouri River, every Mandan village was a loose cluster of domed, growing-grass-covered earth lodges facing toward an open plaza. A D-shaped Okeepa lodge was on the north side & a fenced shrine, called the ark, was in the center. This shrine was sacred to Lone Man, who made the earth with First Creator ~ Coyote & established Mandan culture. A cedar post, painted red, stood at the middle of the shrine to represent Lone Man, surrounded by a cottonwood plank palisade, like the one he used to protect Mandans from the Flood, whose highest level was indicated by an encircling willow branch tied near the top edge.

Lone Man made the world to the east of the Missouri River & First Creator made that to the west. Similarly, Mandans were divided into moieties:

West	Black	Buffalo Bison
East	Red	Corn Maize

Before over 80% of the Mandans died during an 1837 smallpox epidemic, East included six matriclans & West had seven.

Each moiety built, decorated & painted their own half of the Okeepa lodge. Three east side roof supports rested on cornmeal & were painted red. Three uprights on the west rested on buffalo hair & were painted black.

This lodge represented Dog Den Butte "holy home". There Speckled Eagle ~ _Hoita_ once lured & impounded all the bison, causing great hardship. He was tricked to release them, jealously joining with Lone Man at the first human-sponsored Okeepa. In sum, this rite was a world renewal to celebrate a) creation of the earth, b) retreat of the Flood, c) release of the buffalo & d) initiation of boys & men into the tribe. If only one rite were held that year, it occurred after families returned from the summer buffalo hunt. Any more were scheduled before & after this outing.

An Okeepa filled four days, each night concerned with both time, an era of tribal history & space, as a cardinal direction (S E N W). Roles & events depended on owning special bundles, with garments & rights to select the performers who wore them in the Okeepa.

Principals in the rite were Lone Man, Hoita, 8 singers (called Blue Herons), 8 buffalo dancers & Okeepa Maker. He was a man whose vision to host the rite had been approved by Okeepa officers & the community. For a year after pledging to be host, his family amassed over a hundred gifts of robes, elkskin dresses, cloth, shirts decorated with porcupine quills, leggings & knives.[109] His matriclan also gave generously. Every villager contributed something as a gift for participants. Prior to the rite, Okeepa Maker avoided situations where bison were butchered or their entrails eaten so as not to offend their spirits.

Though Lone Man went everywhere, Hoita, like his spirit in Dog Den Butte to the east, remained inside the lodge until the last day. Before the start, residents moved out as that lodge was cleaned, painted & adorned with fresh willows.

Between fifty & a hundred males pledged to fast, pray & suffer. They ranged in age from eight to thirty-five, although most were teenagers & the youngest only fasted for a single day. Older men suffered & endured to the end.

Day 1 Creation ~ South

Before dawn, a crier went through the village announcing the imminent arrival of Lone Man. Chiefs painted their faces black & gathered at the home of the head chief to wait. With the dawn, the man impersonating Lone Man came from the **south**, painted completely white, wearing a wolfskin robe, jackrabbit fur collar & anklets & a headdress of porcupine hair, fringed with jackrabbit fur & topped by a stuffed raven. In his left hand was a pipe & in his right a flat, ashwood club. It was decorated with designs of Moon & Thunderbird on one side & of the Sun & Morning Star on the other.

---

[109] Emphasis on knives during Okeepa may echo Ramey flint blades, cf Osage "cutting" knives.

Members of the Black Mouths, always acting as camp police, met Lone Man. After ascertaining his intentions, they took him to the Okeepa lodge where all the men gathered. There, he recounted the origins of the Okeepa, restating his promise to return yearly for the rite when willow leaves were fully grown.

The head chief sent the crier through the town to warn all women & children to remain inside with their pet dogs. Lone Man wandered through the village retelling stories about creation, impounded buffalo & Flood. At each lodge where a boy or man lived who was about to undergo initiation, Lone Man received knives to take back to the lodge. In exchange for each knife, Lone Man gave a handful of pemmican ~ greased & granulated buffalo meat, often mixed with wild berries.

That evening, Okeepa Maker took all of his amassed gifts into the back of the lodge, along with bags filled either with pemmican or with meal balls. These were made from ground up corn, beans, squash & sunflowers. A singer brought in a dry, rolled-up buffalo robe to serve as a drum. During the night, three singers, painted red & wearing eagle feathers & anklets taken out from their bundles, shifted the drum so it moved from west to east. Two men with rattles sat beside the drum. Lone Man sat in front, smoking his pipe & eating pemmican. Since the first day involved the start of Mandan history, trappings were minimal.

Males entered to fast & undergo ordeals. Each was naked, painted according to personal desires, carrying a shield, quiver & bow in his left hand & his father's medicine bundle in the right. Each boy arranged his own place, with a sage-covered bed & a bison skull pillow, per his moiety & clan membership. His weapons hung behind on the back wall, with the bundle propped up in front.

An altar, north of the fireplace between the moieties, held four human skulls, four bison skulls & four sky posts. Each represented one of the four directions divided between the moieties. Knives filled the center of the altar, placed underneath Bull Dancer outfits.

After all was prepared, Lone Man gave his pipe to Okeepa Maker & directed Hoita to supervise inside of lodge. Whenever drummers sang, boys danced in the lodge. By midnight the drum rested in the east & singing ended. Boys "cried" (prayed) all night long.

At daybreak, boys reversed their robes so the hair was outside to assumed the guise of buffalo impounded by Hoita. Singers took the drum outside, placed it just east of the ark & sat behind it facing the lodge. Rattlers sat behind them, waiting for the Okeepa Maker. He came out painted yellow & wearing an entire antelope skin as an apron. He placed pipe & pemmican in front of the drum, then walked to the south side of the ark. A buffalo cow skull had been placed inside the palisade & a bull skull outside. Standing on the bull cranium, Okeepa Maker placed his hands & forehead against the planks, praying to Lone Man for community wellbeing.

When he finished, drummers sang as the fasters filed out from the lodge. They danced by moiety on either side of the ark before joining together on the south side. The Okeepa Maker continued his weeping prayer as the fasters took on roles as buffalo, pawing the ground & hooking horns at each other. Then all the men crowded back into the lodge. Fasters danced four times the first day – at sunrise, pre-noon, mid-afternoon & pre-sunset. Very young fasters, spared further hardships, often left the lodge after this first day.

At sunset, Lone Man went to the keeper of the sacred turtle drums – rawhide covered frames filled with buffalo hair pellets – which had helped to avert the Flood. Lone Man lifted these powerful emblems to predict future bison hunts by their weight – the heavier the drum, the more buffalo there would be.

Women could not enter the lodge so they left needed firewood outside the door. Those females who were fasting stood on its entry roof until the third sunset.

Day 2 Ordeal ~ East

Okeepa, meaning "look-a-likes," was named for Buffalo Bull Dancers who appeared this day. Before sunrise, green willow branches were delivered to the lodge. Eight large men had been previously selected to embody these bison. Other animal impersonators had also been selected by the owners of appropriate bundles. For example, those with Bird bundles selected Bird dancers & those with River bundles appointed water creatures & snakes, since all rivers were inhabited by Snake spirits.

In all, dancers included eight Buffalo, two Bald Eagles, two Women (wise, foolish), two Swans, two Snakes, Calumet Eagle, Hawk, two Black Bears, two Grizzlies, two Beavers, two Dried Meat Strips, two Nights, two Days, two Wolves, First Creator Coyote, Meadowlark, Fool ~ Owl & many young Antelopes.

For the entire morning, men with proper bundle *puwah* painted & dressed each animal dancer. Bulls wore horned bison head skins & bundled willow branches. Painted on their bodies were stripes & rings of red, black & white as symbols of such strength & potency that their foreskins were tied up & overcaked with white clay.

At noon, women left food outside the lodge for dancers, Lone Man, Hoita & drummers. Inside, fasters & Okeepa Maker avoided all food & water. Okeepa Maker led the dancers out of the lodge, left his pipe & pemmican in front of the turtle drum on the **east** side & resumed his place at the ark to pray.

Pairs of Bulls took up positions at the four directions around that shrine. Dancers went into the plaza eight times that day. Fasters only came out once, after the first Bull dance, because their ordeals now began. Each day, four more dances were added, making a total of 40, the number of days the flood lasted.

Inside, each faster presented himself to men of his father's clan. Using the knife already given to Lone Man, these men poked four holes in his chest or shoulders, implanted two wooden skewers & attached rawhide ropes, used to suspend the boy from roof beams. Skewers inserted in the legs were attached to bison skulls. Fasters stayed suspended in midair for a time. Then men with poles spun them around until they passed out. Once unconscious they were lowered & left to recover. Upon reviving, they crawled over to a masked man & offered their left little finger for amputation. Lack of this finger was a sign of tribal initiation. Other fingers might also be sacrificed, as women often did when mourning. Some suspensions were timed so that returning Bull dancers could hook the boy with their horns, giving him luck for bison hunting.

That night intended animal dancers came to the lodge so each could receive a special stick conferring authority to dance the next day.

Day 3 Returns ~ North

Called "Everything Returns," this day was devoted to high drama. The entire morning, bundle owners painted & dressed their dancers. Before noon, all filed out of the lodge while Okeepa Maker went to the ark. Fasters rested & looked **north** from the south edge of the plaza during four dances. Before the fifth, they returned to the lodge for their ordeals to continue.

Every dancer had an assigned location. Bull dancers paired at the four cardinal (N, S, E, W) directions & then separated to semi-cardinals (NE, N, NW, E, W, SE, S, SW). Day dancers were on the east & Nights on the west. Bears were on the north. Antelopes, boys painted with yellow bodies & white heads, frolicked all over the plaza.

During the first dance, a figure appeared off in the distance. He was painted black with many white & red circles, with a red sun disk on his chest & a red moon crescent on his back. This was the Owl ~ Foolish ~ Fool, son of the Sun who had no respect for sacred things. His clothing was a close-fitting buffalo hide cap decorated with a raven feather, cornhusk necklace, buffalo tail & bison fur anklets. Pure libido, hanging over his bison hair breechclout were a wooden rod & two small pumpkins. He carried an eight foot pole with a red ball of bison fur, representing a human head, tied at one end. A fine thread linked the end of this pole to the tip of the rod between his legs so that when he lifted the pole, the rod arose suggestively.

Understandably modest, women & children acted terrified of him. Moving in a zigzag, he came toward the ark until Okeepa Maker confronted him with the *puwah* of Lone Man's pipe. Subdued, Fool instead acted like a bison bull in rut, approaching two Woman dancers. The Wise one refused him, but the Foolish one did not. Later, he pretended to mount some of the Bull dancers. While the other animals danced twelve times that day, Fool only appeared four times.

After his last appearance, he rushed the lodge doorway, with the pole forced sideways so it broke. Women then mobbed him, splinted the pole & drove him **west** out of the village. Cowering on the ground, the rod & pumpkins were removed & given to a woman, who wrapped them like a baby & displayed them from the lodge rooftop.[110] At the river, Fool dancer washed. Men bound up his cap & necklace into the shape of a doll & hung it from a pole in front of the lodge as an offering to the Sun. Thus, both women & men received powerful, life-giving effigies from vanquished Fool.

The last dance was led by the two Nights, who, acting as Stars, moved very slowly until the first actual stars appeared in the sky, when everyone returned to the lodge & fasters were released from their vows.

Day 4 Hunting ~ West

On "Hunting Day," only the four largest, bravest Bulls danced. Of note, special hunters exercised poles & hoops. New willows refurbished the lodge floor.

The first dance featured only Okeepa Maker, drummers, rattlers & four Bulls. During the day, Bulls danced in honor of each of the clans, thirteen before 1837 & ten afterwards. In all, sixteen dances were held. Okeepa Maker, along with a few brave fasters, suffered on this last day.

Finally, four special songs were sung. Each turtle drum was lifted to predict the quantity of future bison hunts. In four stages, these drums were moved from east to **west** while the men stamped their feet like a bison herd. Everyone followed Hoita out of the lodge, taking their usual positions, as he replaced Okeepa Maker at the south side of the ark, with Bulls further south. Four times, Bulls danced toward Hoita as hunters jabbed into them, drawing blood from their legs as a prayer for hunting success.

Then each Bull stood & bellowed to represent, in order, a season & direction: spring = east, autumn = west, winter = north & summer = south. Finally, gathering around the ark, Bulls removed their masks & danced in frenzy with the hunters. The last fasters were led from the lodge by their father's clansmen, who were painted blue on the right side & red on the left. Then,

---

[110] George Catlin's (1967: 83-85) eyewitness account of the 1832 Okeepa has a fascinating sequence, written in Latin, in which boys's ordeals did not begin until after Fool was castrated & the woman on the roof allowed them to start. On the night after Okeepa ended, this same woman hosted a "walking with the buffalo" to transmit *puwah* between men through their wives (Cf Kehoe 1970). In Melanesia & elsewhere, puberty ordeals for boys do not begin until their mothers, in public, agree to allow these tortures initiating their sons into manhood.

dragging buffalo skulls, these boys ran around the ark, as rapidly as possible, until they passed out. When the last one collapsed, drumming & singing ceased & the hunters threw hoops in the air. When revived, these fasters went back into the lodge. Those on the west rubbed their wounds with cornmeal & those on the east applied buffalo marrow. Later they went home to drink broth & eat sparingly, until they could resume taking food.

Meanwhile, Lone Man gave all the knives to the Missouri River, along with a few robes & seven meal balls. In the lodge, gifts went to all officials, dancers & participating father's clansmen. Later, Okeepa Maker & any fasters who had been blessed with visions assembled medicine bundles according to instructions they received at their ordeals.

Given the enormous cosmic drama that is Okipa & Mandan's continued obsession with chunkey, their significance at Cahokia seems assured.

X X X X X

While Okipa is public, dramatic & complexly involved in world renewal, vital roles by bundles, ranks, clans & clubs ~ cults ~ guilds bespeak wider implications. Again, poles, stone knives, masks & crystals feature, along with tobacco & datura to enter trance, alternative universes, or contemplative stupor. While maize was more important than bison at Cahokia, these herds may well have lured its heirs up the Missouri River.

Cults, many age graded, characterize Omaha, both social & secret; Mandan, featuring turtle drums & corn priests; Hidatsa, both men's & women's; Pawnee, star derived town & earthly personal bundles & especially Osage because so much survives in native language texts, thanks to Omaha Frank LaFlesche. HoChunk show the importance of creation epics ~ tribal genesis saga for validating Chiwere & other esoteric fraternities. Cherokee illustrate yearly cycle of 7 clans & 7 rites immersed in crops, rivers & sky lore. Centuries ago, their *uku* priestly leader lapsed & their abusive priesthood was eradicated, providing negative examples of the overreaching & misuse of *puwah*.

Cityscapes & Cultures

While bonds between Chaco & Keres (& Mexico) are likely, debate surrounds Cahokia's ties, if any, to ethnographic tribes, though most scholars look to Dhegiha & Chiwere Siouians. The error, however, seems to be with the searchers not with the sources. Looking for flat out obvious references to a "city," "big village," "great camp" has not worked & a more native perspective is needed, such as comparison with Aztec Nahuatl, where a city state is metaphorically called an *altepetl*, literally meaning "water mountain" (Lekson 2015). Armed with this image & reviewing a range of Siouian tales, a plausible tie emerges in the Mandan epic of Lone Man's journey in a self propelled canoe to "an island in the ocean off the mouth of a river" (Beckwith 1930: 5, 12) to gain a special food or abalone shells after surviving challenges by chief Manike intended to feast & pipe smoke them to death. Lone Man placed a reed through his body & so was able to safely pass food & smoke into the ground. Carrying off their intended supplies, on their return home, Lone Man instructed everyone in rites & ceremonies around a post surrounded by a barricade fence, enabling all to survive a Flood sent by Manike four years later.

In another Mandan epic, suggestive of chunkey, to which George Catlin reported Mandans were addicted, Lodge Boy ~ *Atutish* is able to capture & tame his twin Spring Boy ~ *Mahash* when they were playing "with gambling sticks & a round stone with a hole bored through" & "the boy got down on his knees to look & see if the ring lay on the stick" (30: 33). Overall, these important twins are matched by others over the millennia, including those sharing the Beaded Cape in Mound 72.

On the last day of Okeepa, special hunters skilled in the use of lances & hoops drew blood from the legs of Bulls, echoing chunkey gear if not also sacrifices toward victory.

Maize had a crucial role in both cities & there are abundant materials on Busk & other corn ceremonialism throughout the Americas. Most telling perhaps is that the ever eclectic Navaho regard their entire religious system as like a maize stalk, with various chants branching off like leaves from the mainstalk of Blessingway ~ *hózhǫ́ǫ́jí* (Farella 1984), the root, stem & font for all.

Shifting locations & migrations seems related to cosmic concerns, with Keresans moving back & forth to their Chaco center from the Dolores in the north to the Puerco in the south, before finally settling in the east on the Rio Grande & San Jose. Similarly, as mound top using Toltec faded in Arkansas, Cahokia rose with mounds of many shapes & functions, including lordly homes & halls. Similarly, in ancient Ohio, Hopewell layouts of circle & square at High Bank earthworks shifted north & turned 90° at the Newark Octagon to better achieve proper longitude for key astronomical alignments (Lepper 2005: 161).

Lastly, while Keres puebloized others by means of their priesthoods grafted into other societies & kinship systems, Cahokia diffused. Humble priests whose main insignia was a left bear paw mitten contrasted with Falcon warrior in flashy copper and shell. Eastern Woodlands mounding rites fractured, according to Robert Hall (1997: 160), into ethnographic rites for fertility ~ world renewal, for adoption ~ succession & for mourning ~ soul release. For historic Plains tribes these became Sun Dance, Calumet & Ghost keeping, whose morphing of ethnographic analogies further complicate archaeological interpretations.

The key dynamic involved blood / bundle ~ people / place harnessing *puwah*. Throughout the arid Southwest, reliance on water & maize encouraged cooperative matrilineal blood ties, especially in adjoining stone households linked into clans, phratries & often moieties, variously named Turquoise / Squash ~ Summer / Winter ~ Land / Water. Along the Mississippi, a mix of wild & field foods ~ farming & hunting, relying on men, encouraged patrilineal organizations.

Complementing blood are bundles, place-based arrays of items sanctified by visions & virtues to provide the basis of personal, clan & cult identities. Osage bundles involved 170 initiations at the tribal level, while many personal bundles are opened at feasts when Thunder first rumbles in the spring, as life-giving *puwah* regrew landscapes. Transmitted through bundles, poles, effigies & artifacts, such as knife blades which draw nourishing blood & deflect thunderstorms, *puwah* is concentrated, redirected & diffused for human & cosmic purposes.

Bundles are foci for various stages of integrations, from whole communities, through clans & cults, to families & individuals. Their 'owners' ~ caretakers thereby derive social & political authority, with personal bundles kept at the bedside & tribal ones kept in temples, shrines, or secluded locales. Among the more remarkable bundles are those composed of the remains – skulls, long bones, hair – of their visionary founders, compounding & concentrating blood & bundle for increased regard, much like the relics of saints in the Roman Catholic & Orthodox Churches infuse reliquaries, shrines, chapels ~ curates, churches ~ priests, cathedrals ~ bishops, basilicas ~ archbishops & Rome ~ pope.

Proofing & advising on the manuscript that became this volume, Blue Clark (2016) noted these universals & parallels for rites across the Americas: Suncentric, 4 ~ 7 directions, priests, ritual song & dance, animals & men, plants & women, fasting ~ feasting, purging, liquid medicines, community harvest, renewal, night long rites, shared new fire, built environs = paths, shrines, plazas, mounds, borders, reverence for ancestors & ancient places

In sum, Chaco & Cahokia emerged from their climates & landscapes, relying on maize economy & rituals, guided by priesthoods with divine celestial sanctions. Earthly leaders assumed personas of orderly sky beings, especially Sun, Moon, Polaris & Venus (both Morning & Evening), but when their worlds disordered, leaders suffered until deposed. Reinforcing their own authority were elite troops (with filed teeth) of warriors ~ bodyguards ~ thugs ~ soldiers, who both kept the regional peace (*pan pax*) & trimmed rival dynasties, whose heirs featured in the next human sacrifice to better serve their lords above & below.

Public theater encouraged elevated stagecraft, often incremental mounds (like 72), witnessing tableaus of bodies, bones & belongings soon deeply buried, though alive in memory. Over time, safe & secure mounds expanded their functions, variously feasting, housing, skywatching & burial. Most dramatically, a thousand years ago, Arizona Hohokam changed from focal oval ballcourts to rectangular house mounds, with their public looking up at leaders after looking down at players.

Blood lines follow universal patterns of lineage, clan, phratry, moiety, tribe; more matrilineal in the Southwest & Southeast, more patrilineal in the heartland & Great Lakes. Bundles are normally a male inheritance, though as in the case of Scattercorn's custody of her father's Mandan corn bundle, proper care is primary over descent. Some bundles have such potency that their assembly is both temporary & hugely public, such as Acoma "Suns" & Mandan "Phallus Baby".

Of ceremonies just reviewed, Busk definitely played a major role at Cahokia, like Corn Dances at Chaco, though pilgrims probably also celebrated at their home fields. Solar & cleansing rites by priestly guilds dominated Chaco, with world renewals "to keep the world moving" foremost. Indeed, as *puwah* amasses & depletes, so must it be renewed & recharged, now as in the past.

Bib

Adair, James 1930 <u>History of the American Indian</u>. Samuel Cole Williams, ed. NY: Promontory Press. [1775, London]

2005 <u>History of the American Indian</u>. Kathryn Holland Braund, ed. Tuscaloosa: University of Alabama Press.

Adams, E. Charles 1991 <u>The Origin & Development of the Pueblo Katsina Cult</u>. Tucson: University of Arizona Press.

Ahler, Steven, ed. 2000 <u>Mounds, Modoc & Mesoamerica ~ Papers in Honor of Melvin Fowler</u>. Illinois State Museum Scientific Papers # 18.

Ainsworth, Caitlin, Patricia Crown, Emily Jones, & Stephanie Franklin 2018 Ritual Depostion of Avifruana in the Northern Burial Cluster at Pueblo Bonito, Chaco Canyon. <u>Kiva</u> 84 (1): 110-135.

Alt, Susan 2001 Cahokian Change & the Authority of Traditon: Ch 9, 141-156. <u>The Archaeology of Tradition ~ Agency & History Before & After Columbus</u>. Timothy Pauketat, ed. Gainesville: University Press of Florida.

Altschul, Jeffrey 1978 The Development of the Chacoan Interaction Sphere. <u>Journal of Anthropological Research</u> 34 (1): 10-146.

Akins, Nancy 1986 A Biocultural Approach to Human Burials from Chaco Canyon, New Mexico. National Park Service, Branch of Cultural Research, Reports of the Chaco Center # 9.

Awakuni-Swetlund, Mark 2001 <u>Dance Lodges of the Omaha Peoples ~ Building from Memory</u>. NY: Routledge.

Bailey, Garrick 1973 Changes in Osage Social Organization 1673-1906. Eugene: University of Oregon Anthropological Papers # 5.

Bailey, Garrick, ed. 1995 <u>The Osage & the Invisible World ~ From the Works of Francis La Flesche</u>. Norman: University of Oklahoma Press.

2004 Continuity & Change in Mississippian Civilization: 83-91. Hero, Hawk & Open Hand ~ American Indian Art of the Ancient Midwest & South. Richard Townsend, ed. New Haven: Yale University Press. .

Barker, Alex & Timothy Pauketat, eds. 1992 Lords of the Southeast: Social Inequality & the Native Elites of Southeastern North America. William Fitzhugh, ed. Archaeological Papers of the American Anthropological Association # 3.

Barnes, RH 1984 Two Crows Denies It ~ A History of Controversy in Omaha Sociology. Lincoln: University of Nebraska.

Beck, Robin 2013 Chiefdoms, Collapse & Coalescent in the Early American South. Cambridge University Press.

Beckwith, Martha Warren 1930 Myths & Hunting Stories of the Mandan & Hidatsa Sioux. Poughkeepsie: Vassar.

Bell, Amelia Rector 1984 Creek Ritual, The Path to Peace University of Chicago: PhD Dissertation.

1990 Separate People: Speaking of Creek Men and Women. American Anthropologist 92: 332-342.

Boas, Franz 1925, 1928 Keresan Texts. Publications of the American Ethnological Society VIII (1 & 2).

Bowers, Alfred 1950 Mandan Social & Ceremonial Organization. University of Chicago Press.

1965 Hidatsa Social & Ceremonial Organization. DC: Bureau of American Ethnology, Bulletin 194.

Brown, James A. 1985 The Mississippian Period. Ancient Art of the American Woodland Indians III: 93-145. David Brose, James Brown & David Penny, eds. New York: Harry N. Abrams, Inc.

1996 The Spiro Ceremonial Center. An Archaeology of Arkansas Valley Caddoan Culture in Eastern Oklahoma. Ann Arbor: Memoirs of the Museum of Anthropology, University of Michigan, # 29, 2 Volumes.

2003 The Cahokia Mound 72-Sub 1 Burials as Collective Representation. A Deep-Time Perspective ~ Studies in Symbols, Meaning & the Archeological Record ~ Papers in Honor of Robert Leonard Hall. The Wisconsin Archeologist 84 (1 & 2): 81-97.

2004 The Cahokia Expression: Creating Court & Cult: 105-123. Hero, Hawk & Open Hand ~ American Indian Art of the Ancient Midwest & South. Richard Townsend, ed. New Haven: Yale University Press.

2006a Where's the Power in Mound Building: An Eastern Woodlands Perspective. Leadership & Polity in Mississippian Society. Brian Butler & Paul Welch, eds. Carbondale: Center for Archaeological Investigation, Occasional Paper # 33.

2006b The Shamanic Element in Hopewellian Period Ritual, Chapter 26: 475-488. Recreating Hopewell. Douglas Charles & Jane Buikstra, eds. Gainesville: University Press of Florida.

2007 On the Identity of the Birdman Within Mississippian Period Art & Iconography. Ancient Objects & Sacred Realms ~ Interpretations of Mississippian Iconography, Chapter 4: 56-106. Kent Reilly & James Garber, eds. Austin: University of Texas Press.

Buffalohead, Eric 2004 Dhegihan History: A Personal Journey. Plains Anthropologist 49 (192): 327-343.

Buikstra, Jane & Douglas Charles 1999 Centering the Ancestors: Cemeteries, Mounds & Sacred Landscapes of the Ancient North American Midcontinent.

Bullard, William 1962 The Cerro Colorado Site & Pithouse Architecture in the Southwest United States Prior to A.D. 900. Peabody Papers # 44 (2).

Burns, Louis 1984a <u>Osage Indian Customs & Myths</u>. Fallbrook, Ca: Ciga Press.
1984b <u>Osage Indian Bands & Clans</u>. Fallbrook, CA: Ciga Press.
2005   <u>Osage Indian Customs & Myths</u>. Tuscaloosa: University of Alabama Press, Fire Ant Books. [1984]

Byers, A Martin 2006 <u>Cahokia ~ A World Renewal Cult Heterarchy</u>. Gainesville: University of Press of Florida.

Catlin, George 1967 <u>O-KEE-PA</u>. A Religious Ceremony & Other Customs of the Mandans. Yale University Press. [Lincoln: University of Nebraska Press, 1976, original 1867].

Chafe, Wallace 1976 The Caddoan, Iroquoian & Siouian Languages. Mouton.

Chapman, Kenneth & Bruce Ellis 1951 The Line Break, Problem Child of Pueblo Pottery. <u>El Palacio</u> 58 (9): 251-289.

Chappell, Sally A. Kitt 2002 <u>Cahokia ~ Mirror of the Cosmos</u>. Chicago: University of Chicago Press.

Chaudhuri, Jean Hill & Joyotpaul Chaudhuri 2001 <u>A Sacred Path</u> ~ The Way of the Muscogee Creeks. Los Angeles: UCLA American Indian Studies Center.

Clark, Blue 2016 Handwritten note of 28 July.

Cloud, Henry Roe ~ *Wa-na-xi-lay Hunkah* 1929 Mythologies of Our Aborigines in Relation to Prehistoric Mound Builders in America. <u>The Ohio Archaeological & Historical Society Publications</u> # 38. 4 May.

Cordell, Linda 1979 Middle Rio Grande Valley, New Mexico. Cultural Resources Overview. Government Printing Office, Bureau of Land Management (BLM).

Crawford, Michael 1978 <u>The Mobilian Trade Language</u>. Knoxville: University of Tennessee Press.

Crown, Patricia & W. James Judge, eds. 1991 Chaco and Hohokam ~ Prehistoric Regional Systems in the American Southwest. Santa Fe: School of American Research Press.

Culin, Stewart 1975 Games of the North American Indians. NY: Dover. [Bureau of American Ethnology, Annual Report # 24 1907]

Curtis, Edward 1909 Mandan, Arikara & Atsina. North American Indian. Cambridge. MA: University Press.

Davenport, William 1959 Nonunilinear Descent & Descent Groups. American Anthropologist 61 (4): 557-572.

Davis, Irvine 1959 Linguistic Clues to Northern Rio Grande Prehistory. El Palacio 66 (3): 73-84.

1963 Bibliography of Keresan Linguistic Sources. International Journal of American Linguistics 29 (3): 289-293.

1964 The Language of Santa Ana Pueblo. Bureau of American Ethnology, Papers 191 (69): 53-190.

De Boer, Warren 1993 Like a Rolling Stone ~ The Chunkey Game & Political Organization in Eastern North America. Southeastern Archaeology 12 (2): 83-92. Winter.

Di Peso, Charles 1974 Casas Grandes. A Fallen Trading Center of the Gran Chichimeca # 1, 2, 3. Flagstaff: Northland Press.

Doyel, David, ed. 1992 Anasazi Regional Organization & the Chaco System. Maxwell Museum of Anthropology, Anthropological Papers # 5.

Dozier, Edward 1967 Hano, A Tewa Indian Community in Arizona. Case Studies in Cultural Anthropology. New York: Holt, Rinehart & Winston.

1970 The Pueblo Indians of North America. Case Studies in Cultural Anthropology. New York: Holt, Rinehart & Winston.

Dutton, Bertha   1938   Łeyit Kin ~ A Small House Ruin, Chaco Canyon, New Mexico. Santa Fe: School of American Research, Monograph # 7.

Drechsel, Emanuel

1997   Mobilian Jargon ~ Linguistics & Sociohistorical Aspects of a Native American Pidgin. UK: Oxford Studies in Language Contact.

2001   Mobilian Jargon in Southeastern Indian Anthropology: Chapter 11, 175-183. Anthropologists & Indians in the New South. Rachel Bonney & Anthony Paredes, eds. Tuscaloosa: University of Alabama Press.

Eastman, Jane & Christopher Rodning, eds.   2001   Archaeological Studies of Gender in the Southeastern United States. Gainesville: University Press of Florida.

Ellis, Florence Hawley 1950 Keresan Patterns of Kinship & Social Organization. American Anthropologist 52: 499-512.

1951   Patterns of Aggression & the War Cult in Southwestern Pueblos. Southwest Journal of Anthropology 7 (2): 177-202.

1952   Jemez Kiva Magic & Its Relation to Features of Prehistoric Kivas. Southwest Journal of Anthropology 8 (2): 147-163.

1953   Authoritative Control & the Society System in Jemez Pueblo. Southwest Journal of Anthropology 9 (4): 385-394.

1959   Outline of Laguna History & Social Organization. Southwest Journal of Anthropology 15 (4): 325-347.

1964   A Reconstruction of the Basic Jemez Pattern of Social Organization, With Comparisons to Other Tanoan Social Structures. University of New Mexico, Anthropological Paper # 11.

1966   The Immediate History of Zia Pueblo as Derived from Excavations in Refuse Deposits. American Antiquity 31 (6): 806-811.

1967   Where Did the Pueblos People Come From? El Palacio 74 (3): 35-43.

Emerson, Thomas   1982   Mississippian Stone Images in Illinois.   Urbana-Champaign: Illinois Archaeological Survey, <u>Circular</u> # 6.

1984 Water, Serpents & the Underworld: An Exploration into Cahokia Symbolism: 45-92 in Galloway, <u>The Southeastern Ceremonial Complex ~ Artifacts & Analysis</u>. Lincoln: University of Nebraska.

1997 <u>Cahokia & the Archaeology of Power</u>. Tuscaloosa: University of Alabama Press.

Emerson, Thomas & Dale McElrath 2001 Interpreting Discontinuity & Historical Process in Midcontinental Late Archaic & Early Woodland Societies: Chapter 12, 195-217. <u>The Archaeology of Tradition</u> ~ <u>Agency & History Before & After Columbus</u>. Timothy Pauketat, ed. Gainesville: University Press of Florida.

Farella, John 1984 <u>The Main Stalk</u> ~ <u>A Syntheses of Navajo Philosophy</u>. Tucson: University of Arizona Press.

Feeling, Durbin 1975 <u>Cherokee – English Dictionary</u>. Tahlequah: Cherokee Nation of Oklahoma. .

Fenn, Elizabeth 2014 <u>Encounters at the Heart of the World</u> ~ <u>A History of the Mandan People</u>. NY: Hill & Wang.

Fletcher, Alice 1994 <u>A Study of Omaha Indian Music</u>. Lincoln: University of Nebraska. [1893, Harvard University, Archaeological & Ethnological Papers of the Peabody Museum 1 (5)]

Fletcher, Alice & Francis LaFlesche 1972 <u>The Omaha Tribe</u>. Lincoln: University of Nebraska Press. [Bureau of American Ethnology, Annual Report # 27 1911]

Fogelson, Raymond, ed. 2004 <u>Southeast</u>. Handbook of North American Indians, 14. DC: Smithsonian Institution Press.

Fowler, Andrew & John Stein 1992 The Anasazi Great House in Space, Time & Paradigm. Anasazi Regional Organization & the Chaco System. Doyel, ed. Maxwell Museum of Anthropology, Anthropological Papers # 5: 101-122.

Fowler, Melvin 1989 The Cahokia Atlas ~ A Historical Atlas of Cahokia Archaeology. Springfield: Illinois Historic Preservation Agency, Studies in Illinois Archaeology # 2. [1997 Revised].

Fowler, Melvin, Jerome Rose, Barbara Vander Leest & Steven Ahler 1999 The Mound 72 Area ~ Dedicated & Sacred Space in Early Cahokia. Springfield: Illinois State Museum, Reports of Investigations # 54.

Fox, Robin ~ JR 1967 The Keresan Bridge. London: Athlone Press, London School of Economics, Anthropological Monograph # 35.

Frazier, Kendrick 1986 People of Chaco ~ A Canyon & Its Culture. New York: W.W. Norton & Company.

Fritz, John 1978 Paleopsychology Today: Ideational Systems & Human Adaptation in Prehistory: 37-59, Chapter 3, in Charles Redman & others, eds. Social Archaeology ~ Beyond Subsistence and Dating. New York: Academic Press.

Gabriel, Kathyrn 1991 Roads to Center Place. A Cultural Atalas of Chaco Canyon & the Anasazi. Boulder, CO: Johnson Books.

Gallay, Alan 2002 The Indian Slave Trade: The Rise of the English Empire in the American South, 1670-1717. New Haven: Yale University Press.

Galloway, Patricia 1984 The Southeastern Ceremonial Complex: Artifacts & Analysis. Lincoln: University of Nebraska.

1995 Choctaw Genesis, 1500-1700. Lincoln: University of Nebraska Press.

2006 Practicing Ethnohistory. Mining Archives, Hearing Testimony, Constructing Narrative. Lincoln: University of Nebraska.

Gilman, Carolyn & Mary Jane Schneider   1987   The Way to Independence ~ Memories of a Hidatsa Indian Family, 1840-1920.   St Paul: Minnesota Historical Society, Museum Exhibit Series # 3.

Gladwin, Harold   1945   The Chaco Branch, Excavations at White Mound & in the Red Mesa Valley.   Gila Pueblo: Medallion Papers # 33. 159pp.

1957   A History of the Ancient Southwest.   Portland, Maine: Bond & Wheelright.

Goldstein, Lynne   2000   Mississippian Ritual as Viewed Through the Practice of Secondary Disposal of the Dead.   Mounds, Modoc & Mesoamerica: Papers in Honor of Melvin L. Fowler.   Steven Ahler, ed.   Springfield: Illinois State Museum Scientific Papers # 18:   193-205.

Grange, Roger   1979   An Archaeological View of Pawnee Origins.   Nebraska History 60 (2): 134-160.

Grebinger, Paul   1973   Prehistoric Social Organization in Chaco Canyon, New Mexico: An Alternative Reconstruction.   The Kiva 39 (1): 3-23.

1975.   Prehistoric Social Organization in Chaco Canyon, New Mexico; Postscript 1975.   15 pp. manuscript.

Gunn, John   1917   Schat-Chin: History, Traditions, and Narratives of the Queres Indians of Acoma and Laguna.   Albuquerque: Albright and Anderson.

Hall, Robert L.   1979   In Search of the Ideology of the Adena-Hopewell Climax. Hopewell Archaeology: The Chillicothe Conference.   David Brose & N'omi Greber, eds.   Kent, Ohio: Kent State University Press.

1997 An Archaeology of the Soul ~ North American Indian Belief & Ritual.   Urbana: University of Illinois Press.

2007 Review of Byer's Cahokia.   Wisconsin Archaeologist 88 (1): 101-106.

Harlow, Francis   1973   Matte-Paint Pottery of the Tewa, Keres & Zuni Pueblos. Santa Fe: Museum of New Mexico.

Harris, Arthur, James Schoenwetter & A.H. Warren 1967 Archaeological Survey of the Chuska Valley & the Chaco Plateau, New Mexico. Santa Fe: Museum of New Mexico Research Records # 4, Part 1.

Hawley, Florence & George Hawley 1938 Classification of Black Pottery Pigments & Paint Areas. University of New Mexico, Anthropological Papers # 321, 2 (4): 1-27.

Hayes, Alden c.1973 Pithouses Y & Z at Shabikeschee (29 SJ 1659). 10 pp. manuscript in the Chaco Center Library, University of New Mexico.

1981   Part One: A Survey of Chaco Canyon Archeology: 1-68 in Hayes, Brugge & Judge. Archaeological Surveys of Chaco Canyon, New Mexico. Washington: National Park Service, Publications in Archaeology # 18A. Chaco Canyon Studies.

Hayes, Alden, David Brugge & W. James Judge 1981 Archaeological Surveys of Chaco Canyon, New Mexico. Washington: National Park Service, Publications in Archaeology # 18A. Chaco Canyon Studies.

Hewett, Edger 1909 The Excavations at Tyuonyi, New Mexico in 1908 American Anthropologist 11 (3): 434-455.

1936 Chaco Canyon & Its Monuments. Albuquerque: University of New Mexico Press.

1943 Ancient Life in the American Southwest. New York: Tudor Publishing Co.

Hoebel, E. Adamson 1952 Keresan Witchcraft. American Anthropologist 54 (4): 586-589.

1953   Underground Kiva Passages. American Antiquity 19 (1): 76.

1968   The Character of Keresan Pueblo Law. Proceedings of the American Philosophical Society, Volume # 112 (3): 127-130.

1969   Keresan Pueblo Law: 92-116 in <u>Law in Culture & Society</u>.   Laura Nader, ed. Chicago: Aldine Publishing Co.

1979   Zia Pueblo: 407-417 in <u>Southwest</u>, Ortiz, ed.

Holder, Preston & T Dale Stewart 1958 A Compete Find of Filed Teeth from the Cahokia Mounds in Illinois.   <u>Journal of the Washington Academy of Sciences</u> 48: 349-357.

Holley, Geroge & Stephen Lekson 1999 Great Towns & Regional Polities in the Prehistoric American Southwest & Southeast: Chapter 3, 39-43.   <u>Great Towns & Regional Polities in the Prehistoric American Southwest & Southeast</u>. Jill Neitzel, ed. Albuquerque: University of New Mexico Press for Amerind Foundation.

Howard, James, with Willie Lena 1984 <u>Oklahoma Seminoles</u> ~ Medicines, Magic & Religion. Norman: University of Oklahoma Press.

Hudson, Charles 1975 Vomiting for Purity: Ritual Emesis in the Aboriginal Southeastern United States. <u>Symbols & Society</u> ~ Essays on Belief Systems in Action. Carole Hill, ed. Southern Anthropological Society, Proceedings # 9: 93-102.

1976   <u>The Southeastern Indians</u>. Knoxville: University of Tennessee Press.

1990   Conversations with the High Priest of Coosa: 214-230. <u>Lamar Archaeology</u>, Mississippian Chiefdoms in the Deep South. Mark Williams & Gary Shapiro, eds.

1997   <u>Knights of Spain, Warriors of the Sun</u>. Hernando de Soto & the South's Ancient Chiefdoms. Athens: University of Georgia Press.

2003   <u>Conversations with the High Priest of Coosa</u>. Chapel Hill: University of North Carolina Press.

Hudson, Charles, ed. 1979 <u>Black Drink</u>. A Native American Tea. Athens: The University of Georgia Press. [2004 Reprint]

Hudson, Travis & Ernest Underhoy 1978 Crystals in the Sky ~ An Intellectual Odyssey Involving Chumash Astronomy, Cosmology & Rock Art. Ballena Press Anthropological Papers # 10: 1-163.

Hunt, Edward Proctor 2015 The Origin Myth of Acoma Pueblo. Peter Nabokov, ed. NY: Penguin Classics. [Stirling 1942]

Irwin-Williams, Cynthia, ed. 1972 The Structure of Chacoan Society in the Northern Southwest ~ Investigations at the Salmon Site 1972. Eastern New Mexico University Contributions in Anthropology 4 (3): 1-144.

Irwin-Williams, Cynthia 1973 The Oshara Tradition: Origins of Anasazi Culture. Eastern New Mexico University Contributions in Anthropology 5 (1): 1-28.

Jackson, Jason 2003 Yuchi Ceremonial Life ~ Performance, Meaning & Tradition in a Contemporary American Indian Community. Studies in the Anthropology of North American Indians. Lincoln: University of Nebraska Press.

Kane, Allen 1989 Did the Sheep Look Up? Sociopolitical Complexity in Ninth Century Dolores Society: 307-361. The Sociopolitical Structure of Prehistoric Southwestern Societies. S Upham, KG Lightfoot & RA Jewett, eds. Boulder, CO: Westview Press.

Kehoe, Alice 1970 The Function of Ceremonial Sexual Intercourse among the Northern Plains Indians. Plains Anthropologist 15: 99-103.
2007 Osage Texts & Cahokia Data: Chapter 10, 246-261. Ancient Objects & Sacred Realms ~ Interpretations of Mississippian Iconography. Kent Reilly & James Garber, eds. Austin: University of Texas Press.

Kelleys, J Charles & Ellen 1975 An Alternative Hypothesis for the Explanation of Anasazi Culture History: 178-223 in The Collected Papers in Honor of Florence Hawley Ellis. Theodore Frisbie, ed. Santa Fe: Papers of the Archaeological Society of New Mexico # 2.

Kidder, Alfred & Samuel Guernsey   1919   <u>Archaeological Explorations in Northeastern Arizona</u>. Bureau of American Ethnology, <u>Bulletin</u> # 65.

Kimball, Geofrey   1994   <u>Koasati Dictionary</u>. Lincoln: University of Nebraska Press.

King, Duane   1975   A Grammar & Dictionary of the Cherokee Language. University of Georgia: PhD Linguistics.

King, Kathleen   1983   <u>Cricket Sings</u> ~ <u>A Novel of Pre-Columbian Cahokia</u>. Athens: Ohio University Press.

Knight, Vernon 1989 Symbolism of Mississippian Mounds. <u>Powhatan's Mantle</u> ~ <u>Indians in the Colonial Southeast</u>: 279-291. Peter Wood, Gregory Waselkov & M. Thomas Hatley, eds. Lincoln: University of Nebraska Press.

   1998 Moundville as a Diagrammatic Ceremonial Center. <u>Archaeology of the Moundville Chiefdom</u>: 44-62. Vernon James Knight & Vincas P. Steponaitis, eds. DC: Smithsonian Institution Press.

   2004   Ceremonialism Until 1500. <u>Southeast</u> 14: 734-741.   Raymond Fogelson, ed. DC: Smithsonian Institution Press.

LaFlesche, Francis 1932 A Dictionary of the Osage Language. DC: Bureau of American Ethnology, <u>Bulletin</u> # 109.

   1939   War Ceremony & Peace Ceremony of the Osage Indians.   DC: Bureau of American Ethnology, <u>Bulletin</u> # 101.

Lange, Charles 1953 Reappraisal of Evidence of Plains Influence Among the Rio Grande Pueblos. <u>Southwestern Journal of Anthropology</u> 92 (2): 212-230.

   1958 The Keresan Component of Southwestern Pueblo Culture. <u>Southwestern Journal of Anthropology</u> 14 (1): 34-50.

   1968a <u>Cochiti</u> ~ <u>A New Mexico Pueblo, Past & Present</u>.   Carbondale: Southern Illinois University Press, Arcturus Books. [1959]

1968b <u>The Cochiti Dam Archaeological Salvage Project.</u> Santa Fe: Museum of New Mexico Research Records # 6, part 1.

1979a Cochiti Pueblo: 366-378 in <u>Southwest,</u> Volume # 9, Pueblos. Alfonso Ortiz, ed. Smithsonian: Handbook of North American Indians.

1979b Santo Domingo Pueblo: 379-389 in <u>Southwest,</u> Volume # 9, Pueblos. Alfonso Ortiz, ed. Smithsonian, DC: Handbook of North American Indians.

Lanoue, Guy 2007 Experiences of Power among the Sekani of Northern British Columbia ~ Sharing Meaning through Time and Space: 10, 237-253. Jean-Guy A Goulet & Bruce Granville Miller, eds. <u>Extraordinary Anthropology</u> ~ Transformations in the Field. Lincoln: University of Nebraska Press.

La Vere, David 2007 <u>Looting Spiro Mounds</u> ~ <u>An American King Tut's Tomb</u>. Norman: University of Oklahoma Press.

Leblanc, Steven 1983 <u>The Mimbres People</u>. Ancient Pueblo Painters of the American Southwest. New York: Thames & Hudson.

Lekson, Stephen, Thomas Windes, John Stein & James Judge 1988 The Chaco Canyon Community. <u>Scientific</u> <u>American</u> (July).

Lekson, Stephen 1994 Thinking about Chaco: 11-42. Peck, Lekson, Stein & Ortiz. <u>Chaco Canyon</u> ~ <u>A Center & Its World</u>. Santa Fe: Museum of New Mexico Press.

1999 <u>The Chaco Meridian</u> ~ <u>Centers of Political Power in the Ancient Southwest</u>. Walnut Creek, CA: Altamira Press.

2015 <u>The Chaco Meridian</u> ~ <u>One Thousand Years of Political & Religious Power in the Ancient Southwest</u>. Lanham: Rowman & Littlefield Publishers.

Lekson, Stephen, ed. 1983 <u>The Architecture & Dendrochronology of Chetro Ketl, Chaco Canyon, New Mexico</u>. Albuquerque: Reports of Chaco Center # 6.

Lekson, Stephen & Catherine Cameron   1995   The Abandonment of Chaco Canyon, The Mesa Verde Migrations & the Reorganization of the Pueblo World. Journal of Anthropological Archaeology 14: 184-202.

Lepper, Bradley, ed. 2005 Ohio Archaeology ~ With Feature Articles Contributed By Over 20 Archaeologists & Scholars. Wilmington, OH: Voyager Media.

Lindberg, Christer   2004   George Catlin's Account(s) of the O-Kee-Pa in Concordance with Other Sources: 185-205 in The Challenges of Native American Studies ~ Essays in Celebration of the Twenty-Fifth American Indian Workshop.   Barbara Saunders & Lea Zuyderhoudt, eds.   Leuven: Leuven University Press.

Longacre, William, ed.   1970   Reconstructing Prehistoric Pueblo Societies. Albuquerque: University of New Mexico Press for the School of American Research.

McKenna, Peter & Wolcott Toll   1992.   Regional Patterns of Great House Development among the Totah Anasazi, New Mexico.   Anasazi Regional Organization & the Chaco System.   D Doyel, ed.   Maxwell Museum of Anthropology, Anthropological Papers # 5: 133-146.

Mallam, Clark   1976   The Iowa Effigy Mound Manifestation ~ An Interpretive Model. Iowa City: Office of the State Archaeologist, Report # 9.

Martin, Jack & Margaret McKane Mauldin   2000   A Dictionary of Creek/Muskogee, with notes on the Florida & Oklahoma Seminole dialects of Creek. Lincoln: University of Nebraska Press.

Martin. Paul   1939   Modified Basketmaker Sites, Ackmen-Lowry Area, Southwestern Colorado, 1938.   Field Museum of Natural History, Anthropological Series # 23 (3).

Mathews, John Joseph 1961 The Osages. Norman: University of Oklahoma Press.

Maybury-Lewis, David 1965 The Savage & the Innocent. Life with the Primitive Tribes of Brazil. New York: The World Publishing Company.

Miller, Jay 1972a Anthropology of Keres Identity. Rutgers University: PhD Dissertation.

1972b Priority of the Left. Man 7 (4): 646-7.

1975 Kokopelli: 371-380 in The Collected Papers in Honor of Florence Hawley Ellis. Theodore Frisbie, ed. Santa Fe: Papers of the Archaeological Society of New Mexico # 2.

1983 Keres Culture & Prehistory. Models of Pueblo Prehistory Symposium C-015-00. XI International Congress of Anthropological & Ethnological Sciences. Phase II (Vancouver). Sunday 21 August.

1989 Deified Mind among the Keresan Pueblos: 151-156 in General & Amerindian Ethnolinguistics ~ In Remembrance of Stanley Newman. Mary Ritchie Key & Henry M. Hoeningswald, eds. Berlin: Mouton de Gruyter.

1996 Changing Moons: A History of Caddo Religion. Plains Anthropologist 41 (157): 243-259.

2001 Keres: Engendered Key to the Pueblo Puzzle. Ethnohistory 48 (3): 495-514 Summer.

2015 Ancestral Mounds ~ Vitality & Volatility Crossing Native America. Lincoln: University of Nebraska Press.

2016 Allied Mounds ~ Amazon Press.

Milner, George R.

1998 The Cahokia Chiefdom ~ The Archaeology of a Mississippi Society. DC: Smithsonian Institution Press.

2004 The Moundbuilders. Ancient Peoples of Eastern North America. London: Thames & Hudson.

Mindeleff, Victor   1891   <u>A Study of Pueblo Architecture</u>:   <u>Tusayan & Cibola</u>. Bureau of American Ethnology, <u>Annual Report</u> # 8: 3-228.

Mochon, Marion Johnson   1972   Language, History & Prehistory: Mississippian Lexico-Reconstruction.   <u>American Antiquity</u> 37 (4): 478-503.

Mooney, James   1891   <u>Sacred Formulas of the Cherokee</u>.   Bureau of American Ethnology, Annual Report # 7.   [1982, Cherokee, NC: Cherokee Heritage Books]

   1982   <u>Myths of the Cherokee</u>.   Glossary.   Cherokee, NC: Cherokee Heritage Books.   [1900, Bureau of American Ethnology, Annual Report # 19]

Morris, Earl   1921-8   <u>The Aztec Ruin</u>.   American Museum of Natural History, <u>Anthropological Papers</u> # 26, parts 1-5.

Morris, Earl & Robert Burgh   1941   <u>Anasazi Basketry</u>:   A Study Based on Specimens from the San Juan River Country.   Washington, DC: Carnegie Publications # 533.

Nabokov, Peter   1986   <u>Architecture of Acoma Pueblo</u>.   The 1934 Historic American Buildings Survey Project.   Santa Fe: Ancient City Books.

   2015a <u>How the World Moves</u> ~ <u>The Odyssey of an American Indian Family</u>.   NY: Viking.

   2015b Introduction: xi-xiv.   Edward Proctor Hunt, <u>The Origin Myth of Acoma Pueblo</u>.   NY: Penguin Classics.

Neitzel, Jill, ed.   1999   <u>Great Towns & Regional Polities in the Prehistoric American Southwest & Southeast</u>.   Albuquerque: University of New Mexico Press for Amerind Foundation.

O'Brien, Patricia   1989   Cahokia: The Political Capital of the "Ramey" State. <u>North American Archaeologist</u> 10: 275-292.

Ortiz, Alfonso   1965   Dual Organization as an Operational Concept in the Pueblo Southwest.   <u>Ethnology</u> 4 (4): 389-96.

1969   The Tewa World. University of Chicago Press.

Ortiz, Alfonso, ed   1972   New Perspectives on the Pueblos. Albuquerque: University of New Mexico Press for the School of American Research.

1979   Southwest. Smithsonian: Handbook of North American Indians, Volume # 9, Pueblos.

Ortiz, Simon   1994   Chaco Canyon ~ A Center & Its World. Peck, ed, with Lekson, Stein & Ortiz. Santa Fe: Museum of New Mexico Press.

Parks, Douglas, Wesley Jones & Robert Hollow, eds.   1978   Earth Lodge Tales From the Upper Missouri ~ Traditional Stories of the Arikara, Hidatsa & Mandan. Bismarck: Mary College.

Parks, Douglas, ed.   1981   Ceremonies of the Pawnee by James Murie. Part I: The Skiri. DC: Smithsonian Contributions to Anthropology # 27.

Parks, Douglas   2001   Pawnee. Plains. Handbook of North American Indians, Volume 13, Part I: 515-547. Raymond DeMallie, ed. DC: Smithsonian.

Parks, Douglas & Waldo Wedel   1985   Pawnee Geography, Historical & Sacred. Great Plains Quarterly 5 (Summer): 143-76.

Parks, Douglas & Lula Nora Pratt   2008   A Dictionary of Skiri Pawnee. Lincoln: University of Nebraska Press.

Parsons, Elsie Clews   1917   The Antelope Clan in Keresan Custom & Myth. Man 17: 190-3, article 131.

1919   Mothers & Children at Laguna. Man 19: 34-8, article 18.

1920   Notes on Ceremonialism at Laguna. American Museum of National History, Anthropological Papers 19 (4): 83-130.

1923   Laguna Genealogies. American Museum of National History, Anthropological Papers 19 (5): 131-282.

1925   The Pueblo of Jemez. Yale University Press.

1928   The Laguna Migration to Isleta.   American Anthropologist 30 (4): 602-613.

1932   Isleta, New Mexico. Bureau of American Ethnology, Annual Report # 47: 193-466.

1933   Some Aztec & Pueblo Parallels.   American Anthropologist 35 (4): 611-631.

1936   Early Relations Between the Hopi & Keres. American Anthropologist 38 (4): 554-60.

1939   Pueblo Indian Religion. 1 & 2. University of Chicago Press.

1940   Relations between Ethnology & Archaeology in the Southwest. American Antiquity 5 (3): 214-20.

1962   Isleta Paintings.   Esther Goldfrank, ed.   Bureau of American Ethnology, Bulletin # 181.

1968   The House-Clan Complex of the Pueblos: 229-31 in Essays in Anthropology Presented to A. L. Kroeber.   Freeport, NY: Books for Libraries. [1936]

Pauketat, Timothy, ed. 2001 The Archaeology of Tradition ~ Agency & History Before & After Columbus. Gainesville: University Press of Florida.

Pauketat, Timothy 2004 Ancient Cahokia & Mississippians. Case Studies in Early Societies. Cambridge University Press.

2009 Cahokia ~ Ancient America's Great City on the Mississippi. NY: Viking Penguin.

Pauketat, Timothy & Thomas Emerson, eds. 1997 Cahokia: Domination & Ideology in the Mississippian World. Lincoln: University of Nebraska Press.

Pauketat, Timothy & Susan Alt   2003   Mounds, Memory & Contested Mississippian History. Archaeologies of Memory: 151-179. R Van Dyke & S Alcock, eds. Oxford: Blackwell.

Pauketat, Timothy & Susan Alt, eds.   2015   Medieval Mississippians ~ The Cahokia World. Santa Fe: SAR Press.

Paytiamo, James   1932   Flaming Arrow's People ~ By An Acoma Indian. New York: Duffield & Green.

Peck, Mary, Stephen Lekson, John Stein, Simon Ortiz   1994   Chaco Canyon ~ A Center & Its World. Santa Fe: Museum of New Mexico Press.

Pepper, George   1906   Human Effigy Vases from Chaco Canyon, New Mexico: 320-334. Boas Anniversary Volume. New York: GE Stechert.
1909 The Exploration of a Burial Room in Pueblo Bonito, New Mexico: 196-252. Putnam Anniversary Volume. New York: GEStechert.
1920 Pueblo Bonito.   American Museum of National History, Anthropological Papers # 27.

Peregrine, Peter   1995   Networks of Power: The Mississippian World-System: 247-265.   Native American Interactions ~ Multiscalar Analysis & Interpretations in the Eastern Woodlands. Michael Nassaney & Kenneth Sassamon. eds. Knowville: University of Tennessee Press. [p253 military power]

Peregrine, Peter & Stephen H. Lekson   2012   The North American Oikoumene. In Oxford Handbook of North American Archaeology. Timothy Pauketat, ed. New York: Oxford University Press.

Perino, Gregory   1967 Additional Discoveries of Filed Teeth in the Cahokia Area. American Antiquity 32 (4): 538-542, Oct.

Plog, Fred 1978 The Keresan Bridge: An Ecological & Archaeological Account: Chapter 15: 349-71 in Charles Redman & others, eds. <u>Social Archaeology ~ Beyond Subsistence & Dating</u>. New York: Academic Press.

Pluckhahn, Thomas 2003 <u>Kolomoki</u> – Settlement, Ceremony & Status in the Deep South, AD 350-750. Tuscaloosa: University of Alabama Press.

2010 The Sacred & the Secular Revisited: The Essential Tensions of Early Village Society in the Southeastern United States: 100-118. <u>Becoming Villagers</u>. <u>Comparing Early Village Societies</u>. Matthew Bandy & Jake Fox, ed. Tucson: University of Arizona Press.

Prentice, Guy 1986 An Analysis of the Symbolism Expressed by the Birger Figurine. <u>American Antiquity</u> 51 (2): 239-266.

Quintero, Carolyn 2004 <u>Osage Grammar</u>. Lincoln: University of Nebraska Press.

2009 <u>Osage Dictionary</u>. Norman: University of Oklahoma Press.

Rankin, Robert

1981 letter of 14 December.

1996 On Siouan Chronology. ms.

2006 Siouan Tribal Contacts & Dispersions Evidenced by the Terminology for Maize & Other Cultigens. John E. Staller, Robert H. Tykot & Bruce F. Benz, eds. <u>Histories of Maize: Multidisciplinary Approaches to the Prehistory, Linguistics, Biogeography, Domestication & Evolution of Maize</u>. Amsterdam: Elsevier Academic Press.

2007 Siouian Tribes of the Ohio Valley: "Where did all these Indians Come From?" 16 May 2007, American Indien Studies Lecture Series, The Ohio State University. <u>http://hdl.handle.net/1811/28545</u> {kb.osu.edu/ dspace/browse ?value = Robert Rankin}.

Redman, Charles & others, eds. <u>Social Archaeology ~ Beyond Subsistence and Dating</u>. New York: Academic Press.

Reilly III, F. Kent & James F. Garber, eds. <u>2007 Ancient Objects & Sacred Realms ~ Interpretations of Mississippian Iconography</u>. Austin: University of Texas Press.

Rice, Glen & Steven LeBlanc 2001 <u>Deadly Landscapes ~ Case Studies in Prehistoric Southwestern Warfare</u>. Salt Lake City: University of Utah Press.

Richards, John D. & Melvin L. Fowler, eds. 2003 <u>A Deep-Time Perspective</u>: Studies in Symbols, Meaning & the Archeological Record. Papers in Honor of Robert L Hall. <u>The Wisconsin Archeologist</u> 84 (1 & 2).

Ridington, Robin & Dennis Hastings ~ *In'aska* 1997 <u>Blessings for a Long Time ~ The Sacred Pole of the Omaha Tribe</u>. Lincoln: University of Nebraska.

Robbins, Lester 1976 The Persistence of Traditional Religious Practices among Creek Indians. Dallas: Southern Methodist University, PhD Dissertation.

Roberts, Frank HH 1929 Shabik'eshchee Village. Bureau of American Ethnology, <u>Bulletin</u> # 92.

1930 Early Pueblo Ruins of the Piedra District, Southwestern Colorado. Bureau of American Ethnology, <u>Bulletin</u> # 96.

1932 The Village of the Great Kivas on the Zuni Reservation. Bureau of American Ethnology, <u>Bulletin</u> # 111.

1939 Archaeological Remains in the Whitewater District of Eastern Arizona. Bureau of American Ethnology, <u>Bulletin</u> # 121. Part I: House Types.

Roe, Peter 1982 <u>The Cosmic Zygote ~ Cosmology in the Amazon Basin</u>. New Brunswick: Rutgers University Press.

Romain, William 2000 Mysteries of the Hopewell. Astronomers, Geometers & Magicians of the Eastern Woodlands. Akron: The University of Akron Press.

2015 Moonwatchers of Cahokia: 33-42. Medieval Mississippians ~ The Cahokia World. Timothy Pauketat& Susan Alt, eds. Santa Fe: SAR Press.

Rooth, Anna Birgetta 1957 Creation Myths of North American Indians. Anthropos 52: 498-508.

Roper, Donna & Elizabeth Pauls, eds. 2005 Plains Earthlodges ~ Ethnographic & Archeological Perspectives. Tuscaloosa: University of Alabama Press.

Salzer, Robert & Grace Rajnovich 2001 The Gottscall Rockshelter: An Archaeological Mystery. Maplewood, MN: Prairie Smoke Press.

Sam, Archie 1976 Interview by Charlotte Capers, Olivia Collins, Elbert Hilliard, HT Holmes. Mississippi Department of Archives & History # OH83-03. August 30.

Santa Ana Damayame 1994 Santa Ana ~ The People, the Pueblo & the History of Tamaya. Laura Bayer, Floyd Montoya & the Damayame, eds. Albuquerque: University of New Mexico Press.

Saunders, Joe, Reca Jones, Thurman Allen, Josetta LeBoeuf & Sunny Meriwether 2008 Indians Mounds of Northeast Louisiana. A Driving Trail Guide. Baton Rouge: Louisiana Division of Archaeology, Ancient Mounds Heritage Area & Trails Advisory Commission.

Shambach, Frank 1996 Mounds, Embankments, and Ceremonialism in Trans-Mississippi South. Mounds, Embankments, and Ceremonialism in the Midsouth. Robert Mainfort and Richard Walling, eds. Arkansas Archaeological Survey Research Series # 46: 36-43.

Schelberg, John Daniel 1982 Economic & Social Development As An Adaptation To A Marginal Environment in Chaco Canyon, New Mexico. PhD Dissertation: Northwestern University.

Schele, Linda & David Freidel 1990 A Forest of Kings. The Untold Story of the Ancient Maya. New York: William Morrow.

Schweitzer, Marjorie 2001 Otoe & Missouria. Handbook of North American Indians, Plains, Volume 13, Part 1: 447-461. Raymond De Mallie, ed. DC: Smithsonian.

Sebastian, Lynne 1991 Sociopolitical Complexity & the Chaco System: 109-134 in Patricia Crown & W. James Judge, eds. Chaco and Hohokam. Prehistoric Regional Systems in the American Southwest. Santa Fe: School of American Research Press.

1992 The Chaco Anasazi ~ Sociopolitical Evolution in the Prehistoric Southwest. Cambridge University Press.

Service, Elman 1968 Primitive Social Organization. New York: Random House.

Sherrod, Clay & Martha Ann Rolingson 1987 Surveyors of the Ancient Mississippi Valley ~ Modules & Alignments in Prehistoric Mound Sites. Arkansas Archaeological Survey Research Series # 28.

Skele, Mikels 1988 The Great Knob: Interpretations of Monks Mound. Springfield: Illinois Historic Preservation Agency, Studies in Illinois Archaeology #4.

Smiley, Terah, Stanley Stubbs & Bryant Bannister 1953 A Foundation for the Dating of Some Late Archaeological Sites in the Rio Grande Area, New Mexico. University of Arizona: Laboratory of Tree-Ring Research, Bulletin # 6.

Spier, Leslie 1917 An Outline for a Chronology of Zuni Ruins. American Museum of Natural History, Anthropological Papers # 18: 207-331.

Spencer, Robert 1940 A Preliminary Sketch of Keresan Grammar. University of New Mexico: Master`s Thesis.

1946 The Phonemes of Keresan. International Journal of American Linguistics 12 (4): 229-236.

Sofaer, Anna, Michael Marshall & Rolf Sinclair 1989 The Great North Road: a cosmographic expression of the Chaco culture of New Mexico: 365-376 in World Archaeoastronomy. Anthony Aveni, ed. Cambridge University Press.

Springer, James Warren & Stanley Witkowski 1982 Siouan Historical Linguistics & Oneota Archaeology. Oneota Studies. Guy Gibbon, ed. University of Minnesota Publications in Anthropology 1: Chapter 5, 69-83.

Squier, Ephraim G. 1851 The Serpent Symbol & the Worship of Reciprocal Principles of Nature in America. New York: George F Putnam. [1975, Kraus Reprint]

Squier, Ephraim G & Edwin Davis 1848 Ancient Monuments of the Mississippi Valley. Smithsonian Contributions to Knowledge 1. [1998 Smithsonian Classics of Anthropology]

Stein, John & Stephen Lekson 1992 Anasazi Ritual Landscapes. Anasazi Regional Organization & the Chaco System. Doyel, ed. Maxwell Museum of Anthropology, Anthropological Papers # 5: 87-100.

Stevenson, Matilde Coxe 1894 The Sia. Bureau of American Ethnology, Annual Report # 11: 3-157.

1904 The Zuni Indians. Bureau of American Ethnology, Annual Report # 23: 3-608.

Steward, Julian 1937 Ecological Aspects of Southwestern Society. Anthropos 32 (1-2): 87-104.

1970 The Foundation of Basin-Plateau Shoshonean Society: 113-151 in Languages & Cultures of Western North America. Earl Swanson, ed. Pocatello: Idaho State University Press.

Sunderhaus, Ted & Jack Blosser 2006 Water & Mud & the Recreation of the World: Chapter 8, 134-145. Recreating Hopewell. Douglas Charles & Jane Buikstra, eds. Gainesville: University of Press of Florida.

Stubbs, Stanley 1950 Bird's Eye View of the Pueblos. Norman: University of Oklahoma Press.

Swanton, John 1911 Indian Tribes of the Lower Mississippi Valley & Adjacent Coast of the Gulf of Mexico. DC: Bureau of American Ethnology, Bulletin # 43. [NY: Dover Reprint, 1998]

1912 A Dictionary of the Biloxi & Ofo Languages. DC: Bureau of American Ethnology, Bulletin # 47.

1922 Tokuli of Tulsa. American Indian Life, by Several of Its Students. Elsie Clews Parsons, ed. New York: BW Huebsch, Inc.

1928a Social Organization & Social Usages of the Indians of the Creek Confederacy. DC: Bureau of American Ethnology, Annual Report # 42 for 1924-25: 23-472.

1928b Religious Beliefs & Medical Practices of the Creek Indians. DC: Bureau of American Ethnology, Annual Report # 42 for 1924-25: 473-672.

1928c Aboriginal Culture of the Southeast. DC: Bureau of American Ethnology, Annual Report # 42: 673-726.

1928d Chickasaw. DC: Bureau of American Ethnology, Annual Report # 44: 169-273.

1928e The Interpretation of Aboriginal Mounds by Means of Creek Indian Customs. Smithsonian Institution, Annual Report 1927: 495-506, 7 plates.

1929 Myths & Tales of the Southeastern Indians. DC: Bureau of American Ethnology, <u>Bulletin</u> # 88.

1931 Source Material for the Social & Ceremonial Life of the Choctaw Indians. DC: Bureau of American Ethnology, <u>Bulletin</u> # 103.

1932 Green Corn Dance. <u>Chronicles of Oklahoma</u> X (11): 170-195.

1998 <u>Early History of the Creek Indians & Their Neighbors</u>. Gainesville: University Press of Florida. [DC: Bureau of American Ethnology, Bulletin # 73, 1922]

Temple, Wayne   1966   Indian Villages of the Illinois Country.   Illinois State Museum <u>Scientific Papers</u> # 2 (2): 1-218.

Teuton, Christopher, ed. 2012 <u>Cherokee Stories of the Turtle Island Liars' Club</u>. by Hastings Shade, Sammy Still, Sequoyah Guess, Woody Hansen. Chapel Hill: University of North Carolina Press.

Thomas, Cyrus   1985   Report on the Mound Explorations of the Bureau of Ethnology. DC: Smithsonian Institution Press. [1894 Bureau of American Ethnology, <u>Annual Report</u> # 12 1890-91]

Timberlake, Lt Henry 2007 <u>Memoirs</u> ~ The Story of a Soldier, Adventurer & Emissary to the Cherokees, 1756-65. Duane King, ed. Cherokee, NC: Museum of the Cherokee Indian.

Toll, H. Wolcott 1991 Material Distributions & Exchange in the Chaco System: 77-108 in Patricia Crown & W. James Judge, eds. <u>Chaco and Hohokam</u>. Prehistoric Regional Systems in the American Southwest. Santa Fe: School of American Research Press.

Toll, Wolcott, Eric Blinman & Wilson Dean   1992   Chaco in the Context of Ceramic Regional Systems. <u>Anasazi Regional Organization & the Chaco System</u>. Doyel, ed. Maxwell Museum of Anthropology, Anthropological Papers # 5: 147-158.

Townsend, Richard 2004 Hero, Hawk & Open Hand ~ American Indian Art of the Ancient Midwest & South. New Haven: Yale University Press.

Turner, Christy & Jacqueline Turner 1999 Man Corn ~ Cannibalism & Violence in the Prehistoric Southwest. Salt Lake City: University of Utah Press.

Trombold, Charles, ed. 1991 Ancient road networks & settlement hierarchies in the New World (sic). Cambridge, UK: New Directions in Archaeology.

Van Dyke, Ruth 2007 The Chaco Experience ~ Landscape and ideology at the Center Place. Santa Fe: School for Advanced Research Resident Scholar Book.

Van Nest, Julieann 2006 Rediscovering This Earth: Some Ethnogeological Aspects of the Illinois Valley Hopewell Mounds: Chapter 22, 402-426 in Recreating Hopewell. Douglas Charles & Jane Buikstra, eds. Gainesville: University Press of Florida.

Van Tuyl, Charles 1979 The Natchez: Annotated Translations from Histoire de la Louisiane ~ A Short English-Natchez Dictionary. Oklahoma Historical Society, Series in Anthropology # 4.

Vega, Garcilasco de la 1980 The Florida of the Inca. John & Jeannette Varner, trans. Austin: University of Texas Press.

Vivian, Gordon 1959 The Hubbard Site & Other Tri-Wall Structures in New Mexico & Colorado. National Park Service, Archaeological Research # 5.

Vivian, Gordon & Tom Mathews 1964 Kin Kletso. Globe, Arizona: Southwestern Monuments Association, Technical Series # 6, Part 1: 1-115.

Vivian, Gordon & Paul Reiter 1965 The Great Kivas of Chaco Canyon. Santa Fe: School of American Research, Monograph # 22.

Vivian, Gwinn 1970 An Inquiry into Prehistoric Social Organization in Chaco Canyon, New Mexico: 5-83 in Reconstructing Prehistoric Pueblo Societies.

William Longacre, ed. Albuquerque: University of New Mexico Press for the School of American Research.

1972 Prehistoric Water Conservation in Chaco Canyon. Final Technical Letter Report to the National Science Foundation. Grant GS-3100.

ms Conservation & Diversion: Water Control Systems in the Anasazi Southwest.

1990 The Chacoan Prehistory of the San Juan Basin. New York: Academic Press.

1991 Chacoan Subsistence: 57-76 in Patricia Crown & W James Judge, eds. Chaco and Hohokam. Prehistoric Regional Systems in the American Southwest. Santa Fe: School of American Research Press.

Vivian, Gwinn & Bruce Hilpert 2002 The Chaco Handbook ~ An Encyclopedic Guide. Salt Lake City: University of Utah Press.

Vivian, R Gwinn, Dulce Dodgen & Gayle Hartmann 1978 Wooden Ritual Artifacts from Chaco Canyon, New Mexico; The Chetro Ketl Collection. University of Arizona, Anthropological Papers # 32: 1-152.

Wheat, Joe Ben 1955 Mogollon Culture Prior to A.D. 1000. American Antiquity, Memoir # 10.

Weigand, Phil 1992 The Macroeconomic Role of Turquoise within the Chaco Canyon System. Anasazi Regional Organization & the Chaco System. Doyel, ed. Maxwell Museum of Anthropology, Anthropological Papers # 5: 169-176.

Weltfish, Gene 1965 The Lost Universe ~ The Way of Life of the Pawnees. NY: Ballantine Books. [1977 University of Nebraska Press].

Wessen, Cameron 2001 Creek & PreCreek Revisited: Ch 6: 94-106 The Archaeology of Tradition ~ Agency & History Before & After Columbus. Timothy Pauketat, ed. Gainesville: University Press of Florida.

White, Leslie   1928   A Comparative Study of the Keresan Medicine Societies. Proceedings of the International Congress of Americanists 2: 604-19.

1932a The Acoma Indians. Bureau of American Ethnology, Annual Report # 47: 17-192.

1932b The Pueblo of San Felipe. American Anthropological Association, Memoirs # 38.

1935 The Pueblo of Santo Domingo.   American Anthropological Association, Memoirs # 43.

1942 The Pueblo of Santa Ana. American Anthropological Association, Memoirs # 60.

1943 New Material from Acoma. Bureau of American Ethnology, Bulletin # 136 (32): 301-59.

1944a A Ceremonial Vocabulary among the Pueblos. International Journal of American Linguistics 10 (4): 161-167.

1944b Notes on the Ethnobotany of the Keres. Papers of the Michigan Academy of Science, Arts & Letters 30: 557-68.

1947 Notes on the Ethnozoology of the Keresan Pueblo Indians. Papers of the Michigan Academy of Science, Arts & Letters 31: 223-43.

1948 Miscellaneous Notes on the Keresan Pueblos. Papers of the Michigan Academy of Science, Arts & Letters 32: 365-73.

1962 The Pueblo of Sia. Bureau of American Ethnology, Bulletin # 184.

1964 The World of the Keresan Pueblo Indians: 53-64 in Culture in History ~ Essays in Memory of Paul Radin. Stanley Diamond, ed. NY: Columbia University Press.

White, Nancy Marie, Lynne Sullivan & Rochelle Marrinan 1999 Grit-Tempered ~ Early Women Archaeologists in the Southeastern United States. Gainesville: University Press of Florida.

White, Tim 1992 <u>Prehistoric Cannibalism at Mancos 5MTUMR-2346</u>. Princeton University Press.

Whitman, William 1937 The Oto. <u>Columbia University Contributions to Anthropology</u> # 28.

   1947 Ioway-Otoe Grammar. <u>International Journal of American Linguistics</u> 13 (4): 233-248.

Will, George & George Hyde 1964 <u>Corn among the Indians of the Upper Missouri</u>. Lincoln: University of Nebraska Press.

Williams, Stephen 1990 The Vacant Quarter & Other Late Events in the Lower Valley: 170-180 in <u>Towns & Temples Along the Mississippi</u>. David Dye & Cheryl Anne Coxe, eds. Tuscaloosa: University of Alabama Press.

   2001 The Vacant Quarter Hypothesis & the Yazoo Delta, <u>Societies in Eclipse</u>: 191-203 in Archaeology of the Eastern Woodlands Indians, AD 1400-1700. David Brose, C Wesley Cowan & Robert Mainfort, eds. DC: Smithsonian Institution Press.

Wilshusen, Richard & Scott Ortman 1999 Rethinking the Pueblo I Period in the San Juan Drainage: Aggregation, Migration & Cutlural Diversity. *Kiva* 64 (3): 369-399, Spring.

Windes, Thomas 1977a Typology & Technology of Anasazi Ceramics: 279-370 in Reher 1977.

   1977b Preliminary Investigations at the Pueblo Alto Complex, Chaco Canyon, 1976. Manuscript (84pp) in the Chaco Center Library, University of New Mexico.

   1978 <u>Stone Circles of Chaco Canyon, Northwestern New Mexico</u>. Reports of the Chaco Center # 5.

   1991 The Prehistoric Road Network at Pueblo Alto, Chaco Canyon, New Mexico: 111-131 in <u>Ancient road networks & settlement hierarchies in the</u>

New World (sic). CharlesTrombold, ed. Cambridge, UK: New Directions in Archaeology.

Windes, Tom & Dabney Ford 1992 The Nature of the Early Bonito Phase:. Anasazi Regional Organization & the Chaco System. Doyel, ed. Maxwell Museum of Anthropology, Anthropological Papers 5: 75-87.

Wilson, Edmund 1960 Apologies to the Iroquois. NY: Farrar, Straus & Cudahy.

Wildschut, William 1975 Crow Indian Medicine Bundles. John Ewers, ed. NY: Museum of the American Indian, Heye Foundation, Contributions XVII.

Wittfogel, Karl & Esther Goldfrank 1943 Some Aspects of Pueblo Mythology & Society. Journal of American Folklore 56 (219): 17-30.

Wood, Peter, Gregory Waselkov & M. Thomas Hatley, eds. 1989 Powhatan's Mantle ~ Indians in the Colonial Southeast. Lincoln: University of Nebraska Press.

Wormington, Hannah Marie 1957 Ancient Man in North America. Denver Museum of Natural History, Popular Series # 4.
1964 Prehistoric Indians of the Southwest. Denver Museum of Natural History, Popular Series # 7.

York, Annie, Richard Daly & Chris Arnett 1994 They Write Their Dreams on the Rock Forever ~ Rock Writings of the Stein River Valley of British Colombia. Vancouver, BC: Talon Books.

Young, Biloine Whiting & Melvin Fowler 2000 Cahokia ~ The Great American Metropolis. Springfield: University of Illinois Press.

Zogry, Michael 2010 Anetso ~ The Cherokee Ball Game at the Center of Ceremony & Identity. Chapel Hill: University of North Carolina Press.

Zuni People 1972 The Zunis ~ Self-Portrayals. Albuquerque: University of New Mexico Press.

Index

A

Acoma, 1f, 7f, 34f, 35f, 39, 44f, 52f, 65f, 126
Adams, Charles, 25 #14, 61
Adena, 66
Akins, Nancy, 21f
Alfred Herrera site (LA 6455), 37
altepetl, 124
American Bottom, 72f, 83, 86
Animas River, 5, 35, 62f
Ant Priesthood, 61
Antelope clan, 52f, 65
Ashlislepah, 56

B

Bandelier National Monument, 31
Basketmaker, 1, 6, 16f, 26f, 34, 44, 57f, 61
Beaded Cape, 124
Beloved Women, 98
Bernalillo, 35
"Big Bang", 69
Big Dipper, 73
Big Moon, 115
Big Mound, 84
Blessingway ~ hózhǫ́ǫ́jí, 124
Blowsnake, Jasper, 108f
Boogers, 994
Boyakya, 45
Broken Flute Cave, 29
Bulls, 94, 107, 110f, 120f
Busk ~ Green Corn, 68, 74, 84f, 87f, 91f, 124f

C

cache pits, 66, 103, 117
Calumet, 116, 120, 125
Cantine ~ Canteen, 74
carbon paint, 8f, 16, 21, 33, 37
Carlsbad Caverns, 45
Casa Rinconada, 5f, 11, 27
Casas Grandes, 1, 43, 60f
Catawbas, 88, 100, 106f
Cebolleta Mesa, 26

cedar post, 79, 106f, 117
Cerrillos turquoise, 13, 60
Chaco Halo, 6
Chaco-McElmo Black-on-white, 8
Chayainyi, 63
Chicagos, 86
Chimayo, 63
Chiwere Oto, 67, 85, 106, 123
Chiwere Siouans, 67
Chota ~ Itsodiyi, 99
Chungishnish, v
chunkey, 13, 69f, 78, 123f
Chuska Mountains, 13, 19
Cibola, 6, 22
clay core, 70
Cochiti, 2, 16, 23, 33f, 44f
Consciousness Deity ~ Thought Woman, 4, 60
Corn clan, 1, 52f, 65
Corn Mother, 67, 85
Crab Supernova 1054, 72
Cricket Sings, 74f

D

deonic, 81
Dhegiha Siouians, iv, 67, 105
districts, 7, 59, 100
Dog Soldiers, 73
Dolores River, 25, 64f, 124
Dozier, Edward, 40

E

Earth Diver, 70, 81
Earthmaker, 108f
Effigy bowls, 83
El Faro, 56
Elati, 100
Ellis, Florence Hawley, 11,
entradas, 37

F

Fewkes, Jesse Walter, 31
First Creator, 117

Flint, 3, 45
Four Pole, 103
Fourmile glaze, 61

G

gatiyo'i, 101
Geese, 83
Giant, 45
gila, 98
Gomaiyawish, 53
Gottschall Cave, 110
Great Knob, 73
Great North Road, 56
Grebinger, Paul, 14
Guillet, Dom Urban, 73
gumbo, 81
Gunn, John, 40

H

Halley's Comet 1066, 72
Halloween, 68
Hewett, Edgar, 5, 31
Hill, Ames, 74
HoChunks ~ Winnebagos, 108f
Hoita, 118f
Hokan, 37
holy grounds, 103
Hosta Butte, 14
hot house ~ *oosi*, 98
hotcanitsa, 16, 44 # 19
Hudson, Dee, 10
Hunt Chief, 40
Hurons, 67

I

Illini-Myaamis, 86f
Inside ~ *Hochaiyanyi*, 40
Isolated Earth, 113f
iyaanyi, vi, 4, 13, 20, 48 # 22

J

jacal, 29f
Jemez, 16
Judd, Neil, 17
Junaluska, 101

K

Kanati ~ hunter, 98
Kashkachrutiya, 4065
Katsina, 25 # 14, 42, 56
Keresic, v, 28 # 15
Kidder, Alfred, 27
kihus, 63
kinship, iv, 108
Kite Hawk, 116
Kituwha, 98f
Kopishtaiya, 40f

L

left, 3, 22 # 12
Lekson, Stephen, 5, 8, 60 # 30
Łeyit Kin, 16
lightning rod, 74
Little Ice Age (1300-1870), v
Lohmann phase, 72,
Lone Man, 117f
Lumpwood, 107

M

Maiyanyi, 11, 25f, 35f
maize ~ corn, iv, vi, 3, 23f, 63, 69f, 74, 81f,
    98f, 103f, 115f, 124f
Maize Model, 82
Mallam, Clark, 81 # 57
Mandan, iv, 67f, 106f, 115f
Manike, 124
Manuelito Canyon, 9, 58
Martin, Paul, 29
Masewi, 2, 46f, 53
matrilineal, iv, 1, 104, 125
matrilocal, 30
mats, 78f, 112
mayordomo, 12
Medieval Warm (950-1250 AD), iv
Mesa Verde, 7, 16f, 37f, 64
Milner, George, 83
mineral paints, 8, 21f, 31f, 35
Mobilian Jargon, v, 67
Mogollon, 6, 27f, 61f
moieties, 10, 65f, 82f, 90f, 110f, 120f
Momentum rites, 40f, 65

Moravians, 101
Morgan, Lewis Henry, 5
Mound, 18f, 41, 56f, 62f, 70f, 80f, 90f
Moundville, iii, v
mudlodges, 102f
Murphy, NC, 99

N

nahiya, 40
Napoleon, 73
nawai, 46f
New Cahokia, 69
New Fire ~ Busk, 74
Newark Octagon, 125
Nikwasi, 99f, 100 # 90
Northeast Corner, 45
Nunnehi, 99
nupka, 117

O

Ohio Valley Siouians, 106
Okeepa, 117f
Okipa, 68
Old Cahokia, 69
Old Dog, 107
Opi, 42f, , 54, 62
Osages, iii, 67, 82, 86, 105, 110f, 125
Oshara tradition, 1, 5, 12, 25f 30f
Outside ~ Sahte Hochaiyanyi, 13, 29, 40
Owl ~ Fool, 120f
Oyoyewi, 2, 47f

P

Pa'ako, 35
Paquime, 63, 64
patrilineal, iv, 29f, 59, 104, 125f
Pe'lush, 16
pemmican, 119f
Peñasco Blanco, 10, 14f, 42, 56
Peoria, Baptise, 86
"pins", 102
Pittsburg, 73
pochteca, 5, 36, 44
Polaris, 73, 75, 106, 126
Pueblo Alto, 5, 10, 15f, 50
Puwamuya, 58

Q

Qualla Boundary, 99f

R

Radin, Paul, 108f
Ramey Incised, 81, 85
Ramey knives, 70, 85
Rave, John, 108
Red Horn, 110f
Red Mesa Phase, 23
Red Sticks, 101
right, 3, 22, 45, 53, 78, 82, 106, 111, 117f, 122
Rito de las Frijoles, 31f
Roberts, Frank HH, 29f
Rocky Mountain beeweed, 33
rotunda, 68f, 98f

S

Sakbe ~ white road, 57 #28, 72 #48
Salmon site, 13, 26
San Juan, 1, 6, 11f, 20f, 34f, 42f
Sebastian, Lynne, 8f, 19
Selu ~ maize, 98
semi-cardinal directions, 103, 121
Sequoya ~ George Guess, 101
Shabik'eshchee, 30
Shaul, David, 43
Shell Robe, 1, 115 # 108
Sherente, 57
Shikame, 45f
Shipop[u], 2f, 7, 40, 56
Shiwana, 25, 35f
Shuratsha, 52f
Shuratsha Lights The Fire, 55f
Sioux City, IA, 108
Skewers, 121
Skunks, 107
Snakes, vi, 58, 70, 94f, 107, 116f
South Bands, 102
Southeast Corner, 30, 45, 103
spider web, vi
Spring Boy ~ *Mahash*, 124
Springplace, GA, 101
Squash, 3, 6, 22, 46f, 65f, 102, 117f, 125

stairways, 19, 41, 56f
Stone Hammers, 107
summer ~ *go•ki*, 99
Sun ~ *oshatsh*, 46

T

Tahlequah, 101
Tamaroa ~ cut tail, 86
Tamaya, 2, 35
tansy mustard, 33
Tellico, 101
Tetilla Peak, 44
Tewa, 7, 26, 33f, 64
Thebes Gap, 70
Thomas, Major Will ~ wilusti, 101
Tiamunyi, 9, 16, 32, 40f, 50f
Timberlake, Lt. Henry, 99
Toloachi, vi
Toltec Module, 69, 75f, 82
Tower kivas, 7, 25, 35, 51
Trappists, 73
trocaderos, 5
Tsali ~ Charlie, 99
Turquoise, 2f, 13f, 46f, 60f, 125
turtle drums, 116f
Twins, 2f, 41, 53f, 68, 76f, 98, 109f, 112
Tysic,viii, 67f, 72 # 48, 98f
Tyuonyi, 9, 31f, 43

V

Vivian, Gwinn, 1f, 12f, 22f

W

Wakonda, 111
Washburn, Cephas, 101
waxo'be ~ sacred, 112
Wenimatsa, 53
white beans, 13
White House, 36, 40f, 52f, 64
Wijiji, 7f
Windes, Tom, 15 #9
winter ~ *go•la*, 99
Wittfogel, Karl, 12
Wonderful Skull, 103
woodhenges, 70f, 82

X

xópini, vi, 115

Y

Yazoo Basin, 76

Z

Zuni, 18 #11

Please Help our Struggles against Typo Gnomes

Sold @ Amazon